Meals That Can Wait

Patricia Brooks

Meals That Can Wait

A cookbook for commuters' wives,
weekend hostesses and other
dependents of the undependable

FUNK & WAGNALLS · NEW YORK

To my dependable commuter
L.J.B.

Contents

Introduction

Too many times dinnertime is not the witching hour, but the bewitched, bothered and bewildered hour, in which nothing works right, and all the tensions of the day accumulate in the kitchen. A loaf of bread, a jug of wine and thou, paugh! Things are not that simple anymore. It is a rare household where dinner is scheduled for a given hour and served on the dot. Most households live by a more spontaneous set of rules, sometimes spelled c-h-a-o-s. (C = coming home late, H = hurrying to the kitchen, A = anguishing at the empty refrigerator, O = ordering someone to set the table, S = scurrying around to improvise *something* for the evening repast. Put them all together and it is indeed chaos.)

There are so many pressures on Madame Homemaker today: civic activities, school obligatons, children's sports and extracurricular programs. All too often, after ferrying to and from dental appointment and dancing class, there is the desperation dash to the supermarket at 5:30 with the frantic query, "What shall I fix for dinner tonight that's fast?" Then home again, home again, jiggedy jig, wth the frenzy of the sorcerer's apprentice and the loneliness of the long distance runner, rushing to make and serve dinner by the time the family congregates at the table. If Madame manages to put a handmade meal on the table, she feels she has scored. The name of the game far too often is frozen TV dinner.

Some people, I will admit grudgingly, are by nature beau-

tifully organized and also have endless time at their dis-
posal. In my envious mind's eye I see them: at 8:30 A.M. they
sit down with coffee and pencil in hand and plan their
week's menus. Then, majestically, dressed in their Country
Casuals, off they go leisurely shopping—to one market for
meats, then across town to the produce specialists, a browse
at the cheese shop for interesting canapé items. Then there
is a visit to still another shop for that special sourdough
bread that George adores. By 3:30 P.M. when the children
return from school, the potatoes are pared and diced, the
soup is merrily simmering, and the pie is contentedly baking in the oven.

Such precise organization isn't total fantasy, but how
many of us in these scattered, broken-up, mobile days have
time for such an orderly pacing of a day? Far too many of
us ping-pong from school to market to divers errands to be
able to operate so efficiently.

It is for the majority of less organized types that this book
is written. To overcome the Hour of Instant Insanity that
often passes for dinnertime, I thought the book should en-
compass meals that are patient, that *like* to be kept waiting,
and that can be planned and prepared ahead, maybe even
a full day ahead in some instances, and set aside until Insanity Hour arrives. I have evolved a system that works for
me (and hopefully for you) and helps to avert those panic-
laden situations that far too often seem part of mobile
modern life.

This book first sprouted as an idea of recipes for commuters, or rather, commuters' wives, those harassed gals
who wait and also stand and serve (but mostly wait, and
wait, and wait . . .). As the wife of a long-time commuter,
who is a not-too-patient rider of New Haven Railroad rails,
I know all the hazards of the course.

Even in the bad old days, the distant days of earlier commuters such as Julius Caesar, I'll bet Signora C. had her
moments of anxiety as she watched her saltimbocca turn
into a Roman ruin or her Caesar's salad wilt, as she waited
for the chariots to return from Gaul. Or imagine Mrs. Co-
lumbus, scanning the horizon, waiting for the ship to come
in, and trying to keep the gazpacho chilled. And I suspect
it was no boon to be in Boonesville when Daniel was late
to dinner. Most likely the burgoo had bur-gone. Mary Lin-

coln would probably have liked to split more than hairs
when her husband, a legendary dawdler, sauntered in for
his evening supper—or what was left of it. The smoke coming from the Lincoln house probably wasn't coming just
from the stove.

While our country has become increasingly urban and
suburban, still not every man commutes to work. On the
other hand, every woman or homemaker, at one time or another, and usually all too often, is faced with the joyful
alternatives of preparing a slapdash Happening in haste at
dinnertime or watching her elaborately prepared dinner become fossilized from oven fatigue because of husband, teen-
ager or guests' delay.

To get down to the nitty-gritty, the recipes in this book
are for meals that can be prepared and/or assembled in
advance, at odd moments in a hectic day, and then shelved
(or refrigerated) until Fall-Apart Time, *i.e.,* the dinner
hour.

At the last minute, the dishes require a mere reheating
or "finishing off." To lapse into the lingo of a former school-
teacher, these "pre-fixes" lend themselves to some measure
of flexibility, so that calmness and reason may prevail at the
end of the day.

There are occasions, in addition to the family dinner
hour, when pre-fixes are even more welcome. Nothing comes
on so strong at a dinner party as a relaxed hostess, who has
the time to warm up the guests (as the dinner is warming up
in the oven) and get the party moving. Often a dinner party
that dies on its feet does so because the hostess is on *hers,*
because she has abandoned her guests for her stove, leaving
complete strangers to grope their way through a conversational maze, often with little success.

To me, the mark of a successful dinner party is one at
which I have time to talk with my guests. By having the dinner, from canapés to soup to main dish to dessert, all set to
pop into the oven (or ready in the refrigerator) before the
first guest arrives, I am ready for the evening.

Dinner usually can be served at a reasonable hour if it is
assembled ahead. Too many dinners become drinkathons
because the hostess is trying too late to do too many things
in the kitchen. Meanwhile, starving guests are devouring
everything devourable in the living room, even the canapé

picks, in a desperate last-ditch effort to survive the cocktail hour, which is fast approaching the eleventh hour, literally. By the time dinner finally staggers to the table, so do most of the guests, in no condition to appreciate the tender loving care the hostess has lavished (far too lengthily) on the food.

I have a friend who begins to chop her first onion for the main course the moment the last guest arrives at her dinner party. We call her dinners Martha's Midnight Madness, because that is the earliest hour at which she manages to serve the meal. Anyone who has survived such refined torture once will fortify himself with a triple-decker sandwich just before leaving for Martha's drink-in.

I savor the cocktail hour as much as anyone, but I also savor good food, and I want my guests to—particularly when the preparation of it has involved a considerable expenditure of time, a commodity I hoard as jealously as a Silas Marner. Please, let the only glazed look at a dinner party of mine be on the carrots or ham. In short, let's have meals that can wait rather than guests who *must* wait.

Many cookbooks err on the side of blandness in seasonings, so I think I should stand up and be counted and say straight out that the seasonings in most of the recipes in this book lean slightly in the other direction. In other words, recipes with garlic or curry might have a bit more than a bland palate would be happy with. So if your palate doesn't like to be tickled, you might temper your spice measurements slightly. An East Indian would most likely find *my* spice measurements bland by *his* standards, although I would categorize them as moderately spicy. In recipes using ham or bacon, however, I go lightly on the salt. Individual hams differ so in saltiness, I recommend playing the saltiness by ear—or taste. Seasoning is highly individual, and one should go about it gingerly. A good cook plays the taste-and-test game as she goes.

Most recipes specify whether fresh or dried herbs should be used. Dried herbs are more concentrated, thus smaller amounts are needed. I would strongly urge any serious cook to establish a flowerpot of basil, for even more than fresh chives or parsley, fresh basil is a totally different animal from the dried variety. Nothing adds quite so much piquancy and excitement to a salad or main course as a few leaves of this wondrous plant. What a pity for housewives everywhere that commercial gardeners don't distribute it as freely as parsley. Heaven knows, it is vastly superior as a flavoring.

To sum up, the recipes in this book, whether for dinner, lunch or breakfast, may all be readied ahead of time. Each recipe is calculated to serve six medium-hungry adult-sized people. I settled on six as a likely number, as I think it is about the average family size, and also a good number for a small dinner party. All the recipes are flexible—they have to be to withstand an unpredictable, make-ahead schedule— and can be expanded or contracted to fit specific situations or expediencies. Without any further pontificating, onward to the kitchen and a future of unhurried, unharried meals— staked out in advance, ready and willing to wait.

Bon Appétit—sooner or later!

Meals That Can Wait

CHAPTER I

Cockles and Mussels and Other Fruits of the Sea

Even before Jacqueline Kennedy Onassis put the White House on a four-course schedule, we Americans had been simplifying our dining habits. It is rare today to find a fish course, except at the fanciest, most formal dinners.

That doesn't mean the consumption of seafood has declined. Quite the contrary. We are probably eating more varieties of seafood than ever before. For instance, in former days in the small inland New England town in which I live, nobody but immigrant Italians ate mussels. Now they are party fare at many a Yankee dinner. Even conchs and squid are available at our local fish market.

1

Of course no seafood surpasses shrimp in current popularity. Part of its appeal, no doubt, is its versatility, the number of ways in which it may be served. As hors d'oeuvre, salad or main course, this little pink delicacy may be combined with so many other foods that its uses seem endless.

There are, however, many other sea delights, and recipes for preparing them ahead of time, as you will find in this chapter.

Curried Seafood Potpourri

Curried dishes, like many made with tomato sauce, improve with age (within limits), making them ideal for early-in-the-day or night-before preparation. The flavors in this dish need a little time to get acquainted. I usually make it early in the morning and refrigerate it all day long. It is very flexible and can be freely adapted to suit the seafood of the season (or what is available in your local market).

3 Tbs. butter
3 cloves garlic, peeled but not chopped
3 scallions, chopped (or 3 Tbs. minced onion)
2½ Tbs. flour
2½ Tbs. curry powder
1½ cups cream
¾ cup chicken stock, broth, or canned consommé (undiluted)

1½ cups fresh cooked shrimp (frozen or canned also permissible)
1 cup fresh cooked or canned crab meat
1 cup fresh oysters, barely cooked
3 Tbs. lemon juice
1½ Tbs. chutney
3 cups cooked rice
½ cup chutney
½ cup almonds, chopped
½ cup raisins, chopped

Any combination of seafood may be used, as long as it equals 3½ cups in all. Lobster, clams or scallops, lightly cooked, may be substituted for the seafoods listed.

Melt butter in top of double boiler. Add garlic and scallion or onion and cook gently over high heat for 5 minutes, or until soft and brown. Remove garlic and discard. Add flour and curry powder to the onion, stir into a smooth paste, and add the cream and stock slowly. Stir and cook over low fire until mixture is thick and smooth. Add seafood, lemon juice and chutney. Mix well. Refrigerate, covered, until dinnertime. When your husband is halfway through his cocktail, remove dish from refrigerator and reheat in saucepan. Serve over hot rice, with side dishes of chutney, almonds and raisins. Serves 6.

Mussels Pilakisi

The ancients may not have been talking about mussels when they referred to ambrosia, but this succulent seafood is *my* idea of ambrosia. Served cold in this Turkish recipe, they make a lovely appetizer or first course at dinner.

36 *mussels*
4 *cups water*
½ *tsp. salt*
½ *cup flour (more if necessary)*
⅛ *cup water (more if necessary)*
¾ *cup olive oil*
1 *large onion, chopped fine*
1 *carrot, chopped fine*
¼ *cup olive oil*
3 *cloves garlic, minced*

1 *small raw potato, chopped fine*
1 *small parsnip, chopped fine*
½ *tsp. sugar*
⅓ *cup water*
½ *tsp. salt (more to taste)*
1 *tsp. flour*
1½ *tsps. tomato sauce*
1 *bunch fresh parsley, chopped*
1 *tsp. dill weed or fresh dill*

To clean mussel shells, first cut beards with kitchen shears, then scrub vigorously with a vegetable brush. Soak briefly in cold water and scrub again. Rinse and drain. Cook quickly in 4 cups water to which you have added ½ teaspoon salt, until shells are steamed open. Cool and drain. Remove mussels from shells and drain them on absorbent toweling. Make a paste of ½ cup flour and ⅛ cup water. Paste should be fairly thick, but not gummy. Add more water if needed. Dip mussels in this paste and fry quickly in ¾ cup hot olive oil. Drain on absorbent paper. Meanwhile, sauté onion and carrot in ¼ cup olive oil in large skillet. After 3 minutes, add garlic, potato, parsnip, sugar and ⅓ cup water. Salt to taste and cook over low heat until all vegetables are tender but not mushy. Mix 1 teaspoon flour with tomato sauce and add to vegetables. Continue cooking until water is absorbed. Add drained mussels and parsley. Cook 5 minutes longer. Mix well and remove from heat. Cool. Fill mussel shells with mixture, sprinkle dill on top and refrigerate until needed. Serve cold. 6 servings.

Middle Eastern Mussels

This appetizer works well cold or hot, but I think there is a little piquancy if served cold.

30 *fresh mussels, well scrubbed*
  and debearded in cold water
¾ *cup white wine, sauterne pre-*
  ferred
1 *tsp. salt*
1 *large onion, chopped fine*
1 *garlic clove, minced*
2½ *Tbs. olive oil*
¾ *cup raw rice*

⅓ *cup pine nuts*
⅓ *cup currants*
1 *tsp. allspice*
⅛ *tsp. oregano*
¾ *tsp. ground coriander*
⅛ *tsp. nutmeg*
½ *tsp. black pepper (more to*
  taste)
3 *Tbs. chopped fresh parsley*

Place well-cleaned mussels in a large kettle. Add 1¼ cups water, along with wine and salt. Steam mussels, covered, approximately 10 minutes, or until shells open. Set kettle aside. In deep large skillet, lightly sauté onion and garlic in heated olive oil. When onion is golden, add rice, stir, and sauté for 2 or 3 minutes. Pour 1¼ cups mussel liquid over the rice. Cover skillet and simmer over low heat 10 minutes until most of the liquid is absorbed. Stir, then add nuts, currants, all seasonings and parsley. Mix well and continue simmering covered for 5 minutes. Remove mussels from shells and stir lightly into rice mixture. Set aside to cool. Stuff mussel shells with mixture and refrigerate *at least* 3 hours. If you prefer serving them hot, set stuffed mussels aside in shallow baking pan covered with aluminum foil. Keep warm in low 250° F. oven until company arrives. Serves 6.

Salade de la Mer

You needn't be vacationing by the shore to enjoy this yummy sea-food salad. I call it Summer Solace, for it can be prepared in the morning before the weather gets too warm and steamy, then pulled out of the refrigerator at serving time. Presto! a delicious main dish for August's dog days. To say nothing of June's or July's.

½ *cup onion, chopped fine*
3 *Tbs. butter*
1½ *cups raw rice*
2¾ *cups chicken broth (or con-*
  sommé)
1 *tsp. turmeric (optional)*
¼ *tsp. dried tarragon*
Salt and pepper to taste
1 *cup large shrimp, cooked and*
  coarsely chopped
½ *cup lobster, cooked and*
  coarsely chopped

⅓ *cup canned tuna, in large*
  chunks
1 *cup mussels, cooked (optional,*
  as not always available)
¾ *cup raw mushrooms, sliced*
  thin
½ *cup green pepper, sliced thin*
6 *Tbs. olive oil*
2 *Tbs. wine vinegar*
2 *hard-boiled eggs, in wedges*
2 *tomatoes, cut in wedges*
6 *ripe olives, whole*
1 *tsp. chopped fresh parsley*

Sauté the chopped onion in melted butter until clear. Add the rice and cook over low heat until rice is yellow. Stir often. Heat chicken broth to boiling and pour over rice, along with turmeric and tarragon. Stir once, cover and gently simmer until the broth is absorbed, approximately 20 to 30 minutes. Add salt and pepper to taste. Set aside and then chill thoroughly. About ½ hour before serving time, remove rice from refrigerator, add all the seafoods, raw mushrooms and green pepper. Mix lightly. Combine olive oil and vinegar and add to the rice mixture. If not moist enough, add a little more oil-vinegar (in 3-to-1 proportions). Arrange in a mound on a platter, garnish with eggs, tomatoes and olives. Sprinkle with parsley. Return to refrigerator until ready to serve. Serves 6.

Sesame Swordfish Steaks

Swordfish is almost impossible to ruin, and, at its best, there is no better fish around. Here's a recipe that shows this fish off superbly.

3 *large swordfish steaks, 1 inch thick*	¼ *tsp. dried tarragon*
3 *Tbs. butter*	½ *tsp. dried thyme*
1 *cup crisp bread crumbs, crumbled fine*	1½ *tsps. salt*
½ *cup butter, melted*	¼ *tsp. black pepper, freshly ground*
	3½ *Tbs. sesame seeds, toasted*

Wash swordfish steaks and pat dry. Place in a well-greased long shallow rectangular pan. Spread 1 tablespoon butter over each steak. Heat in a 350° F. oven until fat oozes on top of steak—approximately 10 minutes. Remove from oven, scrape off fat, turn steaks over, and return to oven. When fat begins to ooze on second side, remove, scrape, and set aside. Meanwhile, combine bread crumbs, melted butter, herbs, salt and pepper. Mix well and add sesame seeds. Pour over the steaks. When guests and husband are midway through their drinks, return pan to oven (350° F.) and bake an additional 15 minutes until lightly browned on top. Delicious with a rice or vegetable casserole and salad. Serves 6.

Kilich Shish, or Turkish Swordfish Kabob

This different way of serving swordfish makes it very appealing for a belated family or company dinner.

3 *lbs. fresh or fresh-frozen sword-*   2 *Tbs. olive oil*
   fish   2 *Tbs. lemon juice*
½ to ¾ *tsp. black pepper, freshly*   2 *Tbs. onion juice*
   ground   6 *whole bay leaves*
Salt to taste

Trim the skin off the swordfish and cut fish into 1-inch cubes. Place cubes on a large flat platter. Sprinkle with pepper and salt. Blend together the other ingredients, except the bay leaves. Mix well, add the bay leaves, and pour the mixture over the swordfish cubes. Refrigerate at least 6 hours, turning cubes occasionally. At mealtime, thread the fish cubes on skewers, ready to be popped into broiler as soon as the errant guests or husband arrive. During the 10 minutes or so it takes the cubes to cook, turn skewers once or twice until fish is browned. Serve with the following Lemon Sauce. Serves 6.

Lemon Sauce

This easy-to-whip-up sauce may be made while the above *Kilich Shish* are in the oven.

¼ *bunch fresh parsley*   1½ *Tbs. olive oil*
1 *large lemon*   *Salt to taste*

Chop the parsley very fine and place in medium mixing bowl. Add the juice from the fresh lemon, olive oil and salt. Whip vigorously with a fork. Pour over hot, broiled *Kilich Shish* at the table.

Crab-Pasta Casserole

I like to serve this easy-to-make dish for dinner on matinee or bridge days. It tastes extra special and conceals the fact that I have *not* been slaving over a hot oven all day. I haven't even been home all afternoon.

3 *cups macaroni or shell pasta,*   1½ *cans king crab meat* (6½ *oz.*)
   cooked   3 *Tbs. chopped parsley*
1 *large onion, chopped coarsely*   ⅓ *cup flour, sifted*
½ *tsp. Tabasco sauce*   ¼ *tsp. Worcestershire sauce*
2¼ *cups milk*   2½ *tsps. paprika*
⅓ *cup butter, melted*   ½ *tsp. dried tarragon*
¾ *tsp. salt*   ¾ *cup soft bread crumbs*
¾ *tsp. dry mustard*   ¾ *cup sharp Cheddar cheese,*
¼ *tsp. white pepper*   *loosely grated*

Grease a 2-quart casserole and line the bottom with the cooked pasta. Place remaining ingredients, except for bread crumbs and cheese, in large mixing bowl and mix together vigorously. Be sure the crab meat is well broken up. Pour mixture evenly over the pasta in the casserole. Sprinkle bread crumbs over the top and grated cheese over the bread crumbs. Cover and refrigerate until dinnertime. At about the time your family is *expected,* remove casserole from refrigerator and allow to stand on top of stove until chill is off the casserole. When your Johnny-come-latelies actually *appear,* place the casserole in a preheated 350° F. oven and bake for 30 to 35 minutes. Serve hot with warm rolls and a green salad. Serves 6.

Crab Mousse

I call this my favorite beach dinner—not to take to the beach, but to have waiting in the refrigerator after spending a hot day at the beach. So nice to come home to (try that orchestrated!). It is also a heavenly choice for a spring or summer luncheon main course.

½ *cup chicken broth*	1½ *Tbs. onion, chopped*
2 *envelopes plain gelatin*	¼ *tsp. dried tarragon*
½ *cup cold water*	¼ *tsp. dried marjoram*
2 *Tbs. sherry*	1 *Tb. chopped parsley*
2 *eggs, separated*	½ *tsp. Tabasco sauce*
1 *can crab meat, flaked (6 ozs.)*	¼ *tsp. Worcestershire sauce*
½ *cup mayonnaise*	1 *cup medium cream*
1 *celery stalk, cubed*	

Heat, but do not boil, chicken broth. Dissolve gelatin in cold water, then slowly add to hot mixture. Pour into blender, add sherry, cover, and blend at high speed for 35 seconds. Add the egg yolks, crab meat, mayonnaise, celery, onion, herbs, Tabasco and Worcestershire sauce. Cover again and blend at high speed 10 seconds longer. Remove cover, keep motor going at low speed, and gently pour in the cream. Turn off motor. Fold mixture into the egg whites, which have been beaten stiff. Pour into a mold and chill. It takes at least an hour for mixture to set, but can be kept chilled all day. Serves 6.

Crab Meat-Stuffed Green Pepper

Some people (like Lester Brooks) will eat green peppers stuffed with ANYTHING. But there are others who disdain stuffed peppers as "leftover improvisations" or "economy meals." Such scornful souls have to be lured to the pepper with promises of exotica. For such cynics, *voilà!*

6 *green peppers, whole*	2 *Tbs. cornstarch*
1 *cup light cream*	½ *tsp. dried tarragon*
¼ *cup butter*	1¼ *tsps. salt*
½ *tsp. nutmeg*	1 *cup rice, cooked*
⅓ *cup dry white wine*	2 *cups cooked crab meat*
1½ *tsps. lemon juice*	½ *tsp. paprika*

Wash peppers, remove tops and seeds. Parboil peppers briefly—approximately 5 minutes. Drain and set aside. Scald the cream and add butter and nutmeg to it. In a mixing bowl combine the wine, lemon juice, cornstarch, tarragon and salt. Slowly add to the cream. Cook over a low heat until thick, stirring constantly. Combine the rice and crab meat in a large bowl. Mix the sauce with them, and then spoon the mixture into the cooled peppers. Place peppers in a snug, well-greased, meatloaf-sized pan. Cover with foil and refrigerate until ready to heat. When the guests are at bay with canapés *cum* cocktails, remove foil, sprinkle the tops of the peppers with paprika, and bake in a preheated (350° F.) oven for 15 to 20 minutes. (If you need to keep the peppers a bit longer, replace foil, and turn oven down to 250°F. for an extra 5 or 10 minutes.) Serves 6.

Deviled Crab Shells

Easy to make, easy to bake, easier to eat—no matter when you serve them.

2 *Tbs. butter or margarine*	*Dash of Tabasco sauce*
1 *large onion, minced*	½ *tsp. salt (more to taste)*
1 *fat clove garlic, minced*	¼ *tsp. black pepper, freshly*
1 *medium green pepper, minced*	*ground*
3 *Tbs. finely chopped parsley*	3 *cups flaked crab meat*
1½ *tsps. sugar*	¼ *cup cracker crumbs*
1 *Tb. catsup*	6 *crab shells or baking shells*
2 *tsps. Worcestershire sauce*	1¼ *cups grated Cheddar cheese*
1 *Tb. (heaping) chili sauce*	

Melt the butter or margarine in a large skillet. Sauté onion, garlic, green pepper and parsley in the skillet until limp. Add the sugar, catsup, and all the seasonings. Simmer over the lowest heat for 10 to

15 minutes. Then add the crab meat and mix well. Add just a little of the cracker crumbs, enough to give body to the mixture in the skillet. Set mixture aside for at least 1 hour, or as long as 4 hours if refrigerated. At the witching hour, when family and/or friends have assembled, mound the crab mixture into crab shells or baking shells. Sprinkle grated cheese over the top of each shell, and bake in a 350° F. oven for 15 minutes, or until nicely brown on top. Serves 6.

Sherried Crab-Stuffed Artichokes

Spain has many attributes, but for gourmets, surely one special aspect of this fascinating country is the prevalence of artichokes. In season, they are as common as peas. For us, the artichoke is still a symbol of special dining, as you will find when you serve this dish—unless of course your guests are Spanish.

6 *artichokes*	2 *small (6½ oz.) cans crab meat,*
2 *Tbs. butter*	*drained*
2 *Tbs. flour*	¼ *tsp. salt*
1 *cup cream (½ milk if you*	¼ *tsp. white pepper*
prefer)	3 *Tbs. grated Cheddar cheese*
1 *Tb. sherry*	

Boil the artichokes in salted water (to cover) 20 to 30 minutes or until tender when a fork is poked into them. Remove from water and drain by inverting the artichokes. When cool, spread the leaves apart, remove the center leaves around the choke, and use a teaspoon to dig out the hairy choke. Make a cream sauce with the butter, flour and cream. Thin with the sherry, keep stirring, and add the crab meat. Mix well, season to taste, and spoon the mixture into the artichoke hollows. Place the stuffed artichokes in a flat baking dish and set aside or refrigerate until needed. Remove from refrigerator and allow to stand at room temperature 15 to 30 minutes before reheating. Then sprinkle grated cheese over the creamed crab meat and bake artichokes in a 350° F. oven for 15 minutes or so, long enough to heat thoroughly and brown ever so slightly. Lovely served with a tossed salad, popovers or hot bread. Serves 6.

Crab Meat Creole

This variation on a familiar seafood theme (I have one friend whose sole party repertoire is Shrimp Creole) is a pleasing change, and easy to manage ahead of schedule.

2 *Tbs. bacon fat*
2 *medium onions, minced*
3 *cloves garlic, minced fine*
1 *Tb. chopped celery leaves*
1 *stalk celery, minced*
1 *green pepper, minced*
3 *Tbs. flour*
1 *cup clam juice or broth*
1 *large can tomatoes (1 lb. 12 ozs.)*
1 *small bay leaf*

½ *tsp. black pepper, freshly*
    ground
½ *tsp. salt (more to taste)*
¼ *tsp. chili powder*
2½ *Tbs. chopped fresh parsley*
¼ *tsp. dried thyme*
⅛ *tsp. Tabasco sauce*
2 *tsps. Worcestershire sauce*
4 *slices bacon, cooked and diced*
1½ *lbs. cooked crab meat*
4 *cups cooked rice*

Melt bacon fat in a large skillet. Sauté onion, garlic, celery leaves, celery, and green pepper for 6 minutes. Blend in flour until a smooth paste is formed. Slowly add clam juice. Stir until slightly thickened. Add canned tomatoes with liquid and keep stirring. Add bay leaf and simmer over low fire. Combine all spices and herbs in a small bowl, add Tabasco and Worcestershire sauces, mix well, and add to skillet. Stir in bacon. Add chunky crab meat and mix thoroughly. Simmer 10 minutes. Cover and set aside. At dinnertime, reheat over lowest heat, and allow to simmer at least 30 minutes, half-covered. If the meal must wait even longer, add a little water (approximately ¼ cup at a time) and stir often. Serve on a bed of fluffy hot rice, or in the center of a rice ring mold. Serves 6..

Crab Soufflé

Dishes that can be prepared hours before the party are always welcome news to harried hostesses. This dish goes even further—it can (and should) be assembled the night before. The result, when it finally emerges from the oven, is ambrosia!

9 *slices white bread, crusts*
    trimmed
2 *small (6½ oz.) cans crab meat*
1 *medium onion, chopped*
1 *Tb. chopped green pepper*
¾ *cup celery, chopped*
⅓ *cup mayonnaise*

3 *large eggs, slightly beaten*
2¼ *cups milk*
¾ *can cream of mushroom soup,*
    undiluted
¼ *cup finely grated sharp Ched-*
    dar cheese
½ *tsp. paprika*

Break 5 slices of the bread into quarter-sized bites and arrange in the bottom of a large shallow baking dish. Mix together the crab meat, onion, green pepper, celery and mayonnaise. Mix well, then spread the mixture over the bread in the casserole. Place remaining bread slices over the mixture. Beat eggs and milk together and pour over the casserole. Cover and refrigerate overnight or for at least 10 hours. Remove from refrigerator ½ hour before baking, to allow casserole to warm to room temperature. (This makes for less baking time.) Place casserole in preheated 325° F. oven and heat for 20 minutes. Remove from oven, pour all the cream of mushroom soup except ¼ can over the top. Return casserole to oven for 45 minutes. If guests show no signs of hunger, pour the remaining ¼ can soup over the top to moisten the casserole, sprinkle the cheese and paprika over all, and return casserole to oven, stretching oven time an extra 15 to 20 minutes. (If guests are predictable, you can pour all the soup over the casserole at one time, sprinkle cheese and paprika over all at the same time and bake a mere 45 minutes.) The beauty of this dish is that it has the texture and appearance of a soufflé, but can dawdle in the oven many minutes longer than a real soufflé. Serves 6.

Scallops en Casserole

It took years, but my husband finally convinced me that scallops were edible. Now one of my favorite games is to find new and fascinating ways to eat them. For instance:

3 *Tbs. butter*	½ *tsp. dried thyme*
1 *small onion, minced*	⅛ *tsp. powdered fennel*
1 *lb. mushrooms, cleaned and*	*(optional)*
sliced	1 *bay leaf*
½ *cup dry white wine*	2 *lbs. scallops, well washed*
⅛ *tsp. nutmeg*	3 *Tbs. butter*
1 *Tb. chopped fresh parsley*	¼ *cup flour*
1½ *Tbs. lemon juice*	1 *cup light cream*
½ *tsp. black pepper*	½ *tsp. Worcestershire sauce*
¾ *tsp. salt*	½ *tsp. grated lemon rind*
½ *cup dry white wine*	½ *cup grated Parmesan cheese*
¾ *cup water*	⅛ *tsp. cayenne pepper*
½ *tsp. dried basil*	

In a large heavy skillet, melt 3 tablespoons butter and sauté onions until limp. Add mushrooms and sauté until butter is absorbed—just a few minutes. Pour in ½ cup wine, nutmeg, parsley, lemon juice, black pepper, and salt. Cook over low fire until wine evaporates. Cover skillet and remove from the heat. In a large saucepan, heat remaining ½ cup wine with water, basil, thyme, fennel, and bay leaf. Just before mixture comes to a boil, add scallops, cover pan, and cook gently for 5 minutes. Lift out scallops and set aside. Strain sauce and set aside. In a second skillet, melt remaining butter, and add flour. Blend into a smooth paste. Stir in 1¼ cups of scallop liquid and 1 cup cream. Stir until blended and thickened. Pour ½ the sauce into the first (or mushroom) skillet, add Worcestershire sauce, lemon rind and mix well. Spread ½ the mushroom mixture in the bottom of a large round greased casserole. Sprinkle ½ the scallops over, add remaining mushrooms, then a last layer of scallops. Stir ¼ cup Parmesan and cayenne pepper into remaining cream sauce, and pour over the top of the casserole. Sprinkle remaining Parmesan over all. Cover and set aside—or refrigerate.

This gala dish sounds more complex than it actually is. It can be assembled hours ahead. Actual heat-up time is brief and last-minute. As husband rounds the corner, place casserole in a preheated 425° F. oven for a 10 to 15 minute warm-up. If his ablutions take longer than that, simply sprinkle a little more Parmesan over the casserole, turn oven down to 325° and keep a few minutes longer. Serve bubbly hot and delicately browned . . . with hot buttered rolls and a tossed green salad. Serves 6.

Shrimp and Avocado Mousse

When two of one's favorite foods are combined in a single recipe, the preparation is sheer bliss—and anticipation. That's how I feel each time I make this special mousse.

1½ Tbs. plain gelatin	2 tsps. lemon juice
⅓ cup cold water	1½ cups mashed avocado
¾ cup boiling water	1 cup cooked shrimp, coarsely
⅛ tsp. curry powder	chopped
1 tsp. salt	½ cup heavy cream, whipped
1½ tsps. Worcestershire sauce	½ cup mayonnaise
1 tsp. chives, chopped	

Soak the gelatin in cold water for 5 minutes to soften it. Then pour boiling water over it to dissolve it. Cool. Combine curry powder, salt,

Worcestershire sauce, chives, and lemon juice. Mix well and add to the gelatin. Stir in the avocado pulp mixed with the shrimp. Mix lightly but well. Refrigerate until mixture begins to thicken. Then carefully fold in the whipped cream and mayonnaise. Place mixture in slightly greased mold and refrigerate again—at least 5 hours. Unmold on a platter with lettuce. Serve and enjoy. Serves 6.

Shrimp Soufflé

This is one of those magical dishes that looks like pure legerdemain, but is easier to prepare than the proverbial apple pie. I call it my "Instant Acclaim" company dish. It is so impressive it dazzles guests, yet is embarrassingly easy to make. Assemble it in the morning, stash it in the refrigerator, then about half an hour before guests arrive, bring it to the surface and let it rest at room temperature. Bake it for half an hour during the final round of cocktails.

9 *slices white bread, crusts trimmed*	⅓ *cup butter or margarine, melted*
¾ *lb. Old English (or very sharp Cheddar) cheese*	4 *large eggs, beaten*
1½ *lbs. shelled shrimp, slightly cooked*	3 *cups milk at room temperature*
	¾ *tsp. dry mustard*
	½ *tsp. salt*

Grease a medium (2 to 2½-quart) casserole. Break the trimmed bread into quarter-sized pieces. Cut cheese into small cubes. Place a layer of shrimp in the bottom of the casserole, add a layer of bread pieces, then a layer of cheese cubes. Alternate layers until the casserole is filled. Pour melted butter or margarine over the top. Beat eggs, add the milk to them, then mustard and salt. Mix well and pour over the casserole. Cover. Refrigerate *at least* 5 hours. Bake 30 to 40 minutes in a medium (350° F.) oven, uncovered.

The beauty of this as a meal-that-can-wait is that the oven time is quite flexible. While the dish looks like a soufflé, it can be served either quite moist and bubbly or slightly browned and a bit drier. If guests dawdle, turn oven down to 300° after the first 20 minutes of cooking. Serves 6.

Shrimpy Peppers

Another stuffed pepper recipe for people who didn't think they liked stuffed peppers.

6 *medium green peppers, whole*
1 *medium onion, chopped fine*
1 *clove garlic, minced fine*
2 *Tbs. butter or margarine*
½ *cup raw rice, well washed*
1½ *cups condensed chicken consommé*

1 *lb. raw shrimp, shelled, deveined and chopped*
⅛ *tsp. dried tarragon*
¾ *tsp. dill seed, crushed*
½ *tsp. salt (more to taste)*
¼ *tsp. black pepper, freshly ground*

Cut tops from green peppers and clean out seeds. Parboil 4 to 6 minutes in boiling salted water. Drain and cool. Sauté onion and garlic in melted butter until golden. Add rice, continue sautéing until yellow, but stir often to prevent sticking to skillet. Heat consommé separately. When hot, add it to the rice-onion mixture. Stir, cover skillet, and continue cooking over low heat. Cook 8 to 10 minutes. Then add chopped shrimp, tarragon, dill seed, salt and pepper, and a little water if needed. Cook another 5 to 7 minutes. Mix well and cool. Use mixture for stuffing peppers. When stuffed, place peppers in a shallow baking pan. Set aside or refrigerate until needed. At dinnertime, allow peppers to stand at room temperature for 15 minutes or so. Then place water in the pan ½ inch deep. Heat peppers in a preheated 325° F. oven for 15 to 20 minutes. Add water if the water in the pan evaporates. If dinner is delayed, lower oven heat to 275° and cover pan. Let remain in oven an additional 10 to 15 minutes. Serve hot with a cream or cheese sauce. Serves 6.

Chilled Shrimp with Herb Sauce

During my days (and nights) in the Philippines, I never ceased being amazed at the hot, heavy, elaborate meals served in that humid tropical climate. As a result, siesta was almost mandatory. There is a theory prevalent there that hot foods help the body combat the heat. I persist in clinging to my theory that cold foods do a summer make—cooler. If you can't beat the heat, don't fight it. Enjoy it with this chilled shrimp.

3½ *lbs. fresh shrimp, cooked*
3 *Tbs. wine vinegar*
6 *Tbs. Creole (horseradish) mustard*
1 *tsp. white pepper*
½ *tsp. garlic salt*
½ *small white onion, chopped fine*

½ *tsp. dill weed*
½ *cup olive oil*
1½ *Tbs. hot paprika*
¾ *tsp. salt*
1 *tsp. chopped parsley*
1 *celery heart, chopped*

Place the cleaned, boiled shrimp in the refrigerator 3 to 4 hours before serving to insure a good deep chill. The herb sauce may be made the night before it is needed. Mix all the remaining ingredients, except the celery heart, together. Put in blender at high speed for 10 seconds. Remove, add celery heart, mix. Keep in refrigerator until needed. Shake and pour over shrimp arranged on lettuce leaves. Makes a really special luncheon main course or part of a cold buffet in the evening. Serves 6.

Jambalaya

So much of what we consider Southern cooking has transplanted African roots. This classic Creole stew is an example. Oysters make it even more special.

1 *bay leaf*	5 *Tbs. butter*
3 *whole cloves*	2 *cloves garlic, minced*
6 *peppercorns*	½ *green pepper, chopped*
¼ *tsp. celery seed*	1 *large onion, chopped fine*
½ *tsp. thyme*	1 *8-oz. can tomato sauce*
¼ *tsp. rosemary*	1 *6-oz. can tomato paste*
½ *tsp. dried red peppers*	1½ *tsps. chili powder*
1 *lb. raw shrimp*	2 *cups raw rice*
18 *oysters*	3¾ *cups water*

Make a *bouquet garni* of the bay leaf, cloves, peppercorns, celery seed, thyme, rosemary and dried red peppers. Tie them tightly in a small square of cheesecloth. Put the *bouquet garni,* along with the cleaned, raw shrimp, into a medium-sized pot of boiling water. Cook at high speed for approximately 10 minutes. Drain, set shrimp aside, but save the water. In a small pot, heat the oysters in their own liquid for 4 to 5 minutes. Save the liquid, but remove oysters to a skillet and sauté them in butter for 2 minutes. Add garlic, green pepper, and onion. Sauté gently for 5 minutes. Slowly add tomato sauce and paste, chili powder, and the oyster and shrimp liquids. Stir well and continue simmering. Meanwhile, cook the rice in 3¾ cups water until quite firm, usually 10 to 12 minutes. When cooked, add rice to tomato sauce-oyster mixture, stirring well. Add shrimp and stir lightly. Remove mixture to a covered casserole (largish) and refrigerate until needed. At dinnertime, allow casserole to dechill for ½ hour before putting it, still covered, into a 325° F. oven. Heat 15 minutes at least before serving. If dinner must wait, turn oven down to 300°, and add a little water or tomato juice to casserole. Serves 6.

Shrimp Creole

There are probably as many versions of this Creole specialty as of Jambalaya. One ingredient is common to all: shrimp, big, luscious, succulent. Y'all try this one now.

3 *lbs. raw shrimp*
½ *tsp. dried thyme*
4 *peppercorns*
3 *whole cloves*
1 *dried red pepper*
1 *large bay leaf*
¾ *tsp. celery salt*
1 *tsp. onion salt*
1 *tsp. garlic salt*
3 *cups shrimp water*
½ *tsp. sugar*
2 *tsps. Creole seasoning or chili powder*

2 *Tbs. bacon fat (or butter; but I prefer the bacon flavor)*
2 *large onions, chopped coarse*
1 *large green pepper, chopped*
2 *fat cloves garlic, minced*
3 *stalks celery, chopped*
1 *cup fresh mushrooms, sliced (optional)*
1 *7-oz. can tomato paste*
2 *fresh tomatoes, quartered*
½ *tsp. salt*
¼ *tsp. black pepper*
4 *cups cooked rice*

Clean the shrimp and boil in 1 quart salted water for 10 minutes. Drain, but save the shrimp water. Plunge shrimp immediately into cold water, drain, and set aside. Add thyme, peppercorns, cloves, dried red pepper, bay leaf, celery salt, onion salt, and garlic salt to shrimp water. Add sugar and Creole seasoning and set aside. In a large skillet, heat bacon fat and sauté onions, green pepper, garlic and celery until golden. Add mushrooms and cook lightly. Slowly add 1 cup shrimp water, tomato paste and fresh tomatoes. Simmer slowly, adding second cup of shrimp water, salt and pepper. Simmer gently for 30 minutes. Add shrimp and mix well. Scoop mixture into a medium-sized casserole, cover and refrigerate until mealtime. Heat in low oven (325° F.) for at least 30 minutes. You can keep this much longer—another 45 minutes anyway—by turning oven to 300° and adding the last cupful of shrimp water little by little. Serve in casserole with boiled rice as accompaniment, or, if you prefer, pour the Shrimp Creole over a bed of rice. Serves 6.

Macaroni-Oyster Casserole

Our twenty-first President, Chester Arthur, enjoyed this dish. He was one of our great gourmet Presidents, so you are in pretty good company. He served it with turtle steak, but I would recommend something a bit less exotic—the oysters are rich enough.

1½ *cups macaroni, uncooked*	1 *cup grated sharp Cheddar*
3 *cups small oysters, uncooked*	*cheese*
1 *tsp. salt (more to taste)*	3 *Tbs. butter*
½ *tsp. white pepper*	¾ *cup soft bread crumbs, lightly*
2 *tsps. paprika*	*buttered*

Cook the macaroni in boiling salted water until tender. Drain and rinse with hot water. Drain again. Place half the macaroni in a greased baking dish. Add a layer of ½ the oysters. Sprinkle salt, pepper and paprika over the oysters. Sprinkle ⅓ cup grated cheese, dot with butter, and then repeat the layers in the same sequence. End up with a top layer of crumbs mixed with grated cheese. Set aside or refrigerate until serving time. Then place in a hot oven (400° F.) for 15 minutes, or until well heated and lightly browned on top. A dish fit for a king—or a President! Serves 6.

Lobster and Mushroom Supremioso

The English language doesn't print the expression of real superlatives, as the Romance languages do. What I want to suggest is that this company dish is more than just supreme. Try it and make up your own superlatives.

½ *lb. noodles, uncooked*	⅛ *tsp. dried thyme*
⅓ *lb. butter*	½ *tsp. dried parsley*
¾ *lb. fresh mushrooms, sliced*	½ *tsp. dried tarragon*
1½ *lbs. lobster meat, diced*	½ *tsp. paprika*
⅓ *cup sherry*	2 *cups milk*
¾ *tsp. lemon juice*	¾ *cup heavy cream*
½ *cup flour*	8 *Ritz crackers, crushed*
1 *tsp. salt (more to taste)*	2 *Tbs. melted butter*
½ *tsp. white pepper*	

Cook the noodles in boiling salted water for 10 minutes. Rinse in warm water and drain. Rinse and drain again. Meanwhile, heat ½ the butter in a deep skillet and sauté mushrooms gently until lightly brown. Remove mushrooms and reserve, but save butter in skillet. In a double boiler, melt 1½ tablespoons butter, add lobster meat, sherry and lemon juice. Mix lightly, cover and let cook approximately 5 to 6 minutes. Set aside. Add remaining butter to that in the skillet and

over a low fire blend in flour, salt, pepper, thyme, parsley and tarragon. Stir until smooth. Sprinkle in paprika and continue stirring. Add
milk and simmer until mixture comes to a boil. Keep stirring to help
thicken sauce and keep it smooth. Add cream and bring to a boil
again. Simmer 5 minutes as you continue to stir. Add mushrooms and
mix well. Lightly blend in lobster mixture. Place ⅓ of the cooked
noodles in the bottom of a deep, well-greased baking dish. Cover with
a layer of the lobster mixture. Repeat until all are used. Mix cracker
crumbs with 2 tablespoons melted butter. Sprinkle ½ the cracker
mixture over the top of the casserole. Cover and refrigerate until
needed. At dinnertime, preheat oven to 350° F. and remove baking
dish from refrigerator. Allow to warm up for 15 minutes or so before
putting into oven. Dish takes approximately 30 minutes in oven to
warm up properly. If you need to keep it longer than that, lower heat
to 300°, sprinkle remaining cracker crumbs over top and heat until
top is browned. Serve with crispy salad, hot rolls or bread. Serves 6.

Clam and Eggplant Specialité

Eggplant is one of those old-fashioned vegetables that, happily, re-
fuses to pass into obscurity. Thanks to the recent popularity of Greek
and Middle Eastern cookery, this adaptable vegetable has come into
its own again. Enjoy it in this Eastern (U.S., not Middle Eastern) dish,
where it is wedded harmoniously with clams.

1 *large eggplant*	2 *cans minced clams (7 ozs. each)*
3 *Tbs. margarine*	2 *cups bread crumbs*
1 *large onion, minced*	1 *tsp. salt (less if you prefer)*
1 *small clove garlic, minced*	½ *tsp. white pepper*
1 *Tb. minced green pepper*	

Wash the unpeeled eggplant and cut into cubes. Place in enough
boiling salted water to cover. Boil 10 minutes. Drain and set aside.
Heat margarine in a large skillet. Sauté onion, garlic and green pepper
until lightly cooked, about 5 minutes. Drain the clams and save the
liquid. Add clams to skillet and mix lightly with the onion-garlic mixture. Grease a medium casserole. Line the bottom with a layer of bread
crumbs. Add a layer of eggplant, then a layer of clam mixture. Season
each layer lightly with salt and pepper. Repeat, ending up with
crumbs on top. Pour clam liquid over all. Dot with a little margarine
and cover. Refrigerate until needed. Remove from refrigerator ½ hour
before putting in a preheated 350° F. oven. Bake 20 minutes. If errant
family is still overdue, reduce oven heat to 300°, add a few more dots

of butter, and continue baking. For the last 5 minutes of baking, remove cover of casserole and allow top to brown lightly. Serves 6.

Tuna Casserole Supreme

Sometimes I suspect there is a favorite tuna casserole for everybody in the United States. If you think that is going to daunt me, you're wrong. Here is *my* tuna delight, easy to make, easy to please your family with.

2 *cups diced celery*	1 *cup fresh mushrooms*
1 *6½-oz. can tuna fish, drained*	1 *tsp. onion salt*
(7-oz. size)	½ *tsp. dried tarragon*
1 *3-oz. can chow mein noodles*	1 *Tb. dried parsley*
¼ *lb. cashew nuts, in big pieces*	1 *Tb. butter*
½ *cup water chestnuts, sliced*	2 *Tbs. flour*
1 *Tb. butter*	1 *cup milk*

Grease a 2-quart casserole. Mix together the celery, tuna, ¾ of the chow mein noodles, the cashews and water chestnuts. Set aside. In a deep skillet melt 1 tablespoon butter and sauté the sliced mushrooms in it. Add onion salt, tarragon and parsley and mix well. Remove mixture when mushrooms are lightly browned and add to the tuna mixture. Add remaining butter to the skillet, slowly stir in flour and ¼ cup of milk. Add remaining milk slowly, and keep stirring until sauce is slightly thickened. (If speed is of the essence, you can fake the sauce by using 1 can condensed mushroom soup blended with ⅓ cup water.) Sauce should be pourable, not too thick. Pour over tuna mixture, stir well, and place in casserole. Cover and set aside until needed. This dish really just needs a heating up. So at dinnertime, ring the bell, pop the uncovered casserole into a 350° F. oven, sprinkle the remaining noodles over the top and, in the time it takes the children to wash hands and comb their hair, dinner will be ready. If they respond slowly to the dinner bell, lower the oven to 325°, add a few more noodles to the top of the casserole, and let it bubble 10 minutes longer. Serves 6.

Emergency Tuna Special

There comes a time in every woman's life when she has rummaged wildly through the cupboards for her standby can of tuna fish and box of noodles, the better to cope with drop-in-and-stay-on-and-on guests with that classic quickie of all kitchens, the tuna-noodle casserole.

Eureka! you are saying, not again! Hardly, but here is a way to make it a little bit different, a little bit special, and a whole lot handier.

1 *Tb. butter or margarine*
½ *cup chopped celery*
¼ *cup minced onion*
¼ *cup minced green pepper*
½ *lb. fresh musrooms (optional)*
1 *7-oz. can tuna fish*
1 *11¼-oz. can cream of mushroom soup, undiluted*
¼ *cup dry white wine*
⅛ *tsp. basil*

¼ *tsp. dry mustard*
¼ *tsp. dried tarragon*
½ *tsp. salt*
¼ *tsp. black pepper, freshly ground*
¼ *tsp. soy sauce*
1 *lb. noodles, cooked and drained*
¾ *cup freshly grated Parmesan cheese*

Heat the butter in a large skillet over a low heat. Sauté celery, onion, green pepper together until lightly cooked. Add fresh mushrooms, sliced thick. Sauté until barely cooked. Add tuna, broken into medium-sized chunks. Mix well and remove from fire. Combine mushroom soup with the wine, herbs, salt, pepper, and soy sauce. Mix well and add to the tuna mixture. Put into greased baking pan. Add noodles and lightly mix all together. Cover and keep refrigerated until baking time. If you anticipate having to hold dinner in the oven, place casserole, covered, in oven for 15 minutes at 350° F. Then lower heat to 325°, remove cover, sprinkle cheese over top, and allow to bake an additional 25 minutes. If you can plan more accurately, just sprinkle cheese on at the moment you first put casserole in oven at 350°, making baking time total 20 minutes. Serves 6.

Swiss Cheese-Salmon Loaf

Half a loaf may be better than none, but this whole loaf is better still. And so simple to fix ahead of time!

2 *cups canned salmon, flaked*
1 *cup grated Swiss cheese*
1 *cup cracker or crusty bread crumbs*
1 *small onion, grated fine*
1 *stalk celery, chopped very fine*
1 *Tb. butter*
1 *Tb. minced green pepper*

1 *egg, well beaten*
¾ *cup milk*
½ *tsp. salt*
¼ *tsp. black pepper*
Dash of cayenne pepper
2 *tsps. finely chopped parsley*
2 *Tbs. butter, melted*
Additional butter

Combine the salmon with the cheese and mix well. Add the cracker crumbs and mix again. Sauté the onion and celery and green pepper in butter until lightly brown. Remove and mix with the salmon. Add the egg, milk and all remaining ingredients and mix thoroughly. Place in a regular loaf pan, oval ring, or, best of all if available, a fish-shaped mold. Dot with butter and cover. Set aside or refrigerate until needed. Then set pan or mold into a greased shallow baking pan and heat in a 350° F. oven for 30 minutes, uncovered. Serve hot with dill-and-buttered new potatoes. For additional garnishing, serve salmon loaf with an Almond-White Wine Sauce. (See below). Serves 6.

Almond-White Wine Sauce

This sauce is lovely with any baked, broiled or boiled fish, but is also a nice embellishment for a salmon or tuna loaf. I usually use the same wine in the sauce that I am serving with dinner—sauterne, Riesling or Chablis is fine.

3 *Tbs. butter*	*Dash of cayenne pepper*
3 *Tbs. flour*	*Salt to taste*
1½ *cups consommé*	¼ *tsp. white pepper*
1 *bay leaf*	⅓ *cup toasted almonds, sliced in*
3 *whole cloves*	*strips*
¾ *cup white wine*	

Melt the butter in the top of a double boiler. When melted, stir in flour carefully, making a smooth paste. Add consommé slowly. Keep stirring as mixture cooks and thickens. Add bay leaf and cloves. Simmer over low heat for 8 to 10 minutes. Remove from heat. Strain the sauce, and add the wine and seasoning. Set aside. Just before serving, reheat and stir in the toasted almonds. Serve at once with hot fish course. Yield: 3 cups.

Almond-Pimiento Sauce

This sauce is especially zesty served with a fiish loaf or mousse.

1½ *cups standard white sauce*	⅓ *cup mayonnaise*
⅓ *cup almonds, toasted*	*Salt and white pepper to taste*
4 *pieces cooked pimientos, cut*	
into small pieces	

The white sauce should be on the thickish side, but not too thick. Add the almonds, sliced into strips, to the sauce, along with the pimientos. Mix well and place in a double boiler. At serving time, stir in the mayonnaise. Thin with a little milk if necessary. Add salt and pepper if needed. Heat and serve immediately over the fish loaf or in a gravy boat accompanying the fish loaf. Yield: approximately 2½ cups.

Herb Sauce for Fish or Shrimp

This may be made ahead and set aside to reheat at the last moment. Poured hot over freshly broiled or baked fish, it adds that little Zing! that fish often needs.

¾ cup butter
1 medium onion, chopped fine
2 cloves garlic, minced fine
1 tsp. lemon juice
¾ tsp. Worcestershire sauce
⅛ tsp. Tabasco sauce
2½ Tbs. minced fresh parsley
¼ tsp. dried oregano

¼ tsp. dried marjoram
½ tsp. dried basil
1½ tsps. paprika
2 tsps. dried green scallions
¼ tsp. dried mustard
½ tsp. salt
¼ tsp. black pepper, freshly ground

Melt the butter in a skillet, add onion and garlic and heat until limp. Remove from heat and stir in lemon juice, Worcestershire sauce, Tabasco, and all the herbs. Mix well and set aside. At serving time, add a little more butter if needed, and heat sauce, stirring well. Pour over fish just before taking it to table. Or, if you prefer, pour sauce in bowl with ladle. Yield: approximately 2 cups.

CHAPTER II

Off the Hoof

Most prepared-ahead dishes are for main courses, and in our nonvege-
tarian society that usually means meat dishes. The following recipes
have one thing in common: they can be prepared, abandoned, and reheated in the nick of time.

Beef, veal, lamb, pork, ham, sausage, all are included. Recipes using
one type of meat are grouped together, thus, all beef recipes, then all
the lamb dishes, and so on. You will find more recipes for beef than
for any other kind of meat, but let's face it, beef is still our favorite
national dish.

Sweet and Sour Pot Roast

The joy of cooking this is that you may begin it in the A.M. while
doing other chores or quick errands, then finish it off at dinnertime. *Or*
you may simmer it late in the afternoon, which makes it ideal for one
of those evenings when Commuter Husband says, "I'm not sure when

I'll be home, better not hold dinner for me." With this treatment, you can hold your dinner and eat it too.

2 *Tbs. fat*
4 to 5 *lbs. chuck roast*
1 *large onion, sliced ¼ inch thick*
½ *tsp. salt (more to taste)*
¼ *tsp. black pepper, freshly*
    ground
¾ *cup white vinegar*

½ *cup cold water*
½ *cup brown sugar*
1 *piece (½ inch thick) ginger root,*
    peeled (optional, but zesty!)
¼ *tsp. allspice*
2 *Tbs. flour*

In a deep pan, heat the fat over a low fire. Add the wiped meat and brown slowly. When brown, add onion slices and cook until they are barely limp—about 5 minutes. Remove pan from heat and let cool a few minutes, then rub meat with salt and pepper. Return pan to low heat. Pour over vinegar and water, add sugar, ginger root, and allspice. Cover pan and simmer 4 hours. Check occasionally and add water first, then a little vinegar if needed. But add liquid sparingly. If meat gets thoroughly tender, but Commuter Husband hasn't arrived yet, turn off heat and keep pan covered. At serving time, remove roast to a platter, and thicken gravy with a little flour mixed to a paste with cold water. Delicious served with noodles or rice. Serves 6.

Baked Sour Cream Pot Roast

To be accurate, this is a Dutch Oven Roast, not a Pot Roast. Call it anything you like, then sit back and watch it cook itself.

5 *lbs. chuck roast*
3 *Tbs. flour*
2 *cloves garlic, peeled and halved*
1 *Tb. lard or salad oil*
1 *tsp. salt*
½ *tsp. black pepper, freshly*
    ground

1 *cup bouillon or beef stock*
½ *cup tomato purée*
1 *Tb. brown sugar*
1 *large onion, minced*
1 *bay leaf*
1 *Tb. flour*
1¼ *cups sour cream*

Wipe meat with a damp cloth. Dredge it with 3 tablespoons flour. Rub Dutch oven well with garlic halves, covering bottom and sides. Heat lard or oil in a large skillet. When hot, quickly brown meat. Remove from heat and cool a few minutes. Then rub meat with salt and pepper all over. Place meat on a rack in Dutch oven. Add bouillon or stock, tomato purée, brown sugar, onion and bay leaf. Cover and roast in a 325° F. oven for approximately 4 hours. If necessary, add a little stock or water to keep the meat moist. When dinner finally seems imminent, remove meat and bay leaf. Place meat on ovenproof platter and keep warm in oven at low 200° F. temperature, while making gravy. Mix remaining tablespoon flour with a little cold water to form a paste. Add to liquid in Dutch oven and make a smooth gravy. Stir in sour cream little by little until well mixed. Add salt and pepper to taste. Heat gently. Pour over the roast and serve. Serves 6.

Beef à la Mode

There are fads in cooking, but some dishes go on forever. This particular one was a favorite in the American colonies, before our Republic was formed. George Washington and Thomas Jefferson were both fond of it. It fits in easily with today's hectic schedules, too.

4 to 5 *lbs. chuck roast*	3 *small stalks celery, quartered*
1 *tsp. salt*	3 *cloves garlic, cut fine*
½ *tsp. freshly ground black pepper*	3 to 4 *sprigs fresh parsley*
2 *cups dry white wine*	1½ *cups canned tomatoes with liquid*
2 *Tbs. salad oil or lard*	1 *large bay leaf*
2 *Tbs. flour*	⅛ *tsp. thyme*
2 *cups meat stock or undiluted bouillon*	4 *medium onions, quartered*
	6 *large carrots, quartered*

Wipe the meat with a damp cloth. Rub salt and pepper into it. Place in a deep bowl and pour wine over it. Cover and refrigerate overnight or at least 6 hours. Remove meat, but save marinade. Heat the lard or oil in a deep kettle. Quickly brown the meat on all sides. Remove meat temporarily and pour off most of the oil. Brown flour in kettle, then add meat, marinade, stock or bouillon, celery, garlic, parsley, tomatoes, bay leaf, and thyme. Bring liquid to boil, cover, then turn fire low and simmer 2 to 3 hours. Skim off fat and add the onions and carrots. Continue simmering for another hour, or until meat is tender. Set aside and reheat if necessary. At the last minute, place meat and vegetables on a serving platter, and add a little more salt and pepper to the gravy if needed. Serves 6 to 8.

Chinese Beef Shank

Whatever you may be thinking about shanks' mare, this isn't it. It is, however, an easy-to-make-ahead Chinesified treatment of a not-used-enough cut of meat.

½ *cup salad or peanut oil*   ¾ *tsp. MSG*
3 *lbs. beef shank (bone in)*   6 *Tbs. soy sauce*
1½ *cups water*   1½ *cups raw rice, well washed*
3 *scallions, whole*   3 *cups water*
1-*inch cut of ginger root, peeled* *Salt to taste (careful! soy sauce is*
1 *Tb. sugar*   *salty)*

Heat the oil in a large skillet. Add the beef and brown quickly over a high fire. Meanwhile, bring just to a boil 1½ cups water. Pour it over the meat, turn heat to a low simmer, and add the scallions, ginger root, sugar, MSG and soy sauce. Simmer slowly for approximately 2 hours, or until quite tender. Add water little by little as needed to keep meat from burning. When meat is almost tender, cook the rice in 3 cups water. When cooked and still moist, remove from heat and place in the bottom of an oblong baking dish. Place meat and sauce on top. Cover and set aside. Half an hour before serving, place the casserole in a 350° F. oven to reheat and finish tenderizing. Salt to taste. Serve with additional soy sauce in a side dish. A cold green bean salad with vinaigrette dressing makes a pleasant accompaniment. Serves 6.

Gingersnap Sauerbraten

Your old Viennese auntie might be shocked at this recipe, but I think the gingersnaps are an easy and successful way to "sassy up" this pleasingly sour Austrian dish.

2½ *tsps. salt*   3 *bay leaves*
1½ *tsps. powdered ginger*   2 *tsps. whole black peppercorns*
4 *lbs. chuck roast*   ½ *cup sugar*
2 *cups wine vinegar*   2 *strips lemon rind*
3 *cups water*   6 *whole cloves*
2 *cloves garlic, peeled*   2 *Tbs. lard*
2 *Tbs. pickling spices*   6 to 8 *gingersnaps, crushed*
2 *large onions, sliced thin*

Mix the salt and ginger together. Wipe meat with a damp cloth and rub the salt-ginger mixture all over the meat. Place in a large bowl. Set aside. In a large pot, combine vinegar, water, garlic, pickling spices, onions, bay leaves, peppercorns, sugar, lemon rind, and cloves. Bring to a boil and simmer five minutes. Pour liquid over the meat. Cover and refrigerate *at least* 2 days, preferably 3. Turn meat over once a day. When ready to prepare, remove meat from pickling liquid, but save the liquid. Heat lard in a deep heavy kettle. Brown meat slowly on all sides. Remove, and place a rack in the kettle. Place meat on rack and pour in 1 cup of pickling liquid, along with ½ the onions and spices. Cover and simmer at lowest heat at least 3 hours, or until meat is tender. If liquid is absorbed, add additional liquid to kettle. When ready to serve, remove meat to platter. Strain liquid in the kettle and add remaining pickling liquid to make 2 full cups. (If there isn't enough, add water to equal this amount.) Skim excess fat. Simmer slowly, adding gingersnaps to thicken. Pour into a gravy boat and serve as accompaniment to the thinly sliced meat. Mashed potatoes or buttered noodles make a good complementary side dish. (If meat is ready before the family is, set aside and reheat at appropriate moment.) Serves 6.

French-Style Flank Steak

It's the French dressing and Roquefort cheese that give this a Gallic air. Unlike Caesar's Gaul, this is divided into 6 parts, or servings.

4½ Tbs. flour	⅛ tsp. lemon juice
1½ tsps. salt	⅓ cup water
½ tsp. black pepper	½ cup Roquefort or blue cheese,
¼ tsp. dried thyme	crumbled
¼ tsp. dried oregano	1 tsp. Maggi
3 lbs. flank steak	1 tsp. Worcestershire sauce
5 Tbs. cooking oil	3 Tbs. light cream
½ cup homemade French	1 small bunch fresh watercress,
dressing	chopped coarse

Combine flour, salt, pepper, thyme, and oregano. Mix well. Score the steak and rub flour mixture into it. Heat cooking oil in heavy skillet, and brown steak quickly on both sides. Remove to roasting pan. Pour French dressing, lemon juice and water over the steak. Cover, and bake in 350° F. oven approximately 1 hour. Remove meat from oven. Mix together the Roquefort, Maggi, Worcestershire and cream. Smooth into a loose paste, and spread evenly over the top of the steak. Cover and let stand until needed. Thirty minutes or so before you *think* the family will be ready to eat, return the meat to oven, uncover, and bake at 350° until tender. Baste to prevent drying out. If there is a delay, turn oven to 250°, add water to bottom of pan, cover, and allow to cook slowly until ready. Serve on a platter, decorated with chopped watercress, and slice meat diagonally. Serves 6.

Stracotto Pasta

In Italian, I am told, "stracotto" means "overcooked," which is precisely what you must do with this dish. It is really an unusual and delicious way to serve spaghetti.

1 *lb. top grade beef*	½ *cup undiluted bouillon*
½ *cup butter*	½ *cup dry Marsala wine*
2 *medium onions, minced*	2 *tsps. grated lemon rind*
1 *large stalk celery, chopped fine*	1 *tsp. salt (more to taste)*
1 *large carrot, peeled and minced*	½ *tsp. freshly grated black pepper*
½ *cup finely chopped parsley*	⅛ *tsp. cayenne pepper*
¼ *cup chopped fresh mushrooms*	1 *lb. spaghetti*

Trim fat off meat. Chop meat into tiny, *tiny* cubes (or if you prefer, put it little by little through the coarse blade of a meat grinder). Place meat in heavy kettle, add butter and heat over low fire. When butter melts, add onion, celery, carrot, and parsley. Cook 5 minutes, stirring constantly. Add mushrooms, bouillon, Marsala and lemon rind. Season to taste with salt, pepper and cayenne. Stir well, then cover and simmer 3½ hours. Stir occasionally and add just a little more bouillon, then Marsala if necessary. Set aside. Before serving, boil spaghetti in boiling salted water 10 to 15 minutes. Drain and rinse well with hot water. Reheat sauce over lowest heat for 10 to 15 minutes (while spaghetti is cooking). Pour sauce over drained spaghetti and serve hot with a crisp green salad. Serves 6.

Korean Steak

This highly spiced steak is a fascinating way to serve a solid American standby. And it is an easy recipe to prepare ahead. As with so many spicy dishes, the secret lies in the length of time of the marinating.

1½ to 2 *lbs. sirloin steak*
3 *Tbs. finely chopped green onion*
2 *Tbs. sugar*
6 *Tbs. soy sauce*
3 *Tbs. sesame seeds*

3 *cloves garlic, minced*
2 *tsps. black pepper, freshly ground*
2 *Tbs. finely chopped celery*
5 *Tbs. sesame seed oil* *

Bone and slice the steak into very thin slices, approximately ¼ inch thick. Combine all the remaining ingredients except 2 tablespoons oil and mix thoroughly. Pour over the meat in a shallow baking dish or cake pan. Turn meat to be sure it is all covered with the sauce. Let stand *at least* 2 hours, preferably 3 or 4. At cooking time, heat the remaining 2 tablespoons oil in a large iron skillet over a medium fire. When oil is hot, place steak slices in skillet and cook quickly, turning frequently until cooked. Serve immediately with a side dish of rice. Koreans love pickled vegetables so, to be semiauthentic, you might serve a cold cooked vegetable salad, laced with an oil-vinegar dressing. (Keep meat in marinade until belated guests arrive. Cooking time is so brief it can be accomplished during the course of a single martini.) Serves 6.

Peruvian Steak

This highly spiced dish is a welcome change for steak lovers, and easy as falling off a llama to prepare ahead.

5 *tbs. wine vinegar*
½ *tsp. ground cardamom*
1 *tsp. salt (more to taste)*
4 *cloves garlic, minced*
1½ *tsps. ground cumin*
1 *tsp. black pepper, freshly ground*
¼ *tsp. celery seed*
¾ *cup fresh coriander leaves or 1 tsp. ground coriander*

3 *large onions chopped coarse*
1 *small hot red pepper cut in strips*
6 *shell steaks approx. ½ inch thick*
3 *Tbs. olive oil*
3 *Tbs. butter*
2 *green peppers cut in strips*
½ *cup condensed bouillon or beef broth*

Mix together the vinegar, cardamom, salt, garlic, cumin, pepper, celery seed, coriander, onions and red pepper. Place steaks in flat pan and pour mixture over them. Marinate 4 hours at least, preferably

---

* Corn oil may be substituted, though there is a distinct difference in flavor. Sesame oil is available in Chinese markets and some gourmet food shops.

overnight. Turn occasionally to be sure marinade covers and permeates fully. Heat oil and butter together in a large skillet. Sear steaks on both sides. Add additional salt and pepper if needed. Add green pepper, cover skillet and cook over low heat for 30 minutes. Set aside. 15 minutes before serving, reheat. Add bouillon, little by little. Turn fire as low as possible. Cover pan and turn heat off if necessary. Serve with hot rice or noodles, and a crisp green salad. Serves 6.

Hungarian Gulyas

Sometimes I think there are as many recipes for this dish as there are Hungarians. But that's because it is ideal for improvisation. This is a delicious version, but feel free to amend, add or subtract as you choose. That's the beauty of *gulyas*.

1 *strip bacon or salt pork*	1½ *tsps. salt*
3 *lbs. chuck beef or veal, cut into*	¼ *tsp. black pepper*
2-inch cubes	2 *Tbs. paprika (the real Hun-*
2 *large onions, chopped coarse*	*garian is incomparable)*
2 *cloves garlic, minced*	¼ *tsp. thyme*
1 *large green pepper, chopped*	3½ *cups canned tomatoes (#2½*
coarse	*can)*
¼ *cup flour*	1 to 1½ *cups sour cream*
2 *bay leaves*	

Brown bacon and set aside, reserving the bacon fat. Use fat for browning the meat cubes on all sides. When brown, add onions, garlic, and green peppers. Cook lightly. Slowly blend in flour and seasonings. When well mixed, add tomatoes. Allow to simmer over low heat for approximately 1 to 2 hours, or until meat is tender and the sauce has thickened. Before sauce becomes *too* thick, remove pan from heat. Cover and set aside (or store in refrigerator in a container until dinnertime). *Then,* for *serving,* return dish to large skillet, simmer gently over low heat until warm. If sauce gets too thick, thin with water added sparingly. Continue heating until sauce thickens nicely. As husband walks in the door, stir in sour cream and crumbled bacon. Mix well, and the dish is ready to serve. Serve in a large bowl or over a bed of hot, buttered noodles. Pumpernickel bread and a tossed green salad complete the picture nicely. Serves 6.

Beef and Rice Curry Casserole

This is an all-in-one-dish curry, which makes it a natural meal that can wait. It only improves with age—up to a point of course.

2 *large onions, chopped fine*
2 *Tbs. butter*
3 *lbs. stewing beef, cubed*
2 *Tbs. curry powder, hot variety*
1 *#2 can (1 lb. 12 ozs.) tomatoes*
    or 3 large fresh ones
1 *cup water*
1 *Tb. coconut, chopped, not*
    grated

1 *Tb. chutney*
2 *Tbs. white raisins*
1 *large apple, diced*
2 *tsps. salt*
1 *tsp. ground cumin*
3 *cups consommé, diluted*
1½ *cups raw rice, washed*
½ *cup peanuts, chopped fine*
2 *Tbs. grated coconut*

Over a low fire, sauté the chopped onions in butter until golden brown. Add the beef and brown well. Add curry (to taste), tomatoes with their own liquid, water, coconut, chutney, raisins, apple, salt and cumin. Simmer slowly until meat is tender—possibly an hour. Bring consommé to a boil, add rice, and cook covered over a low heat until rice is barely tender, not mushy. Remove from pot and place rice in bottom of an oblong 9 x 13-inch baking pan. Pour meat mixture over rice, cover and set aside or refrigerate until needed. At your projected dinnertime, place pan in 350° F. oven and heat, covered, 30 to 40 minutes. If husband and/or guests are tardy, add a little consommé or water sparingly to keep dinner moist. If necessary, turn oven off and coast a few minutes. Serve hot with peanuts and grated coconut sprinkled over the top. A side dish of chutney is optional, but adds zing if readily available. Makes 6 servings.

Limas with Creamed Beef

Creamed beef devotees will swoon over this. Wives of creamed beef devotees will join them—it's so easy to prepare.

2 *Tbs. butter*
2 *Tbs. flour*
⅛ *tsp. salt*
½ *tsp. black pepper*
1 *cup cream*
⅓ *lb. dried beef*
¼ *tsp. soy sauce*

1½ *cups cooked lima beans*
    (canned will do)
1 *cup buttered and toasted bread*
    crumbs (use 1 tsp. butter)
½ *cup grated Cheddar cheese (the*
    sharper the cheese, the better)

Melt the butter slowly in the top of a double boiler. Mix the flour, salt and pepper together and add slowly to the butter, making a paste. Add the cream, little by little, stirring constantly to keep the sauce smooth. Cook 10 minutes, stirring often. Meanwhile, cover the dried beef with hot water, let stand 8 to 10 minutes, drain, and separate the meat into pieces. Add to the cream sauce and continue cooking for 5 minutes. Pour mixture into a greased casserole. Mix the soy sauce with the undrained cooked lima beans, and add to the casserole. Mix well and top with bread crumbs tossed lightly with the grated cheese. Cover and set aside until serving time. Thirty minutes before dinner heat the casserole in a 350° F. oven until nicely browned. Serves 6.

French Meat Loaf

This commuter's delight turns meat-loaf loathers into meat-loaf lovers. It is as delicious served cold as hot.

1 *large onion, chopped*	1 *cup milk*
½ *large green pepper, chopped*	¾ *cup crumbled blue cheese*
2½ *Tbs. butter*	¾ *tsp. salt*
2½ *Tbs. water*	½ *tsp. sage*
½ *cup chili sauce*	¼ *tsp. pepper, freshly ground*
2 *lbs. ground beef*	2 *eggs, slightly beaten*
⅓ *lb. sausage meat*	1 *tsp. chopped parsley*
2½ *cups dry bread crumbs,*	
crumbled fine	

Sauté the onion and green pepper in melted butter until lightly browned—approximately 5 minutes. Add the water and ¼ cup chili sauce and heat for 3 to 4 minutes longer. Pour mixture into the bottom of a regular meat loaf pan. Mix the meat with the remaining chili sauce, add all the other ingredients and mix well. Press into the pan on top of the first mixture. Sprinkle parsley on top, cover and refrigerate until baking time. Bake in 375° F. oven approximately 1 hour. Serve warm. Leftovers (if any) are good sliced thin in sandwiches next day. Serves 6 to 8.

Hamburger Spoon Bread

There are those who can make a meal out of spoon bread. We do at our house—by cheating a bit and turning the spoon bread into a modified hamburger casserole, as follows:

1 *lb. ground beef*	¾ *cup corn meal (water-ground)*
1 *tsp. salt*	3 *cups milk*
1 *medium onion, chopped*	2 *tsps. salt*
1 *tsp. poultry seasoning*	3 *large eggs, well beaten*

Sauté beef lightly in skillet. Drain the fat. Add 1 teaspoon salt, on-ions, and the poultry seasoning to the beef and set aside. In a saucepan mix the corn meal with 1½ cups milk and the remaining salt. Heat over a low fire until thickened, stirring constantly. When thickened, set aside to cool. Add the rest of the milk (at room temperature), the beaten eggs, and the beef mixture. Mix thoroughly and pour into a greased 2-quart casserole or glass baking dish. Set aside for an hour or so until dinnertime. Then cook in a preheated 400° F. oven approxi-mately 25 minutes. When lightly browned, but not *too* firm, serve from dish. Delicious with butter added. Serves 6 to 8.

Cheeseburger Loaf

This peppy version of meat loaf is a good appetite reviver when winter menu planning seems bleak and dreary. It is simple and can be put together in the morning and ovened at the dinner witching hour.

1½ *lbs. ground beef*
6 *Tbs. wheat germ or rolled*
    cracker crumbs
1 *large egg, beaten slightly*
1 *large onion, grated*
½ *tsp. pepper, freshly ground*
¼ *tsp. poultry seasoning*

1 *tsp. salt*
1 *Tb. Worcestershire sauce*
¾ *tsp. prepared mustard*
¼ *cup tomato sauce*
¼ *lb. Old English or processed*
    American cheese, or good
    sharp Cheddar

In a large mixing bowl mix the beef, wheat germ (or finely ground crackers), egg and grated onion. Add all the seasonings and tomato sauce and mix thoroughly. Grate the cheese and stir it into the mix-ture, blending well. Place in a loaf pan and refrigerate until needed. At dinnertime, bake for 40 minutes to 1 hour in a 350° F. oven. Serve hot as is. Good also with heated tomato sauce accompanying it. To prolong the waiting time, keep adding a thin layer of tomato sauce over the top and turn oven down to 300°. Serves 6.

Moussaka

This Greek classic is a delightful main dish, but try it sometime, cut into small squares, as a hot appetizer. If Patient Penelope had ever made this, I'll bet Ulysses wouldn't have been away from home so long.

2 *medium eggplants, peeled*
1 *cup flour (approximately)*
¾ *cup salad oil*
¼ *cup butter or margarine*
4 *cloves garlic, minced*
1 *large onion, minced*
2 *tsps. salt*
½ *tsp. black pepper, freshly
    ground*
¼ *tsp. oregano*

½ *lb. ground pork (or lamb),
    very lean*
1 *lb. ground beef, lean*
1 *large fresh tomato, diced*
1 *cup canned tomato purée*
1½ *tsps. lemon juice*
¼ *tsp. nutmeg*
½ *cup cold water*
½ *cup freshly grated Parmesan
    cheese*

Slice eggplant lengthwise into ½-inch slices. Dip each slice in flour. Heat salad oil in large heavy skillet, and sauté eggplant until golden brown. Place ⅓ of the eggplant in the bottom of a greased oblong casserole. Reserve remaining eggplant. In another skillet, melt butter and sauté garlic, onion, salt, pepper and oregano. When onion softens, add pork and beef and brown lightly. Then add tomato, tomato purée, lemon juice, nutmeg and water. Mix well and simmer 15 minutes. When well mixed, remove from heat. Spoon a layer of the meat mixture over the eggplant in the casserole. Cover with another layer of eggplant. Continue until both mixtures are used up. Sprinkle Parmesan evenly over the top. Preheat oven to 350° F. and bake *moussaka* 25 minutes or so, until well heated and crusty on top. If dinner is delayed, turn oven down to 300° and place pan of boiling hot water under casserole. Cover casserole and keep warm in low oven. If delay turns into desperation, just turn oven off. To serve, cut *moussaka* into generous squares and served accompanied by a gusty salad with succulent ripe Greek olives and thick, crusty bread. Serves 6 generously.

Midwestern Eggplant Special

Eggplant is a favorite vegetable in the Middle East, but when a recipe calls for Grape Nuts, grown in our own Middle West, it should appropriately be called a Middle Western Eastern. Whatever you call it, chances are your family will call *for* it a second time around.

3 *medium eggplants*
1½ *Tbs. olive oil*
2 *medium onions, chopped fine*
3 *cloves garlic, minced*
1 *lb. ground beef*
¼ *tsp. thyme*
1½ *tsps. chopped parsley*

¼ *tsp. basil*
2 *tsps. salt*
¼ *tsp. freshly ground black
    pepper*
2 *cups canned tomatoes, drained*
1¼ *cups Grape Nuts cereal*
2 *eggs, slightly beaten*

Cut each eggplant in half and scoop out insides, leaving ½-inch shell all around. Reserve inside pulp and set aside. Parboil the shells in boiling, salted water for 5 minutes. Drain on absorbent paper. Chop eggplant insides into small cubes. Heat oil in large skillet and sauté eggplant cubes, onion, and garlic. Mix well, and add meat. Cook meat until lightly brown, crumbling it with a fork to mix it well with other ingredients. Add thyme, parsley, basil, salt and pepper. Remove from heat. In mixing bowl, combine tomatoes, Grape Nuts and eggs. Add meat mixture and stir well. Spoon mixture into eggplant shells. Place in shallow baking pan with ¼ inch water all around. Set aside until needed. When you can estimate the family's arrival time, place pan in preheated 400° F. oven for approximately 30 minutes. If meal is delayed, add water to pan, cover pan with foil, turn oven to 250° and let bake for an additional 15 minutes. Serve hot with a crispy salad. Serves 6.

Indian Koftas

These highly spiced meatballs make unusual hot hors d'oeuvres. Only the heating up is a last minute job. They are also divine served on rice as a main course. But remember, they're hot-hot!

1 *large onion, minced*	¼ *tsp. black pepper, freshly*
6 *cloves garlic, minced*	*ground*
1 *green pepper, minced*	¼ *tsp. caraway seeds*
½ *tsp. ground coriander*	½ *tsp. ground cardamom*
1 *egg, well beaten*	¼ *tsp. ground cloves*
1 *lb. ground beef or lamb, lean*	⅛ *tsp. cinnamon*
½ *tsp. chili powder*	½ *cup salad oil*
2 *tsps. salt*	

Combine the onion, garlic, green pepper and coriander. Mix well and add to beaten egg. Mix again and work into the ground meat. Mix chili powder, salt, pepper, caraway, cardamom, cloves and cinnamon together and work into meat mixture. Take time to mix thoroughly. Then form meat into 1-inch balls. Refrigerate until needed. When Papa arrives home for dinner, begin sautéeing meatballs in heated oil in a large iron skillet over a medium heat. Turn to brown lightly. Takes about 10 to 15 minutes for meat to cook thoroughly. Serve with canapé picks and with a bowl of chutney and a bowl of sour cream as dips. Serves 6.

Irish-Cuban Meatballs

This not-strictly-authentic national dish was a contribution from a friend who happens to be—you guessed it—Irish and Cuban. Whatever the mixture, the result in this delicious meatball dish is superb. It is less work than Swedish meatballs, and, in my opinion, far surpasses that better-known concoction .

2 *lbs. lean ground round*	½ *cup chopped parsley*
8 *slices rye bread with caraway seeds (white bread* may *be used, but rye with seeds adds piquancy)*	¼ *tsp. black pepper, freshly ground*
	½ *tsp. salt (more to taste)*
2 *eggs, slightly beaten*	2 *cups grated sharp Cheddar cheese*
4 *fat cloves garlic, minced*	½ *cup flour (more if needed)*
2 *medium onions, grated*	¼ *cup olive or salad oil*
1 *lb. fresh spinach or 2 pkgs. frozen spinach (10 ozs. each), cooked and drained*	1 *can tomato paste (7 ozs.)*
	1 *can V-8 juice (6 ozs.)*

Mix together the raw ground beef, bread (crumbled), eggs, garlic, onions, spinach, parsley, pepper, salt, and grated cheese. Mix thoroughly and form into 1-inch meatballs. Dip each one into flour, then brown them in oil and drain on absorbent paper. Combine the tomato paste and V-8 juice. Place meatballs in a deep casserole. Cover with sauce. Keep covered in refrigerator until ready to bake. Bake, still covered, in a 350° F. oven from 30 to 50 minutes. If you need to keep them warm longer, lower oven temperature to 300° and add a little more V-8 juice to casserole, mixing it in a little as you add it. Serves 6.

Curried Beef and Tomato Casserole

Sometimes I suspect we get too compartmentalized in our cooking, thinking for instance that water chestnuts can only be used in Chinese dishes (try them sometimes in a tossed green salad) or curry in Indian recipes. Here is a rather folksy recipe using curry to enliven such old familiars as ground beef, tomatoes, and corn. A meeting of East and West Indians!

2 *Tbs. olive oil*
3 *cloves garlic, minced*
2 *lbs. ground beef*
2 *Tbs. chopped onion*
2 *tsps. brown sugar*
1 *Tb. hot paprika*
1½ *Tbs. hot curry powder*
1½ *tsps. salt*
¼ *cup butter*

¼ *cup flour*
2 *cans tomatoes (1 lb. each)*
2 *cans whole kernel corn, drained*
  (1 lb. each)
½ *tsp. black pepper, freshly*
  ground
1 *tsp. salt*
1 *cup tomato juice*

Heat olive oil in a large heavy skillet. Add garlic. Sauté for 1 quick minute, then add ground beef and sauté until lightly browned, about 10 minutes. Stir to prevent sticking. Then add the onion, brown sugar, paprika, curry and 1½ teaspoons salt. Stir well, and remove from heat. In a saucepan, melt butter and slowly stir in flour until a smooth paste is formed. Add tomatoes and simmer slowly until thickened slightly. Add drained corn, pepper and remaining salt, and bring to a boil. Remove from heat. Place meat mixture in a greased baking dish, and pour the corn mixture around and over it. Cover and refrigerate until needed. (Even overnight is permissible.) Half an hour before baking, remove casserole from refrigerator and let stand at room temperature. Heat uncovered in a 375° F. oven 20 minutes. If the dinner must linger in the oven, add a little tomato juice to the top. Keep adding it as time goes by. Serves 6.

Individual Orange Meat Loaves

Hamburger seems to outdistance every other meat as a favorite with children. I suspect that mine, if put to the test, would willingly eat hamburgers for breakfast, lunch and dinner. To vary the hamburger menu, this recipe even has adult appeal.

6 *Tbs. brown sugar*
½ *tsp. dry mustard*
6 *orange slices, unpeeled*
1½ *lbs. lean ground beef*
1 *large egg, beaten*
1 *large onion, grated fine*
1 *medium green pepper, chopped*

2 *cups soft bread crumbs*
½ *cup orange juice*
2 *Tbs. lemon juice*
¼ *tsp. black pepper, freshly*
  ground
1 *tsp. salt*

Put 1 tablespoon brown sugar in the bottom of 6 greased individual baking dishes. (If you do not have individual casseroles, use one large one, not too deep, or a 9 x 13-inch baking pan. If you use one single casserole, place 6 tablespoons of brown sugar in separate little mounds around the bottom of the pan.) Sprinkle mustard over each tablespoon of sugar and top with an orange slice. Mix together the beef, egg, onion, green pepper, bread crumbs, juice and seasonings. When well mixed, divide into six equal parts and mold into each baking dish. (If you use a single dish, simply press the meat mixture over the entire dish. Do not try to keep the 6 mounds separate.) Set aside or refrigerate, overnight if necessary. When ready to go, bake in a 350° F. oven for 40 to 60 minutes. If the train is late, remove from oven at the halfway mark, then return to oven for final half hour. To keep a little longer after being cooked, put foil over casseroles and turn oven off. Reheat at low temperature when family finally assembles. When ready to serve, turn casseroles upside down on individual heated plates or a heated platter. The orange slices will be on top, molded into the beef, with a slightly glazed effect. Very pretty—and tasty too! Serves 6.

Oriental Beef Casserole

This dish is so tasty it would have brought Genghis Khan home to dinner on time if he had sampled it.

2 *cups half-cooked rice (Just remove it from heat before it is thoroughly cooked)*
1½ *lbs. ground beef*
2 *large onions, sliced thin*
2 *Tbs. sliced water chestnuts (optional)*
1 *10½-oz. can beef bouillon*

5 *Tbs. soy sauce*
½ *tsp. powdered ginger*
¼ *cup sherry*
½ *tsp. MSG (or Accent)*
½ *cup water*
1½ *cups fresh frozen green beans (uncooked, right from freezer)*
1 *16-oz. can bean sprouts, drained*

Mix rice and ground beef thoroughly. Add onions and water chestnuts and mix again. Combine bouillon, soy sauce, ginger, sherry, MSG and water. Mix well and add to meat mixture. Lightly add green beans and mix well. Place mixture in a deep covered casserole and bake in a preheated 425° F. oven approximately 20 minutes. Remove and set aside, still covered. When family begins to assemble and look hungry, add bean sprouts to casserole. Mix well, and reheat in a 400° oven an additional 20 minutes. Serve piping hot with a green salad. Serves 6.

Cavolo Pacco (Cabbage Bundles)

This is an impressive version of pigs-in-a-blanket and can be ready to go hours ahead of schedule and willing to wait for errant guests.

1 *large head cabbage (about*	¼ *tsp. black pepper, freshly*
3 lbs.)	*ground*
1 *cup water*	¼ *tsp. nutmeg*
1 *cup spinach, cooked*	1 *cup freshly grated Parmesan*
¾ *lb. ground beef*	*cheese*
(or veal or lamb)	2½ *Tbs. chopped parsley*
2 *eggs, slightly beaten*	⅓ *cup olive oil*
½ *tsp. salt (more to taste)*	¼ *cup Parmesan cheese*

Wash the cabbage and discard any wilted or bad leaves. Core the cabbage with apple corer about 1 inch deep, in order to remove 12 or 15 of the large outside leaves. Boil 1 cup salted water. Drop loose cabbage leaves into the boiling water and boil 2 or 3 minutes until limp but barely cooked. Remove and drain. Add the spinach to ground meat, beat in the eggs, and then add salt, pepper, nutmeg, cheese and parsley. Mix well. Place 2 large tablespoons of the meat mixture on the center of each cabbage leaf. Fold like a bundle, so the meat mixture is completely enclosed and secure in the rolled up leaf. Tie with soft white twine, or place leaf open end down, to prevent stuffing from falling out. Arrange the bundles in a shallow 9 x 13-inch baking pan. Refrigerate or set aside until needed. When ready to bake, pour olive oil over the top, cover, and bake in a 325° F. oven for approximately 25 to 30 minutes, or until cabbage leaves are tender. If dinner is ready but your family is not, add a little water or diluted consommé to pan to keep leaves from drying out. Turn off oven, and at the last minute turn it on again to 300° to warm up. Sprinkle remaining Parmesan over top. Serves 6.

Stuffed Peppers and Tomato Ensemble

Stuffed green pepper lovers may not agree, but sometimes it is a pleasant change to serve stuffed pepper along with stuffed tomatoes, as in this highly seasoned Middle Eastern recipe. It is delicious served chilled as a change, too.

3 *large green peppers*
3 *large fresh tomatoes*
1 *Tb. butter*
½ *lb. lean ground beef*
1 *medium onion, chopped fine*
½ *cup water*
2 *Tbs. raw rice*
½ *bunch fresh dill (or ½ tsp.*
  dill weed)

1 *tsp. black pepper, freshly*
  ground
½ *tsp. seasoned salt*
¼ *tsp. dried oregano*
1 *small bunch fresh parsley,*
  chopped
2 *Tbs. butter*
1 *cup water*

Wash peppers and tomatoes. Cut off tops and remove pulp. Discard pepper seeds, but keep tomato pulp. Melt 1 tablespoon butter in a skillet and sauté ground beef and onion until lightly browned. Add ½ cup water and rice. Cover and simmer until rice is cooked. Add chopped dill, black pepper, salt, oregano and parsley. Mix well. Mixture should be soft, but not watery. Spoon mixture into peppers and tomatoes. Place in a large shallow baking pan, approximately 9 x 13 inches. Melt remaining butter in skillet, add chopped tomato pulp, 1 cup water, and salt to taste. Mix and pour into the baking pan surrounding the peppers and tomatoes. Bake in a medium 350° F. oven for 20 minutes. At dinnertime, while your husband is relaxing with a drink and canapés, reheat dish for 15 minutes, adding just a little water if the mixture surrounding the peppers and tomatoes looks dry. Serves 6.

Spaghetti Pie

When I first visited England in 1949, the English were still on a rationed, high starch diet, and a mainstay of it seemed to be spaghetti on toast. Ugh! I thought then, and Ugh! is probably what you are thinking now when you see Spaghetti Pie listed. But read on! Pie is perhaps a misnomer. This is actually spaghetti fixed in layers, lasagna style, and it is definitely not Ugh! but Ummmm!!!! Honest!

7-*oz. pkg. spaghetti, uncooked*
1 *lb. lean ground beef*
1¼ *tsps. butter*
2 *cans tomato sauce (8 ozs. each)*
½ *tsp. salt (more to taste)*
½ *tsp. black pepper, freshly*
  ground
½ *lb. cottage cheese*

¼ *cup sour cream*
8-*oz. pkg. cream cheese*
⅓ *cup finely chopped scallions*
1 *medium green pepper, chopped*
  fine
3 *cloves garlic, minced*
2 *tsps. butter*
⅓ *cup grated Parmesan cheese*

Cook the spaghetti in boiling salted water and drain when cooked thoroughly. Set aside in colander. Meanwhile, sauté the beef, broken into small pieces, in 1¼ teaspoons butter until brown. Add homemade or prepared tomato sauce, with salt and pepper to taste. If you use a commercial tomato sauce, add 1 teaspoon chopped basil, 1 teaspoon oregano and 1 tablespoon parsley in addition. Mix well with meat and let simmer for ten minutes. In a large mixing bowl combine the cottage cheese, sour cream and cream cheese. Mix well, then add scallions, green pepper and garlic. Mix again thoroughly. Grease a 2-quart casserole and cover the bottom with a layer of drained spaghetti. Then place a layer of the cheese mixture. Spread a thin layer of the meat-tomato sauce over. Repeat until the layers are finished, ending with a heavy layer of meat sauce on top. Pour 2 teaspoons melted butter over the top, sprinkle with Parmesan cheese and cover. Refrigerate 3 to 6 hours. Before reheating, remove from refrigerator and let stand at room temperature at least ½ hour. Bake in 350° F. oven 30 to 45 minutes. Serve with crisp salad and crusty Italian bread. Serves 6 to 8.

Beef-Noodle Pan Casserole

This is a layered dish prepared in a skillet on top of the stove—and is it good! Well, be a Missourian—try it and see.

3 Tbs. butter or margarine	⅛ tsp. cayenne pepper
2 onions, minced	1 Tb. Worcestershire sauce
1½ lbs. lean ground beef	½ tsp. dried thyme
1 pkg. noodles (8 ozs.), uncooked	1 tsp. salt (more to taste)
4½ cups tomato juice	Dash of Tabasco sauce
1½ tsps. celery salt	1½ cups sour cream
¾ tsp. black pepper	

Melt butter in large heavy skillet. Sauté onion in butter until lightly yellow. Push aside, and add meat. Brown. Mix with onions. Drain excess fat (but keep a little). Spread noodles over beef and onions. Add tomato juice. Mix seasonings together and sprinkle over tomato juice. Do not stir as you add each layer. Cover tightly and simmer 15 minutes. Set aside until serving time. Twenty minutes before serving, return skillet to low heat and simmer. Stir once or twice carefully. Just before serving, stir in sour cream. Serve at once. Serves 6.

Beef and Noodle Casserole

I have always tended to view with a somewhat jaundiced eye recipes for main courses that use breakfast food or dessert toppings. Maybe it's my past experience working for a major food company, but I can visualize the sales manager exhorting the home economists, "But you must *find* a way to make a marshmallow meat loaf." Or, "What's the matter with a Shredded Wheat-Béarnaise sauce for steak?" There are exceptions, however, and this is one of them.

1 *Tb. minced onion*	2 *Tbs. sugar*
2 *cloves garlic, minced*	1½ *tsps. seasoned salt*
2 *Tbs. butter, melted*	¾ *tsp. black pepper*
1 *lb. ground beef*	1 *pkg. noodles (8 ozs.), cooked*
½ *lb. lean ground pork*	¼ *lb. whole fresh mushrooms*
2 *cans condensed tomato soup*	1 *cup salted almonds, chopped*
(10 ozs. each)	1 *cup Corn Flakes*
1½ *Tbs. Worcestershire sauce*	1 *Tb. butter*
⅛ *tsp. Tabasco sauce*	

Sauté onions and garlic in 2 tablespoons melted butter until lightly browned. Add meat and brown. Drain excess fat. Add tomato soup, Worcestershire sauce, Tabasco sauce, sugar, salt and pepper. Simmer for 10 minutes. Place noodles in a greased medium-large casserole. Add meat-soup mixture and toss well, coating noodles with sauce mixture. Set aside until needed. Twenty minutes before dinner, sauté mushrooms, almonds and Corn Flakes in 1 tablespoon butter. Sprinkle over top of casserole. Bake in 350° F. oven until heated clear through. Makes a hearty Sunday night supper. Serves 6.

Eggplant and Sour Cream Casserole

If you're beginning to think I have a thing about eggplant, you're right. It really is a very adaptable vegetable, good with so many other foods, as for instance in this ground beef and sour cream dish.

1 *large eggplant*	½ *tsp. dried basil*
2 *Tbs. olive oil*	½ *tsp. dried thyme*
1½ *lbs. ground beef*	¼ *tsp. dried oregano*
1 *medium onion, chopped*	3 *cups cubed Cheddar cheese*
1 *tsp. salt*	½ *cup sour cream*
½ *tsp. black pepper*	

Prick the eggplant with a fork and place in a hot 425° F. oven for 10 to 15 minutes. When slightly tender, remove. Heat oil and sauté beef and onion. Place a layer of eggplant (sliced ½ inch thick) in the bottom of a greased casserole. Sprinkle a mixture of salt, pepper, basil, thyme and oregano over the eggplant. Top with a layer of the beef-onion mixture, crumbled and well mixed. Then add a layer of Cheddar sprinkled over. Begin again with another layer of eggplant, more herb mixture, then beef-onion, and end up with the Cheddar. Set aside. At mealtime, spread sour cream over the top and bake in a 350° F. oven for 20 minutes, or until heated thoroughly. If you must hold dinner, turn oven down to 275°, add a thin layer of sour cream to keep dish moist and wait. Serves 6.

Meatballs in Sour Cream

You can dress up the humble meatball in this rich and tangy sauce. You can also make it wait until you are good and ready to eat.

1½ *lbs. lean ground beef*	¼ *tsp. black pepper*
1¼ *cups soft bread crumbs*	1 *tsp. Maggi*
1 *egg, beaten slightly*	¼ *cup margarine*
⅓ *cup milk*	1 *green pepper, chopped fine*
¼ *tsp. nutmeg*	3 *Tbs. flour*
1 *small onion, minced*	1 *#2 can (1 lb. 12 ozs.) tomatoes*
2 *cloves garlic, minced*	*with liquid*
1½ *tsps. grated lemon rind*	1½ *cups sour cream*
½ *tsp. salt*	1½ *cups rice, cooked*

Combine meat, bread crumbs, egg, milk, nutmeg, onion, garlic, lemon rind, salt, pepper, and Maggi. Mix well and shape into small balls. (Make them multiples of 6, either 24 or 30.) Melt margarine in large skillet. Brown the meatballs on all sides and remove from skillet. Sauté green pepper in remaining fat until lightly browned. Stir in flour until smooth. Add remaining ingredients and mix well. Put meatballs back in skillet, cover and keep until needed. Twenty minutes before serving, bring to a boil, turn fire low, and simmer until heated through. Stir to keep from sticking. Serve on a bed of hot rice or green noodles. Serves 6.

Hot Tamale Pie

This stretchable is easy to make ahead, economical, and sure-fire. You can modify the seasonings if you like, but the Brookses are Mexicanos at heart (or at palate).

1½ lbs. ground beef	2½ Tbs. chili powder
¼ cup olive oil	½ cup yellow corn meal
1¼ cups chopped onion	1 cup water
3 cloves garlic, minced	1 cup pitted olives
¾ cup chopped green pepper	1½ cups milk
1 #2 can (1 lb. 12 ozs.) tomatoes	2 Tbs. butter or margarine
with liquid	3½ tsps. salt
1 16-oz. can whole kernel corn,	½ cup corn meal
drained	1 cup grated Cheddar cheese
1 tsp. salt	2 eggs, beaten slightly
½ tsp. black pepper	

Sauté the ground beef in olive oil until lightly browned. Then add onion, garlic, and green pepper and continue browning. When lightly cooked, add tomatoes, corn, 1 teaspoon salt, pepper and chili powder. Mix well and simmer for 5 minutes. Mix ½ cup corn meal with the cup of water, slowly to prevent lumping. Add to the simmering mixture and continue cooking for 10 minutes. Add olives and pour mixture into a large oblong baking dish. Set aside, Heat milk, add butter and remaining salt to it. Slowly stir in remaining corn meal. Cook slowly until mixture is thickened. Remove from the heat and slowly add cheese and beaten eggs, folding in carefully. Pour mixture over the meat in casserole. Do *not* mix. Cover and refrigerate until needed. Heat in 375° F. oven for 50 to 60 minutes. If you remove casserole from refrigerator ½ hour ahead of baking time, you can cut off 15 to 20 minutes in the oven. Serve hot with salad and rolls or French bread. Serves 6.

Stuffed Manicotti

Many Italian dishes, particularly those with tomato sauce as a base, deserve to be made a day ahead. It takes time for the various flavors to learn to live together harmoniously. I find this particularly true of manicotti. Make it today, bake it tomorrow night! As with many Italian dishes, the secret lies in the sauce. Everyone has a favorite tomato sauce. This is mine.

1 *lb. lean ground beef*
1/4 *cup olive oil*
1 *large onion, chopped coarse*
1/2 *green pepper*
1 *cup fresh mushrooms, sliced*
2 *medium cloves garlic, minced*
2 *Tbs. chopped parsley*
1 *tsp. dried marjoram*
1 *Tb. fresh basil (1½ tsps. dried)*
1 *tsp. dried oregano*
1 *tsp. dried thyme*
1 *tsp. ground fennel*
2 *tsps. salt*

1/2 *tsp. black pepper*
1/2 *cup fresh ripe olives, chopped*
1⅓ *cups tomato paste (2 cans,*
   6 ozs. each)
2 *cups water*
1 *box manicotti (8 ozs.)*
1 *egg, beaten*
1/2 *to* 3/4 *lb. ricotta cheese*
2 *Tbs. chopped parsley*
1/4 *tsp. salt*
1/4 *tsp. black pepper*
3/4 *cup freshly grated Parmesan*
   cheese

Brown meat lightly in olive oil. Add onion, green pepper, chopped mushrooms. Stir until lightly browned. Then add garlic, 2 tablespoons parsley, marjoram, basil, oregano, thyme, fennel, 1½ teaspoons salt, pepper, olives, to the mixture. Stir and add tomato paste and water. Mix well and simmer over lowest burner approximately 1½ hours. When sauce is almost ready (add a bit more water if needed), cook the manicotti in boiling salted water until lightly tender. *Do not overcook.* Drain, rinse in cold water and set aside for stuffing. *To make stuffing:* Mix egg with ricotta, parsley, 1/4 teaspoon salt, 1/4 teaspoon pepper, and 1/4 cup Parmesan. Mix thoroughly. Stuff into manicotti with a teaspoon or a pastry tube. Then spoon 1/2 the tomato sauce into a long deep, rectangular baking dish. Sprinkle with 1/4 cup Parmesan. Place the stuffed rolls of manicotti on top. Then spoon remaining sauce over the top. Sprinkle remaining 1/4 cup Parmesan over the top. Cover, place in refrigerator overnight, the better for savoring. Bake in 350° F. oven for 30 minutes. Serves 6.

Spicy Stuffed Veal Breast

Breast of veal is still one of the best meat buys around, and when "fancied up" can make a delicious and rather special dinner. A favorite treatment in our house is this.

6 *Tbs. margarine*
2 *medium onions, chopped*
1 *egg, beaten slightly*
1 *cup cooked rice*
3 *cups raw spinach, chopped and*
   packed firm
1/8 *tsp. nutmeg*

1½ *tsps. salt*
1/4 *tsp. black pepper*
1/2 *tsp. chopped parsley*
3/4 *tsp. dried thyme*
3 *or 4 lbs. veal breast, boned*
3 *strips bacon, uncooked*

Melt margarine in heavy skillet. Add onions and sauté 5 minutes over a low heat. Combine egg with rice, spinach, nutmeg, salt, pepper, parsley and thyme. Mix well and add to skillet. Cook for 2 to 3 minutes. Cool. Wipe meat and place flat on counter. Spread the skillet mixture over the meat. Roll meat up and fasten with skewers or tie with cord. Place veal on a rack in a shallow baking pan. Cover with bacon strips. Bake in 325° F. oven approximately 2½ hours, or until just tender when tested with a fork. Remove from oven and set aside until serving time. Reheat 20 minutes before serving. To serve, slice meat on the bias, like flank steak. Delicious with a fruit salad or tossed greens. Serves 6.

Burgundy Veal Loaf

When common garden variety of meat loaf palls, try this veal loaf for a change of pace. It can be partly baked hours ahead and finished off at the last minute—happy news on busy days!

1 *lb. ground veal*	1 *cup soft bread crumbs*
¼ *lb. lean pork, ground*	1½ *tsps salt*
1 *large onion, chopped fine*	½ *tsp. black pepper, freshly*
3 *cloves garlic, minced*	*ground*
1 *egg, beaten*	2 *Tbs. red Burgundy wine*
½ *cup milk*	3 *Tbs. grated Cheddar cheese*

Mix together the veal and pork. Add the onion and garlic and mix well. Add the beaten egg to the milk. Stir bread crumbs into the egg-milk mixture. When well mixed, add to the meat and stir again. Add seasonings and wine, and finally the cheese. Mix thoroughly and pack the mixture into a greased meat loaf pan. Bake in a hot (400° F.) oven for 20 minutes. Lower heat to 350° and bake an additional 20 minutes. Remove from oven and set aside until dinnertime. Then reheat in 350° oven for an additional 20 minutes. (This is delicious served cold. If you prefer it as a summer dish, finish off the baking at one time and refrigerate until ready to serve.) Garnish with parsley sprigs and serve. Serves 6.

Hungarian Veal Casserole

I was an adult before I discovered the joys of Hungarian cooking. My children won't have to wait so long, though they are not old enough yet to identify dishes by nationality. They simply know what they like—and this is an example.

3 *Tbs. butter or shortening,*
  melted
1 *lb. lean veal, cubed*
1 *large onion, chopped*
1 *small clove garlic, minced*
¼ *tsp. rosemary*
Salt and pepper to taste
1 *cup water*

1 *cup sliced fresh mushrooms*
  (or 1 8-oz. can cooked mush-
  rooms, drained)
¼ *cup sherry*
12-oz. *box wide noodles*
1 *cup sour cream*
1 *cup bread crumbs*

Heat the shortening in a skillet. When melted, add the veal and brown it quickly. Lower heat, add onion, garlic, spices and water (approximately 1 cup) and let meat simmer slowly until tender, about 40 minutes. Near the end of the cooking time, add mushrooms and sherry. Meanwhile, cook noodles in briskly boiling water for 3 to 5 minutes, or until wilted but not limp. Drain. Add noodles to meat mixture. Stir in sour cream and transfer the mixture to a deep baking dish. Cover with a thin layer of sour cream, sprinkle on bread crumbs, cover and set aside or refrigerate. When ready to serve, bake for 30 minutes in a medium 350° F. oven. To hold, turn oven down to 275°, add another sprinkling of bread crumbs. Serves 6.

Easy Veal Parmigiana

This Italian favorite is a cinch to prepare and "brighten up" at the last minute.

6 *veal chops*
2 *eggs, beaten lightly*
1½ *tsps. salt*
½ *tsp. black pepper*
¼ *tsp. oregano*
1½ *cups crusty bread or cracker*
  crumbs

6 *Tbs. butter*
6 *Tbs. flour*
3 *cups milk*
1 *cup grated Parmesan cheese*
1 *lb. mozarella cheese*

Tenderize the veal chops with a meat pounder until they are quite flat (or eliminate this step by buying the best cut of veal chops). Put the eggs, salt, pepper and oregano in a bowl, the bread crumbs in another bowl. Dip each chop first in the egg mixture and then in the crumbs. Heat 2 tablespoons of butter in a large skillet. When butter is melted, add the chops and brown over a medium heat for 15 to 20 minutes. Transfer chops to a large low casserole or oblong cake pan. Melt remaining butter in the skillet and blend flour into it with a wire whisk. Add the milk slowly and keep whisking until the mixture thickens smoothly. Add the Parmesan cheese and blend again, taking care to keep the sauce smooth. Cover the chops with the sauce and set aside, covered, until needed. Thirty minutes before serving, uncover the casserole and cover chops with thick slices of mozarella cheese. Place casserole in 275–300° F. oven to heat thoroughly. Five minutes before serving, place under broiler to be sure cheese is fully melted and lightly browned and bubbly. Serves 6.

Veal Paprikash

Hungarian cuisine is surely one of the world's greatest. This classic is an example. And has the added bonus of being adaptable to a do-it-ahead formula.

2 *lbs. veal, sliced very thin*	3 *Tbs. paprika*
3 *Tbs. butter*	⅛ *tsp. dried thyme*
½ *cup fresh mushrooms, sliced*	1 *cup water*
2 *fat cloves garlic, sliced thin*	1 *pt. sour cream*
½ *tsp. salt*	1 *pkg. noodles (10 ozs.)*

Cut the veal into 3-inch squares. Pound it hard with a meat pounder or wooden pestle. Heat the butter in a skillet over a medium fire and sauté the mushrooms and garlic lightly. Add the pounded veal, turn up heat, and brown quickly over a high fire. Add the salt, paprika, thyme and water. Simmer, covered, over a gentle heat for 45 minutes to 1 hour. When meat is tender, remove skillet from fire, cover, and let stand until needed. Fifteen minutes before serving time, turn fire on low, stir in sour cream, additional paprika, and warm thoroughly. Serve hot over a bed of buttered noodles or with hot rice and a crispy green salad. Serves 6.

Jellied Veal Loaf with White Wine

The kitchen, no matter how attractive, is rarely inviting during July and August heat waves. For summer eating, there is nothing as appealing as a cool main course—easily prepared in the cool of the morning, before the thermometer takes off. This one is something special.

1 *lb. veal shoulder, boned*
3 *cups boiling water*
1 *large onion, halved*
1 *bay leaf*
1 *Tb. plain gelatin*
¼ *cup cold water*
½ *cup white wine (sauterne)*
1 *large carrot, chopped fine*
¼ *tsp. thyme*

¼ *tsp. black pepper*
1 *cup sour cream*
2 *Tbs. finely chopped green
    pepper*
1½ *tsps. salt*
2 *stalks celery, chopped fine*
1 *cup frozen peas, barely cooked*
¼ *tsp. marjoram*

Cut the veal into 1-inch cubes. (Better still, let your butcher do it for you.) Wipe with a damp cloth and place cubes in a large kettle of boiling salted water. Add onion and bay leaf and cook over medium fire until tender—¾ to 1 hour. Add water if needed. When done, remove meat. Strain stock and save. Cut any gristle or fat off meat and put it through meat grinder. Set aside in large mixing bowl. Dissolve gelatin in cold water. Heat 1 cup veal stock and slowly add gelatin mixture to it. Stir until dissolved. Add wine, stir, and remove from heat. When cool, place in refrigerator approximately 1 hour, until slightly thickened. Remove and add to veal in mixing bowl. Add all remaining ingredients and mix thoroughly. Place in a loaf pan and chill until needed. Serve inverted on lettuce on a platter. Decorate with crisp radish roses and carrot curls. Green Goddess dressing or mayonnaise may be served in an accompanying dish. Serves 6.

Stuffed Lamb Breast à la Helen of Troy

Well, we can't prove Helen ate this, but it is popular in Turkey, which is where Troy is, and Helen was certainly a commuter of sorts, wasn't she? Besides, it sounds good—and tastes even better.

2 *lamb breasts, with opening
    slits cut*
½ *tsp. salt*
¼ *tsp. black pepper, freshly
    ground*
¼ *cup olive oil*

2 *Tbs. grated onion*
¼ *cup raisins, softened in water*
¼ *tsp. dried thyme*
¼ *cup pine nuts*
1½ *cups cooked rice*
2 *Tbs. tomato sauce*

Wipe lamb and rub it with salt and pepper mixed. Sauté lamb in oil until browned all over. Set aside. Drain excess fat. Sauté the onions in the same skillet until lightly cooked. Add raisins (drained), thyme, pine nuts and cooked rice. Mix well and continue cooking for 5 minutes. Cool. Fill slits in lamb breasts with stuffing. Skewer closed. Place lamb in flat 9 x 13-inch baking pan. Bake in low (300° F.) oven until meat is tender, several hours. Turn occasionally. Baste with water if necessary. Set aside when just tender. At mealtime, add tomato sauce and a bit more water to keep meat moist. Cover pan and heat thoroughly—about 15 minutes minimum. To keep for tardy diners, add water little by little so lamb stays moist. Serve with a vegetable casserole and tossed salad. Serves 6.

Lamb with Raisin Sauce

This is another of those recipes that takes the "lamb" out of lamb—the too-strong flavor—through judicious seasoning.

2½ Tbs. flour	½ cup raisins
3 lbs. breast of lamb	1½ Tbs. currant jelly
2 Tbs. margarine	½ tsp. dill weed
¼ cup sherry	1 cup sour cream
1 can condensed chicken broth	2 tsps. salt
1 large bay leaf	½ tsp. freshly ground black
2 Tbs. margarine	pepper
¼ lb. fresh mushrooms, sliced	

Pat flour onto the lamb breast and sear quickly in the margarine in a large, deep kettle. Add sherry, chicken broth and bay leaf. Cover kettle and simmer over low heat for approximately 1½ to 2 hours, or until meat is well done. Set aside until needed. At dinnertime, reheat meat (add water if necessary) over very low fire. If the dinner hour is postponed, keep kettle covered, but turn off heat. When family finally assembles, remove meat to a hot platter and keep warm in oven. Meanwhile, melt remaining margarine in skillet and lightly sauté mushrooms and raisins. Add jelly, dill weed and sour cream. Mix well and pour into kettle with remaining liquid. Heat and stir. Add salt and pepper, then pour slightly thickened sauce over the lamb, and serve piping hot. Buttered noodles complement this dish well. Serves 6.

Lamb and Apple Curry

Apple and curry are not all that uncommon, but this three-way combination is a bit unusual—and delicious. Like all curries, it loves to be kept waiting.

3 *Tbs. curry powder*
2 *tsps. paprika*
½ *tsp. salt*
½ *tsp. chili powder*
½ *tsp. sugar*
¼ *tsp. cumin*
⅛ *tsp. ground cardamom*
1 *tsp. dried ginger*

5 *Tbs. salad oil*
3 *cloves garlic, minced*
2 *large onions, chopped fine*
1½ *lbs. stewing lamb, cut in 1-inch cubes*
1 *12-oz. can tomato paste*
Boiling water
3 *cups peeled and chopped apples*

Mix together curry powder, paprika, salt, chili powder, sugar, cumin, cardamom and ginger. In deep skillet, heat salad oil and sauté garlic and onion until golden. Add spice mixture, stir well, and cook lightly until brown. Push to one side, and add lamb. Brown meat all over. Add tomato paste and enough boiling water to cover meat. Cover skillet and simmer gently 30 minutes. Set aside until needed. At mealtime, add apples and simmer 20 to 30 minutes. If you are playing the Waiting Game, add just enough water to keep curry moist. Turn heat low and keep skillet tightly covered. Serve on bed of rice, with green salad accompaniment. Serves 6.

Lester's Lamb Stew

As a brand-new bride, I could make smashing brownies, presentable scrambled eggs, and none-too-neat club sandwiches. That exhausted my repertoire. My groom, on the other hand, with several years experience "batching it" with three roommates, prided himself on Beef Stroganoff, Veal Marsala, and endless numbers of improvised *specialités,* such as this lamb stew. In due time I learned. But Lester's Lamb remains a family favorite.

7 to 8 *lbs. stewing lamb (inexpensive cut)*
3 *slices bacon*
1 *large onion, chopped coarse*
¼ *cup sherry*

Salt and pepper to taste
½ *cup water*
1½ *Tbs. lemon juice*
¼ *tsp. marjoram*

Cut the meat into 1-inch cubes. Fry the bacon in a large skillet, drain and set aside. Brown the lamb in 2 tablespoons bacon fat. When brown on all sides, add onion and lightly brown. Drain excess fat. Add sherry, salt, pepper and water. Simmer gently for 1 hour. When lamb is tender, set skillet aside. At dinnertime, reheat lamb, adding water little by little to prevent burning. Keep on the lowest heat possible, adding mixture of sherry and water if dry. When family finally appears, add lemon juice and marjoram. Stir well, cook 1 minute, then serve over hot noodles or with baby new potatoes with basil butter. Serves 6.

Midwinter Lamb Ragout

Hale and hearty, this is a one-dish meal good for a stormy winter's night (though it's tasty anytime!). Overheating can't possibly hurt it.

1 *cup dried white beans*	½ *tsp. oregano*
¼ *cup bacon fat*	½ *tsp. dried basil*
2½ *lbs. lamb shoulder, boned*	2 *tsps. salt*
and cubed	½ *tsp. black pepper*
3 *small onions, sliced thick*	2 *tsps. paprika*
3 *cloves garlic, minced*	1 *bay leaf*
1 *large (1 lb. 12 ozs.) can tomatoes*	3 *Tbs. flour*
1½ *cups chicken broth*	

Wash beans, cover with water and let stand overnight. Simmer beans in soaking water 1 hour or until tender. Heat bacon fat in large skillet. Add cubed lamb and brown lightly. Push to one side of skillet, add onions and garlic and brown them quickly. Place contents of skillet in large deep casserole. Add tomatoes and mix. Heat chicken broth and add oregano, basil, salt, pepper, paprika and bay leaf. Pour immediately over lamb in casserole. Add drained and rinsed beans—but save cooking water. Mix well, cover casserole and bake in preheated 350° F. oven approximately 2 hours. Set aside when lamb is tender—or turn off oven and let casserole stand covered. At serving time, reheat casserole. Meanwhile, blend flour with ¼ cup cold water until smooth paste. Heat in saucepan 1 cup of the bean cooking water. Thicken with flour paste mixture. Stir until smooth, and blend into the heated lamb casserole. Return to oven for 15 minutes or until piping hot. Serve with buttered rolls and a tossed salad. Serves 6.

Lovely Leftover Lamb

Dressed up with sherry and mushrooms, leftover lamb roast revives its spirits beautifully. And it's easy to fix ahead.

¾ *lb. fresh mushrooms, sliced thick*	1½ *cups leftover lamb gravy*
	Salt and pepper to taste
3 *Tbs. margarine*	12 *thin slices leftover lamb roast*
1 *medium onion, minced*	3 *Tbs. sherry wine*
2 *cloves garlic, minced*	¼ *cup grated Parmesan cheese*
¼ *tsp. dried oregano*	

Sauté mushrooms lightly in melted margarine in large skillet. When mushrooms are lightly browned, add onion and garlic and sauté until golden. Add oregano, lamb gravy and salt and pepper to taste. Mix well. Add lamb, cover with sauce mixture, cook 15 minutes and set skillet aside. Twenty minutes before serving, transfer lamb and sauce to flat baking pan. Add sherry, sprinkle cheese over top, and heat for ½ hour in 300° F. oven. Serve with Noodles Supreme or hot buttered noodles or rice. To hold for late arrivals, add more sherry to prevent meat from drying out, sprinkle more cheese over the top, and cover tightly. Turn oven off for the interim wait, then reheat briefly for 10 minutes when guests or family finally arrive. Serves 6.

Leg of Lamb with Yogurt

This is a simple and refreshing way to serve a young leg of lamb. Unlike many young things, this is willing to wait.

3 to 4-*lb. leg of lamb*	6 *small whole onions (or 3 me-*
1 *Tb. margarine or butter*	*dium onions, quartered)*
¾ *cup water*	2 *bunches fresh dill (or ½ tsp.*
½ *tsp. salt*	*dill weed)*
¼ *tsp. black pepper*	1 *pt. yogurt*

Brown the leg of lamb in a large skillet in the melted shortening. Brown on all sides. Transfer lamb to large kettle, and add water, salt and pepper. Check often and add more water if needed. Simmer for approximately 1½ hours. Add onions when lamb has cooked 1 hour. Set aside. Thirty minutes before serving, reheat lamb, adding dill or dill weed at this time. *Just* before serving, stir in the yogurt, mix well and serve. Serves 6 to 8.

Creole Leg of Spring Lamb

This Creole treatment is a great way to jazz up leg of lamb.

⅓ *cup dry red wine*	¼ *tsp. cayenne pepper*
1½ *Tbs. tarragon vinegar*	¾ *tsp. salt*
¾ *cup beef bouillon*	½ *tsp. black pepper*
2 *medium onions, minced*	1½ *Tbs. olive oil*
3 *large cloves garlic, minced*	2 *tsps. sugar*
⅓ *cup chili sauce*	6-lb. *leg of lamb*
1 *bay leaf*	

Combine wine, vinegar, bouillon, onions, garlic, and chili sauce. Mix thoroughly. Add seasonings, olive oil and sugar. Wipe lamb and pour marinade over it. Chill in refrigerator overnight. Turn leg from time to time to be sure sauce covers it. To roast, remove lamb from marinade and place it on a rack in a large roasting pan. Brush marinade over lamb. Place lamb in 325° F. oven and bake uncovered 3½ to 4 hours, brushing marinade over lamb occasionally. Do not let meat dry out. If you use up marinade and lamb becomes dry, add boiling water to roasting pan little by little. Remove lamb when done and set aside until needed. Reheat for 20 to 30 minutes before serving. Place lamb slices on hot platter and thicken the sauce in the pan. Pour over lamb and serve. Hot noodles or rice marry well with this. Serves 6 to 8.

Glazed Leg of Lamb

If your oven has a time-bake element, this is an easy way to have a gloriously prepared leg of lamb ready and waiting for you when you come home from an afternoon of bridge (oh, frivolity!) or den-mothering a covey of Cub Scouts (oh, duty!).

1 7-lb. *leg of lamb*	5 *or 6 cloves garlic*
1 *tsp. salt*	3 *Tbs. currant jelly*
½ *tsp. pepper*	3 *Tbs. brown sugar*
½ *tsp. dried thyme*	1½ *Tbs. wine vinegar*

Trim off only excessive lumps of fat from the lamb, but do not remove the thin skin covering the leg. Wipe the leg with a damp clean cloth. Mix salt and freshly ground pepper together with the thyme and rub over the meat. With a sharp knife, make 5 or 6 deep punctures in the leg, evenly spaced. Poke a garlic clove into each hole. Place the leg in a shallow baking pan, fat side up, skin side down. Roast uncovered in a 325° F. oven for 3 to 3½ hours, depending on whether you like your lamb medium rare or well done. During the roasting time, the lamb can be forgotten. But approximately 20 to 25 minutes before needed, pour a mixture of the jelly, brown sugar and wine vinegar over the lamb. Continue the roasting as before. Serve the glazed lamb hot or oven warm, with hot rice or whipped potatoes and a marinated vegetable salad. For company dinner, Noodle-Mushroom Supreme makes a splendid accompaniment. (See page 121.) Serves 8.

Pan-Glazed Sauterne Lamb Chops

This top-of-the-stove delight can simmer merrily while you do your morning chores, then be set aside and quickly reheated at dinnertime. Yet it is impressive enough to satisfy even a Caesar—no mean commuter himself, from Rome to Gaul and back.

6 *shoulder lamb chops*	1 *large onion, chopped coarse*
4½ *Tbs. olive oil*	¼ *tsp. rosemary needles*
1 *tsp. salt (more to taste)*	½ *tsp. grated lemon rind*
½ *tsp. black pepper*	6 *carrots, peeled and quartered*
3 *cloves garlic, peeled*	6 *medium potatoes, peeled and*
1 *10½-oz. can consommé, un-*	*halved*
diluted	1 *stalk of celery, trimmed*
1¼ *cups sauterne*	

Trim excess fat off each chop. Cut "darts" into each chop to prevent the edges from curling during the cooking. Wipe with a damp cloth. Place the chops in a large skillet in which the oil has been heated. Sprinkle with salt and pepper and brown lightly. Add the garlic cloves, cut in half. Brown the garlic for 5 minutes, then remove. Turn the chops over, add the consommé, wine and chopped onion. Taste and add more salt and pepper if desired, as well as the rosemary and lemon peel. Cover the skillet and allow to simmer over very low fire until tender, usually about 1½ hours. Lift cover, add the carrots, potatoes and celery and cover again. Set skillet aside until 30 minutes before serving time. Then return skillet to very low fire and reheat, allowing vegetables to cook until tender but not mushy. If the liquid has evaporated, add a little more wine diluted with water. Remove and discard celery and serve your one-pan dinner piping hot. Serves 6.

End-of-the-Month Lamb Stew

In my childhood B.A.A. (Before the Affluent Age), the end of the month usually meant Economize! The pay check had been stretched to the breaking point, and many families "enjoyed" a rather starchy-stewy diet until payday. I always think of stew as an inexpensive way to dine—but it can be glamorized today. Here is one way:

3 *lbs. lamb shanks, cut small*	1/4 *tsp. rosemary*
3 *Tbs. flour*	2 *cups water*
1 *tsp. salt*	1 *cup red wine*
1/2 *tsp. black pepper*	1 *tsp. salt*
1/2 *tsp. chili powder (more to*	2 *bay leaves*
taste)	12 *tiny onions, peeled*
2 *Tbs. salad oil*	6 *carrots, diced*
1 *can (15 ozs.) tomato sauce*	3/4 *lb. fresh string beans, halved*
1 *large clove garlic, peeled*	6 *small potatoes, peeled*

Wash the lamb shanks and lightly dry with a damp towel. Mix the flour, salt, pepper and chili powder well. Dip the lamb in this mixture and brown quickly in the heated salad oil in a large skillet. Drain off excess liquid and add the tomato sauce, garlic, rosemary, water and wine, remaining salt and bay leaf. Simmer over lowest heat for approximately 1 hour (until tender). Add the onions, carrots, beans and potatoes, and continue simmering gently for 25 to 35 minutes, or until all vegetables are cooked. Do not overcook to the mushy stage. Pour the skillet contents into a greased casserole, cover and set aside for several hours. (If longer, refrigerate.) Twenty minutes before serving, bake casserole in a 375° F. oven. A meal unto itself! Serves 6.

Lamb Braised in Sour Cream

Lamb and sour cream make an unexpectedly successful combination. This recipe, using lamb neck, is a thrifty day-before-payday special.

3 *lbs. lamb neck, trimmed*	3 *Tbs. butter or margarine*
1/3 *cup flour*	2 *medium onions, minced*
1 *Tb. salt*	2 *cloves garlic, minced*
1/2 *tsp. black pepper*	1 1/2 *cups sour cream*
1/4 *tsp. dried thyme*	3 *Tbs. lemon juice*
1/4 *tsp. rosemary*	1/4 *cup dry white wine*
1/2 *tsp. caraway seeds*	3 *bouillon cubes*
1/2 *tsp. dried tarragon*	1 1/2 *cups boiling water*

Wipe meat and cut into 1-inch pieces. Combine flour, salt, pepper, thyme, rosemary, caraway, tarragon. Mix well. Dredge meat with this dry mixture. Melt butter in large deep skillet. Add lamb and brown quickly. Add onions and garlic and brown. Lower heat, add sour cream, lemon juice, white wine, and cover skillet. Dissolve bouillon cubes in boiling water and add to lamb mixture in skillet. Simmer over lowest heat 1½ hours. Set aside. Before serving, reheat for ½ hour. Serve over bed of hot rice or noodles, or with side dishes of fluffy mashed potatoes and green peas. Serves 6.

Turkish Eggplant Delight ⟨

This is one of those magical dishes that you can prepare at 10 A.M., take an all-day trip, and return to pop it into the oven for a final heat-up, and serve to dazzled guests in the twinkling of an eye (yours).

1 *lb. lamb shoulder*
¼ *cup olive oil*
2 *or 3 small eggplants (or 1 large)*
½ *cup raw rice*
1 *large onion, minced*
3 *cloves garlic, minced*
½ *green pepper, diced*
½ *cup pine nuts*
2 *small tomatoes, diced*
1 *tsp. salt (more to taste)*

¼ *tsp. celery salt*
½ *tsp. black pepper*
⅛ *tsp. cinnamon*
⅛ *teaspoon nutmeg*
½ *tsp. dried oregano*
½ *cup red Burgundy*
1 *cup Feta (Greek goat cheese)*
  or ¾ cup grated Parmesan
  cheese

Cut the lamb into cubes and brown in the oil in a heavy skillet. Add a little water, cover, and simmer until tender. While lamb is simmering over low fire, parboil the eggplants whole in boiling salted water for 10 to 15 minutes, depending on size. Drain, cool, and then cut the eggplants in half lengthwise. Hollow out the meat, leaving a ¼-inch-thick shell. Chop the eggplant meat and set aside. Boil the rice in 1 cup water 10 min. Set aside. When the lamb is almost tender, add the onion, garlic and green pepper to the skillet. When meat is thoroughly cooked, add the pine nuts, tomato, chopped eggplant, salt, celery salt, pepper, cinnamon, nutmeg and oregano. Mix well and pour in the wine. Mixture should be loose but not runny. If too loose, let simmer a bit longer till liquid evaporates a bit. Fill the eggplant shells with the mixture, top with the Feta cheese crumbled into pieces, cover, and refrigerate until mealtime. Place eggplant shells in a baking pan and bake, uncovered, for 30 minutes in a 350° F. oven. Three minutes before serving, place under broiler to brown the cheese slightly. Serves 6.

Indonesian Lamb (Saté Kambing)

This is another one of those delicious dishes that demand marinating, the longer the better. I sometimes begin marinating the meat the night before, although in a pinch two hours ahead of time is long enough for flavor to set in.

¾ tsp. cumin seed, crushed	4 cloves garlic, minced
2 tsps. ground coriander	2 Tbs. Japanese soy sauce
½ to ¾ tsp. saffron	½ cup water
½ tsp. dried chili peppers	2½ lbs. lamb shoulder
1 tsp. powdered ginger	¾ cup wine vinegar
1 tsp. black pepper, fresh ground	½ cup peanut oil

Mix together well the cumin, coriander, saffron, chili peppers, gingers, black pepper and garlic. Add soy sauce and just enough water to make a paste. Cut away the bone from the lamb and cut lamb into 1-inch cubes. Roll the cubes in the spice mixture and place in large bowl. Pour vinegar and ¼ cup peanut oil over the lamb. Allow to marinate at least 2 hours, preferably longer. Turn pieces from time to time. When ready to cook, drain liquid from bowl. Heat the remaining ¼ cup oil in a skillet and add the spiced lamb. Brown quickly. Then add water, cover and simmer over very low heat until tender, approximately 20 minutes. Serve hot on a bed of fluffy rice. Serves 6 to 8.

Turkish Kabobs

Turkey shares the Middle Eastern fondness for meat on a stick. And the longer the meat is marinated, the tastier the kabob. Try marinating the meat beginning the night before, to give the flavors a better chance to permeate the meat.

Small leg of lamb, trimmed of all bone, fat and gristle	½ tsp. black pepper freshly ground
½ cup olive oil	¼ cup lemon juice
½ tsp. Worcestershire sauce	3 large cloves garlic, minced
1½ tsps. salt	2 Tbs. chopped chives
3 Tbs. chopped parsley	1 Tb. dill weed

Cut the lamb into large cubes. Mix all the other ingredients together in a large mixing bowl. Stir well. Add the lamb cubes, cover and leave standing for 1 hour. Stir and turn the cubes to be sure all are covered with marinade. Recover and refrigerate for 3 to 4 hours *minimum,* preferably overnight. When ready to broil, thread the meat on skewers. Broil over a charcoal grill or in the oven. Baste with marinade to keep meat from drying out. If dinner is postponed, hold the threaded skewers in abeyance, broiling at the last minute, during cocktail time. Serve with rice or rice-stuffed cabbage leaves, as well as a green salad. Serves 6.

Braised Lamb Shanks

It is so easy to fall into the steak-chops-ground meat habit, but there are many interesting things that can be done with more offbeat cuts of meat. Take lamb shanks for instance, as in this delicious waitable recipe.

6 *lamb shanks*
1 *lemon, cut in half*
1/2 *cup flour*
2 1/2 *tsps. salt*
3/4 *tsp. freshly ground black*
   pepper
1/2 *tsp. oregano*
1/4 *cup salad oil*
3 *large cloves garlic, minced*

2 *large onions, chopped coarse*
1/2 *cup coarsely chopped celery*
1/2 *cup chopped peeled carrots*
1 *cup red Burgundy*
1/4 *tsp. nutmeg*
1 *can consommé, undiluted*
2 *bay leaves*
2 or 3 *fresh mint leaves*

Trim the meat and rub each piece with lemon. Set aside in a bowl for 10 to 15 minutes. Combine the flour, salt, pepper and oregano. Mix well and pour into a brown paper bag. Put the meat in the bag and shake well, as you would with chicken. Heat the oil in a skillet and add the meat. Set the bag aside for the moment. Sauté meat until brown, then remove it to a deep large casserole. In the skillet sauté the garlic, onion, celery and carrot for 5 minutes. Add remaining flour in bag and brown it lightly. Slowly add the wine, nutmeg and consommé. Heat 2 minutes and pour entire mixture over the lamb in casserole. Scatter the bay and mint leaves over the top and cover casserole tightly. Simmer over lowest heat possible on top of stove for 1 hour—or until just slightly tender. Set aside until needed. An hour before your estimated dinnertime, place casserole, covered, in a 375° F. oven and bake until very tender. If dinner must be delayed, reduce oven heat to 325° and add a mixture of Burgundy and consommé to prevent casserole from drying out. Serves 6.

Turkish Lamb Casserole

This Turkish equivalent of a lamb stew is best if prepared in an earthen crock, for it requires long cooking, and there is something special about a dish that has been allowed to bake slowly in a clay pot. It is the next best thing to being cooked over coals or in a wood fire. This dish may be started early and happily bake through twilight into the dinner hour.

2 to 3 *lbs. lamb shoulder*	2½ *tsps. paprika*
6 *big roasting potatoes, peeled*	1 *bay leaf*
3 *large fresh tomatoes*	2 *tsps. dill weed*
1 *red pepper, chopped fine*	½ *tsp. salt*
6 *cloves garlic, chopped*	¼ *tsp. black pepper, freshly*
12 *small onions*	*ground*
2 or 3 *small scallions*	¼ to ½ *cup water*

Cut the lamb off bone into large egg-sized pieces and place in large earthen casserole. Quarter the potatoes and add to the casserole. Add tomatoes, cubed, red pepper, garlic, onions and scallions. Mix lightly, then sprinkle over the top paprika, bay leaf, dill weed, salt and pepper. Mix again. Add water, cover and bake for 3 hours in 300° F. oven. Check after 2 hours to see if liquid need be added. If so, add water sparingly, but do it gingerly. Makes 6 servings.

Middle Eastern Lamb Patties

Lamb is the ubiquitous meat of the Middle East, from Greece to Egypt and on to Morocco. Lester Brooks decided that lamb was not for him—until he followed this route. Now, prepared with spices to soften the strong lamb flavor, this meat plays a starring role at table. The setting may not be as exotic as Tangiers, but the food is good.

1½ *lbs. lean lamb, cubed*
2 *cups water*
2½ *Tbs. fresh mint*
3 *cinnamon sticks*
1 *tsp. peppercorns*
1¼ *tsps. salt*

1½ *cups canned chick peas*
2¼ *Tbs. yogurt*
3 *Tbs. minced onion*
3 *Tbs. chopped fresh tomato*
2½ *Tbs. chopped fresh ginger*

Cut off all fat from the lamb cubes. Place the cubes in a large saucepan, along with water, mint, cinnamon sticks, peppercorns, salt and drained chick peas. Boil at high speed until all the water is gone, then remove pan from the fire. Discard the cinnamon sticks. When cool, put the mixture through a meat grinder, grinding as fine as possible. Add yogurt to the meat and mix well. Form the meat into 12 patties. Into each patty fold a little onion, chopped tomato, and ginger. Fold over the patty, so filling is mixed inside. Place patties on plate, cover and refrigerate several hours, or until needed. Broil quickly in kitchen broiler, as you would hamburger. Serve with hot buttered rice or wheat pilaff, and a big green tossed salad with ripe olives and pimientos in it. Serves 6.

Lamb and Lima Casserole

A homey and delicious way to serve limas with an inexpensive but hearty cut of lamb! Begin it the night before, finish it off the morning of your dinner. Then reheat at the last minute.

2 *cups dried lima beans*
6 *small lamb shanks (or one large breast)*
3 *Tbs. salad oil*
3 *Tbs. bacon fat*

1½ *tsps. salt (more if needed)*
½ *tsp. black pepper*
½ *tsp. rosemary*
2 *medium onions, sliced*
½ *cup red wine*

Soak the dried limas in 4 cups cold water for *at least* 4 hours. (I usually put them to soak just before bedtime, then they are ready for use the next morning.) Early on in the day, brown the lamb in oil and bacon fat over a medium heat. Remove the meat when nicely browned to a good-sized baking dish, sprinkle with ½ teaspoon salt, the pepper and rosemary, and pour over all 1½ cups hot water. Cover the baking dish and bake in a 350° F. oven for 1 hour. At that time, remove the meat, pour off excess fat, pour in the limas and their soaking water, along with the onion, and additional salt. Put the lamb back on top of the beans, add the wine, cover and bake another 1½ hours. Remove from oven and let stand until dinnertime. Half an hour before serving, return baking dish to oven (350° again) and reheat until most of the liquid has been absorbed. Serve with baby new potatoes boiled with dill weed, or fluffy rice. Serves 6.

Pork Chops with Mushroom Stuffing

Another pocketful of dreams, this dish happily sits and waits.

6 *thick pork chops, loin cuts*	¼ *tsp. black pepper*
½ *lb. fresh mushrooms*	¼ *tsp. salt*
1½ *Tbs. butter or margarine*	¼ *tsp. dried marjoram*
½ *cup dry bread crumbs*	¼ *tsp. summer savory*
¼ *tsp. dried thyme*	1½ *Tbs. butter or margarine*
¼ *tsp. sage*	

Cut, or have your butcher cut, fairly deep pockets in each chop, in the leanest part. Wash the mushrooms and cut the stems off. Chop the stems fine and put them in a saucepan with 2 to 3 cups of water. Let simmer over a low fire until half the liquid has cooked away. Meanwhile, slice half the mushroom caps and set aside. Chop the other half very fine and sauté the chopped ones in a large skillet in butter until lightly browned. Then mix with bread crumbs and all the seasonings. Stuff the mixture into the pork chops. Thread a skewer through the pocket sides to keep opening closed during cooking. Place the chops into the same skillet you used for the mushrooms and brown quickly on both sides. Pour off the pork fat, then add the mushroom liquid with stems included and let chops simmer over a low fire, covered, for 1 full hour. When tender, place chops in flat baking pan and set aside until needed. Save the pan gravy in the skillet. Thirty minutes before serving time, place the casserole in the oven at 325° F. Heat the sauce in the skillet, add remaining butter and sauté the remaining sliced mushroom caps. When they are brown, thicken the sauce slightly with flour, add a little more water if necessary, and pour over the chops in the casserole. When chops are heated through, serve. A sweet potato casserole and fruit salad make harmonious accompaniments to this family dish. Serves 6.

Pork Chop Jambalaya

It may be taking a liberty to call this zesty pork chop casserole Jambalaya, but it is a close relative of that tasty Creole dish. I call this my casserole for people who claim they don't like casseroles (are you there, Jim Brooks?). By keeping the chops intact, one can *pretend* it isn't a casserole. Only we casserole lovers will know for sure. And we'll be too busy eating to tell.

½ cup raw rice
6 small pork chops, medium thick
2 cups cubed canned ham
2 tsps. salt
½ tsp. black pepper
2 large onions, sliced ½ inch thick
3 fresh tomatoes, sliced

1 large green pepper, sliced
⅓ tsp. marjoram
½ tsp. thyme
¼ tsp. dried basil
⅛ tsp. celery salt
1½ cans consommé, undiluted
¼ cup sherry
1 Tb. chopped parsley

Place the rice in the bottom of a fairly deep and wide casserole. Lightly brown the pork chops in a skillet over a medium heat. Add ham and cook 5 minutes longer. Place on top of the rice. Pour drippings from skillet over the rice. Sprinkle just a little salt and pepper over the chops and ham. Then place a layer of onions over the meat, then a layer of tomatoes. Sprinkle more salt and pepper. Add a layer of green pepper. Mix together marjoram, thyme, basil, celery salt with the consommé and sherry. Pour over the casserole. Sprinkle parsley on top. Cover and refrigerate overnight. At mealtime, casserole should bake in 350° F. for approximately 1 hour, but it doesn't mind waiting if you turn oven down to 300° and add a bit more liquid to keep it from getting dry. Serve with fruit or gelatin salad and crusty bread. Pickled apples or spiced applesauce make a compatible side dish. Serves 6.

Pork and Apple Casserole

Basic, hearty autumn fare, this is an ideal company dinner for Halloween or any time. It suggests harvest and winter a-comin'.

6 *thick lean pork chops or slices*   ½ *tsp. dried thyme*
   from a pork roast   1½ *tsps. salt*
6 *fat yams*   ¾ *cup sherry wine*
2 *large onions, grated*   ¾ *cup water*
3 *large MacIntosh apples, peeled*
   and sliced thick

Brown the pork in a skillet in a little cooking oil. Trim all the fat off. Parboil the yams (or sweet potatoes) for 10 or 15 minutes. Cool, then peel and slice into 2-inch squares. Place in the bottom of a large casserole, cover with the pork slices. Top the pork with the onion, then the apple slices. Add the seasoning, then the sherry and water mixed together. Cover casserole and refrigerate until needed. Bake in 350° F. oven, covered, for 30 to 35 minutes. A meal in itself, delicious with cole slaw or a tossed salad, hot rolls or Italian bread. Serves 6.

Pork with a Stuffed Pocket

There are many variations of this, but this recipe is a favorite of mine, and so easy to fix ahead of time. The "finishing off" is just reheating.

1 *pork shoulder, about 5 lbs.*   ¾ *Tb. sugar*
1 *tsp. salt*   ½ *tsp. dried thyme*
½ *tsp. black pepper*   ¼ *tsp. cinnamon*
¾ *cup apples, peeled and*   2 *Tbs. butter or margarine*
   chopped   2 *cups Chablis or other dry white*
¼ *cup walnuts, chopped coarse*   *wine*
¾ *cup seedless raisins*

Ask your butcher to cut a sizable pocket in the pork shoulder. Wipe meat with a damp cloth, then rub it with salt and pepper. Mix together the apples, nuts, raisins, sugar, a pinch of salt, thyme, and cinnamon. Fill the pork pocket with this mixture. Brown the shoulder in margarine in a deep skillet or Dutch oven. When nicely browned, add 1 cup wine to the pan and continue simmering over a low fire. It should take several hours for the meat to be really tender. During this time, add more of the wine. When the meat is done, set aside until needed (or refrigerate). Half an hour before serving, transfer meat to a baking dish and allow to reheat in a 325° F. oven. Add a little wine or hot water to keep meat from drying out. Serves 6.

Blanketed Pigs en Casserole

This piquant version of pigs-in-blankets is easy to fix ahead—and easy to enjoy too.

1¼ lbs. lean pork, boneless
1 Tb. butter
1 large onion, minced
1½ Tbs. salad oil
1 can tomato soup, undiluted
1 cup water
¾ cup raw rice, washed

⅛ tsp. dried thyme
½ tsp. dried basil (or 1 tsp. fresh)
¼ tsp. dried oregano
2 tsps. salt (more to taste)
½ tsp. black pepper
12 fresh cabbage leaves

Cut pork into ½-inch cubes. Sauté on all sides in melted butter in a skillet. Remove pork from skillet to a mixing bowl, but save remaining butter. Sauté onion in butter, with salad oil added, about 5 to 6 minutes, or until limp and translucent. Add soup and 1 cup water to onion. Simmer for 5 minutes. Set aside. Meanwhile, combine pork with raw rice, thyme, basil, oregano, salt and pepper. Cook cabbage leaves in boiling salted water until just barely limp. Cool. Spread leaves flat and fill each leaf with a portion of the pork-rice mixture, using it all up. Roll each cabbage leaf loosely and place, top side down, in a rectangular baking dish (lasagne dish). Pour onion-soup liquid over the cabbage rolls. Cover baking dish securely and bake in 375° F. oven for 1 hour. Remove and set aside until needed. To reheat, set oven at 350° and bake an additional 30 minutes, covered. Serve with a fruit salad and hot rolls or warmed cheese bread. If you have to play the Waiting Game in earnest, turn oven off, add additional onion-soup liquid to keep "Pigs" moist, and keep tightly covered. At last minute, reheat briefly. Serves 6.

Lima, a Most Versatile Bean

If you are accustomed to serving lima beans merely as a side vegetable dish, consider a moment. Limas in a casserole add substance and serve often as a potato or rice substitute in starch content. Further, the texture of limas makes them a welcome contrast and complement to many other foods. The following is one of my make-it-ahead lima favorites:

Lima-Pork Chop Casserole

2 *cups dried lima beans (canned*	½ *cup tomato purée*
may be substituted)	*Salt to taste*
6 *small pork chops*	½ *tsp. black pepper*
3 *Tbs. butter*	½ *tsp. dry mustard*
1 *large onion, minced*	½ *cup canned pineapple, diced*
1 *Tbs. brown sugar*	*(optional)*

Soak the dried beans in 4 cups cold water for 2 hours (or overnight). Cook them in their own liquid until barely tender—approximately 30 to 40 minutes. Drain all but ½ cup water from beans. Place beans and remaining liquid in shallow casserole. Set aside for the moment. Now brown the chops in butter in a skillet, and add the onions. Continue cooking until onions are golden. Transfer chops and onions to casserole on top of the beans. Mix together brown sugar, tomato purée, salt, pepper, and mustard. Place the pineapple around and over the chops. Pour sugar-tomato mixture over all. Cover casserole until evening. Bake 1 hour in a medium (325° F.) oven. (Or if you prefer, bake for ½ hour in the A.M., set aside. Then at dinnertime, simply reheat for ½ hour.) Delicious with a crisp salad and corn muffins or heated Italian bread. Serves 6.

Claret-Baked Corned Pork

Corned pork seems to be going the way of the icebox, but when you can get it, it makes marvelous eating. (The solution is to pickle or corn your own pork shoulder at home, but that takes time.) Easy fixing too.

1 *corned pork shoulder*	¾ *cup brown sugar*
Whole cloves, as needed	*Dash of Tabasco sauce*
2 *cups claret wine*	1½ *Tbs. cornstarch*

Place corned pork in a deep kettle and cover with cold water. Bring to a rapid boil over high heat. Skim the top, cover kettle, and then let the pork simmer over low heat approximately 3 hours, or until tender when a fork is stuck into it. Set aside until cool. Remove pork and take off skin and excess fat. Score meat and stick a clove in each scored square. Place meat in baking pan. Pour claret over meat and bake in fairly hot (375° F.) oven for 45 minutes. Baste often with the claret in the pan. After 45 minutes, turn off oven, open door, and let pork settle in oven until needed. When family arrives, make a paste of brown sugar, Tabasco, cornstarch and just enough water to form paste. Spread paste onto the pork. Heat in 350° oven until pork is well glazed, basting often. This is delicious served cold too. If you opt for cold, the glazing may be done immediately after the meat is fully baked. It may then cool in the oven and be refrigerated overnight. Serves 6 amply.

Teriyaki Pork Kabobs

The basic do-it-ahead aspect of this Japanese dish is the marinade. At mealtime, it is a quick proposition to broil the skewered meat and serve. I usually expedite the proceedings by threading the skewers shortly before cooking time.

3 *lbs. pork shoulder*
1½ *cups soy sauce*
½ *cup sugar*
¼ *cup sherry (or sake if available)*
4 *cloves garlic, chopped*

1 *slice raw ginger (or 1 tsp.*
   powdered)
2 *green peppers, cut in chunks*
2 *tomatoes, sliced thick*
18 *tiny onions, peeled*
1 *can (1 lb. 4 ozs.) pineapple cubes*

Trim the pork of fat and cut meat into 1-inch cubes. Mix together the soy sauce, sugar, sherry (or sake), chopped garlic and ginger. Pour mixture over the cubed pork in large mixing bowl. Refrigerate over-night or at least 6 hours. Turn occasionally in marinade. When ready to broil, thread meat onto skewers alternately with chunks of green pepper, tomatoes, onion, pineapple cubes. Baste frequently with mari-nade. Broil for 30 minutes, turning skewers several times during broil-ing process. Serve with hot rice and a crispy salad. (If dinner has to be held unexpectedly, turn oven off, reheat briefly at the last minute, basting with additional marinade all the while.) Serves 6.

Sauerkraut and Fresh Ham Goulash

My father always disdained goulash in a restaurant, fearful of all the leftovers that might be thrown into it. Of course that's what makes it such a blessing at home—you can improvise as you go along. How to empty the refrigerator in one fell swoop: GOULASH! This one isn't exactly improvised, but it's good anyhow.

3 *lbs. sauerkraut*
⅓ *cup corn or salad oil*
4 *cloves garlic, minced*
4 *medium onions, chopped coarse*
1 *small green pepper, chopped*
  fine
3 *lbs. fresh ham (or pork shoul-*
  der), cut into 1½-inch cubes
1½ *tsps. salt (more to taste)*

¾ *tsps. black pepper*
2½ *Tbs. Hungarian paprika*
2 *Tbs. caraway seeds*
1½ *tsps. MSG*
3 *cups canned tomatoes*
1½ *cups sour cream*
2½ *Tbs. flour*
1 *cup water*

Rinse and drain sauerkraut for 2 to 3 hours. Heat oil in large skillet and sauté garlic, onions, and green pepper until onions become limp and golden. Add cubed meat and brown lightly. Season with salt, pepper, paprika, caraway seeds and MSG. Add tomatoes and "mush" them up, mixing well with other ingredients. Lower heat and simmer until meat is tender, about 1 hour. If dinner threatens to be late, this is the moment to turn off stove, cover skillet and wait. The moment husband appears at the door, add sauerkraut and turn burner low, cooking mixture until sauerkraut is cooked but not mushy. Meanwhile, combine sour cream, flour and 1 cup water, and whisk well with wire whisk. When well blended, add to the skillet. Stir and simmer 3 or 4 minutes, then transfer goulash to a large heated serving bowl. Serve immediately with a side dish of baby new potatoes, boiled and topped with parsley butter. Serves 6 generously.

Indonesian Sate Babi

This Javanese delight must be made ahead. The longer you marinate it, the better it is. Skewered, broiled and served with rice and a green salad, it is a simple, but unusual party dish.

3 *lbs. pork loin (rib end pork*
  roast is economical and good
  for this dish)
1 *cup salted peanuts*
1 *Tb. ground coriander*
½ *tsp. freshly ground black*
  pepper
½ *tsp. ground ginger*
1½ *tsps. crushed red pepper*

1 *Tb. ground cumin or cumin*
  seeds
1 *cup thinly sliced onion*
5 *Tbs. soy sauce (heavy, Japanese*
  imported variety is best)
1 *Tb. lemon juice*
½ *cup salad oil* (not *olive oil*)
2 *Tbs. brown sugar*

Cut the pork into fairly even-sized cubes,* trimming off as much of the fat as possible, as well as all bones and sinews. Set aside. Chop peanuts in electric blender until finely ground. Add all spices and onion slices and blend for 10 seconds. Place pork cubes in a flat pan. Mix the blended spices, onions and nuts with soy, lemon juice, oil and brown sugar. Mix well. Pour over pork, and let marinate at least 6 hours, preferably overnight, turning and stirring every few hours. At mealtime, thread pork on to skewers, arrange them in a flat baking pan, and then begin the Waiting Game. The moment Husband arrives, pop the pan under the broiler. Turn skewers once, then within 10 to 15 minutes they are ready to serve. Place skewers on a bed of hot rice, and serve individual side dishes of soy sauce for dipping. Serves 6.

Ham and Spinach Casa Brooks

At the time of my marriage there was only one Brooks who could cook—my husband. This recipe is one of his early bachelor concoctions which is now part of our family culinary lore. It is a good recipe for using up leftover ham.

2 *large ham steaks (or leftover meat)*	½ *tsp. tarragon*
	Salt to taste (careful!)
½ *cup butter, melted*	8 *eggs*
2 *cups fresh mushrooms, sliced*	¾ *cup grated Parmesan cheese*
2 *cups cooked spinach*	

Brown the ham lightly in a small portion of the melted butter. Then remove it from the skillet and cut into fairly large chunks. Lightly sauté the sliced mushrooms in remaining butter and set aside. Place cooked spinach in the bottom of a greased medium-sized casserole. Mix tarragon with butter and mushrooms. Add just a pinch of salt and pour over the spinach. Place ham on top. At this point, the casserole may be covered and refrigerated until needed. When ready to bake, beat the eggs lightly and pour them over the casserole. Top with a sprinkling of grated cheese. Heat in a 350° F. oven 20 to 30 minutes. If there is a delay, turn oven off and put foil over top of casserole (in oven). At serving time, reheat oven, remove foil, sprinkle a little more cheese over the top, and heat 5 minutes or so at 350°. Served with boiled, baby new potatoes with a topping of parsley butter, this is a delicious casserole. Serves 6.

* Pork cut into 1-inch cubes requires less broiling time to cook thoroughly.

Honeyed Apple and Ham Casserole

If you'll pardon the expression, this is a honey of a family dish. It can be assembled ahead and be all set to pop into the oven when you hear the train whistle or the car in the driveway.

¾ tsp. dry mustard	2 medium eggs, beaten
1 small onion, minced	¾ cup milk
⅛ tsp. ground ginger	1½ cups soft bread crumbs
⅓ tsp. ground cloves	5 small apples, peeled, cored and
¼ tsp. salt (more to taste)	sliced
¼ tsp. black pepper	⅓ cup honey
4½ cups finely ground cooked	3 Tbs. margarine
ham	

Mix mustard, onion, ginger, cloves, salt, pepper together. Add ham and mix again. Combine egg, milk and bread crumbs. Add meat mixture and blend well. Pat into a shallow 9 x 13-inch baking pan. Place sliced apples evenly over the top. Spread honey over the apples and dot with margarine (or butter). Casserole is now ready to go when needed. If you live in the land of the closely watched trains, commuter type, pop the casserole into a preheated 375°F. oven the moment the train whistle greets your ears. Casserole should bake 30 minutes or so, until well heated and firm. Serves 6.

Scalloped Ham and Potato Casserole

This is a jazzing up of an old favorite—scalloped potatoes. It can be made ahead and reheated, or made at mealtime and held in the oven if there is a dinner delay.

6 cups thinly sliced raw potatoes	¼ tsp. dried thyme
3 Tbs. flour	3 Tbs. butter, melted
1 large onion, minced fine	1 large ham slice (about 3 lbs.)
1 tsp. salt (more to taste)	2¼ cups hot milk
¼ tsp. black pepper, freshly	1 tsp. paprika
ground	

Dredge potatoes with flour. Then mix with onion, salt, pepper and thyme. Mix well. Pour melted butter over all. Cut ham into small serving-sized pieces and place in bottom of a flat 9 x 13-inch baking dish.

Pile potato mixture on top of ham and spread. Pour hot milk over potatoes. Sprinkle with paprika. Cover and bake in preheated 375° F. oven for 30 minutes. If there is a delay in dinner, baking dish may be removed from oven and set aside. Reheat, uncovered, an additional 15 minutes when dinner looms imminent. Casserole is ready when it becomes lightly crusty and bubbly. Serves 6.

Ham and Eggs Creole

This makes an attractive luncheon dish or Sunday night supper. (It's so tasty, I've even known people who have eaten it for breakfast.)

3 *Tbs. butter or margarine*	½ *tsp. Worcestershire sauce*
1 *large onion, minced*	⅛ *tsp. dried chili peppers*
1 *large green pepper, diced*	*Salt to taste (careful with the ham)*
3 *Tbs. flour*	1½ *cups grated Cheddar cheese*
1 *can tomato soup*	8 *eggs, hard-boiled*
1¼ *cups beef stock*	1½ *cups diced cooked ham*
½ *tsp. white pepper*	¾ *cup soft bread crumbs*
⅛ *tsp. dried thyme*	3 *Tbs. butter or margarine*
⅛ *tsp. Tabasco sauce*	

In a large heavy skillet, melt 3 tablespoons margarine and slowly sauté onion and green pepper until limp and golden. Add flour and blend into margarine until smooth. Pour in tomato soup and beef stock slowly, stirring until smooth. Bring mixture to slow boil, stirring all the while. Add white pepper, thyme, Tabasco, Worcestershire, chili peppers and a pinch of salt. Mix well. Add grated cheese and continue stirring 2 minutes. Remove from heat. In a greased baking dish, slice the hard-boiled eggs (not too thin) and mix lightly with the ham. Pour sauce over and mix egg and ham with it. Sprinkle bread crumbs on top. Dot with remaining butter. Cover and set aside (or refrigerate) until needed. At mealtime, preheat oven to 350° F. and place baking dish, uncovered (and warmed up to room temperature if it has been in refrigerator), inside. Bake for 15 to 20 minutes, or until heated thoroughly with the bread crumbs nicely toasted on top. Serves 6.

Four Blessings Layered Casserole

No cooking under false colors—I cannot tell a lie, this is not an ancient Chinese recipe as the name implies—just a quartet of blessings of ham, cauliflower, onions and cheese.

1 *large cauliflower*	½ *tsp. salt (more to taste)*
1 *large bunch spring onions*	1 *cup milk*
3 *Tbs. flour*	¾ *lb. grated Cheddar cheese*
3 *Tbs. butter*	1 *cup diced cooked ham*

Wash cauliflower and break into individual flowerets. Cook in boiling salted water approximately 10 minutes. Do not *over*cook. Cut tops off onions and cook them in a separate pan of boiling salted water—also 10 minutes. Make a cream sauce with the flour, butter, salt and milk. When thickened, add grated Cheddar and stir until cheese is melted and mixed. In a greased baking dish, place first a layer of drained cauliflower, then a layer of drained onions, then ham, and finally the cheese sauce. Set aside or refrigerate until needed. Heat for 30 minutes in a preheated medium (350° F.) oven and serve. (This is also a delicious vegetable casserole, *sans* ham, to be served as accompaniment to a roast or meat loaf.) Serves 6.

Spinach-Stuffed Ham Slices

I sometimes think Stuffed Overshoe would be well received at our house, but even for families less addicted to stuffed dishes this is particularly pleasing. And it thrives on being prepared, then ignored until mealtime.

2 *large center-cut, ready-to-eat, ham slices (about 3 lbs.), 1 inch thick*	½ *lb. fresh spinach, washed and drained*
30 *whole cloves*	⅛ *tsp. ground mace*
1 *bunch green onions, chopped*	½ *tsp. black pepper, freshly ground*
1 *egg, well beaten*	⅛ *tsp. cayenne pepper*
¼ *cup diced celery*	3 *Tbs. chopped fresh parsley*
¾ *cup chopped celery leaves*	1 *tsp. soy sauce*

Wipe ham and score edges. Insert whole cloves in fat of each slice. Combine onions, egg, celery, celery leaves, spinach, and toss. Mix mace, pepper, cayenne, parsley and soy. Add to spinach mixture. Mix thoroughly. Pile stuffing mixture on to one ham slice, spread all over it. Cover with second ham slice. Skewer sides of ham slices to keep them together. Place on rack over a shallow baking pan or jelly roll pan.

Bake in preheated 325° F. oven 1 hour. Set aside. Reheat in 325° oven for ½ hour at serving time. Serve with baked or mashed potatoes. Serves 6.

Cauliflower and Ham Layered Casserole

This is a festive and unusual company dinner—but that doesn't mean the family won't gobble it up too.

1 *large head cauliflower*	¼ *tsp. salt (more to taste)*
2 *cups diced cooked ham (smoked*	⅛ *tsp. nutmeg*
ham is best)	⅛ *tsp. mace*
2 *Tbs. butter or margarine*	1½ *tsps. paprika*
1¼ *cups sour cream*	¼ *tsp. white pepper*
¼ *cup chopped green onions*	½ *cup grated sharpest Cheddar*
2 *egg yolks, slightly beaten*	*cheese*

Cook cauliflower in boiling salted water until just barely tender. Drain, rinse with cold water, drain and cool. Break into 2-inch flowerets. Place a layer of the flowerets in the bottom of a deep greased casserole. Top with a layer of ham. Keep making layers until cauliflower and ham are used up. Dot butter over the top. Set aside. Combine sour cream with green onions, mix well, then add egg yolks. Stir in salt, nutmeg, mace, paprika and pepper. Mix thoroughly and pour over the casserole. Cover and bake in preheated 375° F. oven until mixture begins to bubble, approximately 25 to 30 minutes. If the dinner bell is not ready to ring, remove from oven and set aside until all the company are assembled and happily chatting over drinks and canapés. Then return casserole to oven, remove cover, top with grated Cheddar, sprinkle with dash of paprika and bake, again at 375°, until cheese melts and browns slightly—about 10 minutes. Serves 6.

NOTE: To make dish even more festive, add 1 cup sliced fresh mushrooms to recipe. Sauté them lightly in butter first, then add a layer between cauliflower and ham layers. Marvelous!

Cheese and Almond Ham Casserole

My husband claims I would eat an old shoe if it were sprinkled with almonds. I do have a weakness for them I admit. But even almondo-phobes will find this dish appealing. If you *really dis*like almonds (inconceivable!), it's still a good cheese-ham dish, simple to assemble too.

5 *Tbs. butter*
4 *Tbs. flour*
2½ *cups milk*
¼ *cup onion, minced*
½ *cup grated Parmesan cheese*
½ *tsp. dry mustard*

¼ *tsp. black pepper*
Salt to taste
6 *generous slices cooked ham*
¾ *lb. Swiss cheese, sliced*
¾ *cup toasted blanched almonds*

Make a cream sauce by combining melted butter with flour, whisking it smooth. Add milk slowly and keep stirring. Cook over low heat in a saucepan until mixture comes to a boil and begins to thicken. Stir in onion, Parmesan cheese, mustard and pepper. Stir until well mixed. Add just a pinch of salt. Spoon a little sauce over the bottom of a flat baking pan. Place ham slices on top of sauce, then more sauce and a layer of Swiss cheese. Cover with remaining sauce. Set aside until mealtime. Then sprinkle with almonds and bake in a preheated 350° F. oven for 10 to 20 minutes, or until top is lightly browned. May be served on toast if you like or as is. Serves 6.

Sausage-Stuffed Onions

This simple country dish (call it provincial if you feel that adds a flair) is a fine recommendation for a return to the farm.

6 *large mild onions*
1 *box frozen chopped spinach*
½ *lb. sausage (pork generally
    used, but to "fancy recipe
    up" I sometimes used sweet
    Italian sausage)*

2 *tsps. lemon juice*
½ *tsp. ground fennel*
*Salt and pepper to taste (seasoning
    depends on spiciness of
    sausage)*
1 *cup cheese sauce (optional)*

Peel the onions, cover with boiling salted water, and cook 15 to 20 minutes. Do not overcook, as onions will begin to fall apart. Drain and cool. Cut off root end and remove the centers from the root end. Set onions aside, but chop fine the centers removed. Cook spinach briskly and drain. Sauté the sausage in a skillet until brown. Break and crumble the sausage as much as possible. Drain excess fat and add the chopped onion, spinach, lemon juice, fennel, salt and pepper to taste. Mix well and cook 2 to 3 minutes. Let cool and stuff onions with this mixture. Place onions in a greased baking dish and set aside until needed but at least 4 hours. If you use a cheese sauce (page 204), pour it over the onions just before reheating. Bake in a 350° F. oven 20 to 30 minutes. Fine family fare! Serves 6.

Salchicha Soufflé

This may seem a highfalutin' way to say sausage, but this dish is so special it deserves a fancier word than the lowly "sausage." This dish does prove, though, that nothing is too lowly for an inventive cook. Spectacular for a special luncheon or company dinner.

6 *slices white bread, crusts*
    trimmed
1 *lb. pork sausage in bulk, not*
    links
1 *tsp. prepared mustard, moder-*
    ately hot
¼ *lb. Swiss cheese*
3 *eggs, beaten slightly*

1¼ *cups milk*
¾ *cup light cream*
1 *tsp. Worcestershire sauce*
¼ *tsp. black pepper, freshly*
    ground
½ *tsp. salt (more to taste)*
⅛ *tsp. ground nutmeg*

Grease generously a 2½-quart casserole, preferably a long flat one. Pull bread apart into fourths. Place flat on the bottom of the casserole, forming a layer. Extend it along the sides if all the pieces do not fit on the bottom. Break the sausage up, as you would hamburger for spaghetti sauce. Brown it lightly, draining off the grease completely. Stir in the mustard and mix well. Spread the mixture evenly over the bread. Shred the cheese and sprinkle it over the sausage mixture. Combine the eggs and milk. Add cream and seasonings and pour over the cheese in the casserole. Cover. Refrigerate (I make this a full day ahead, though 4 hours is adequate time). Before cooking, let stand at room temperature at least 40 minutes. Bake until firm and fluffy— approximately 35 minutes in a 350° F. oven. Serves 6.

Sausage Casserole En Famille

I am not all that mad for pork sausage, but it is a steady favorite with children, and makes a good family meal prepared this way. If you want to liven it up a bit for the "old folks," *i.e.,* your husband, self and company, substitute a rousing Spanish or Italian sausage. Then watch the chameleon change colors!

1 *lb. pork sausage (not links)*   *Salt and pepper to taste*
1 *medium onion, chopped*   1 *large can tomatoes (#2½)*
1 *large green pepper, chopped*   1 *package thin noodles (8 ozs.)*
4 *bay leaves*   ½ *cup freshly grated Parmesan*
¾ *tsp. Worcestershire sauce*   *cheese*
1½ *tsp. paprika*

Brown sausage slowly in deep skillet, crumbling it as it cooks. Remove from skillet and drain on absorbent paper. Sauté onion and green pepper in sausage fat until golden and glossy. Add seasonings, and tomatoes and stir well. Simmer over low heat for 5 minutes. Set aside. Boil noodles in salted water, drain, and place them in a well-greased large cassereole. Mix the sausage with the onion-pepper mixture, add to the noodles and mix well. Add salt and pepper if necessary. Cover top with Parmesan. Keep covered in refrigerator until needed. Bake uncovered in preheated 350° F. oven 30 to 40 minutes. To keep longer, cover and turn oven off. Just at serving time, turn oven on again, add a little water if needed, stir mixture in casserole, add a spoonful more Parmesan to the top, and heat thoroughly. Serve hot with additional bowl of Parmesan, a hearty green salad, hot rolls or Italian bread. Good autumn fare! Serves 6.

Christmas Eve Casserole

It may be misleading to give such simple fare a fancy-sounding title. But in our house, the night before Christmas is usually hectic, and meal preparations are rather slapdash. Hence, I have evolved a do-it-ahead dish that leaves ample last minute time for all the holiday chores, gift wrapping, tree trimming, et al. Actually this might just as well be called a Too-Busy-To-Cook Casserole, but I'll stick to my family title, for it is, you see, red and green—and what could be more festive?

¾ *lb. green noodles*   ¼ *tsp. black pepper*
3 *cups water*   ½ *tsp. chopped parsley*
2 *Tbs. butter or margarine*   1½ *cans condensed tomato soup*
1 *large onion, chopped fine*   3 *Tbs. Worcestershire sauce*
1 *clove garlic, minced*   ⅛ *tsp. Tabasco sauce*
1 *small stalk celery, minced*   ½ *lb. shredded sharp Cheddar*
1½ *lbs. wieners*   *cheese*
¾ *tsp. salt*

Boil the noodles in boiling salted water for 10 minutes. Drain well. Heat butter in large skillet and brown the onion, garlic and celery in it. Slice the wieners lengthwise, then in half crosswise, and brown them in the skillet too. Add the salt, pepper, parsley, soup, Worcestershire and Tabasco to the skillet and mix well. Finally, add the cheese, and stir often to prevent burning, until cheese melts. Place mixture in a greased casserole. Add noodles and toss lightly. Set aside until needed. Then bake for 20 minutes in a hot oven (375° or 400° F.). Serves 6.

Baby-Sitter's Delight

This may sound weird to anyone over thirty, but the kids love it. I often make it ahead when we Over Thirties are going out to dinner, and let the Sitter pop it into the oven at the appropriate moment. Good for Sunday night supper too.

¼ cup brown sugar, packed tight
¼ tsp. salt
⅛ tsp. cinnamon
⅛ tsp. nutmeg
⅛ tsp. grated lemon rind
3 cups apples, peeled and sliced thick

3 large sweet potatoes, boiled, peeled and sliced thick
1 lb. frankfurters, slit down middle and halved
1½ tsps. lemon juice
½ cup buttered bread crumbs

Mix together brown sugar, salt, cinnamon, nutmeg and grated lemon rind. In shallow, flat baking pan place a layer of sliced apples. Top with a layer of sweet potatoes, then a layer of frankfurters. Sprinkle spice mixture over that. Then add alternate layers of apples, potatoes and frankfurters, and another sprinkling of spice until all ingredients are used up. Top with spice mixture. Sprinkle lemon juice over all and crumbs on top of *that*. Cover and set aside. At baking time, heat oven to 375° F. and bake covered for 40 minutes. Remove cover and continue baking an extra 5 to 10 minutes. Serves 6.

CHAPTER III

Duck, Rabbit, and the Infinitely Varied Chicken

Of all creatures that grace the table, chicken is without doubt the most versatile. And that explains, I hope, why the recipes in this chapter are so heavily weighted on the side of that gangling, clipped-winged, comical-looking bird.

A good argument can be made for the delicacy of pheasant, the savoriness of duck, the joy of rabbit and other game. With such opinions I concur wholeheartedly. But for sheer adaptability nothing approaches chicken. Wine, sherry, brandy, bourbon, tarragon, rosemary, sage, *any* herb, vegetables, rice, potatoes, pasta, fruits, raisins, nuts, what food does *not* find chicken an agreeable mate? What palate does not respond to chicken à *la* You-Name-It. And what cook does not enjoy working with such a flexible creation?

Chicken Teriyaki

This Japanese classic suffers no sea change when served on our shores. Further, it adapts beautifully to a meal-that-can-wait formula.

You may marinate the chicken for 6, 8, 10 hours, even overnight if you like. The only last minute work is the broiling, and this should be done rapidly *after* the errant guests have arrived and have drinks firmly in hand.

1 or 2 *fryer chickens, about 4 to*	2 *Tbs. Bourbon or other whiskey*
5 *lbs. in all*	2 *thick slices raw ginger root*
¾ *cup soy sauce*	2 or 3 *cloves garlic, peeled*
4 *Tbs. sugar*	

Clean chicken and cut into individual serving pieces. Combine soy sauce, sugar and whiskey, and mix well. Pare ginger root. (You *may* substitute 2 teaspoons powdered ginger, but make the attempt to use ginger root, as the flavor is *much, much* better.) Add ginger and garlic to the marinade. Pour over chicken, covering every piece. Let stand in a deep mixing bowl. Turn pieces occasionally. When ready to cook, remove chicken pieces from marinade, place in broiler and broil 20 minutes or so, basting frequently with marinade. If chicken becomes dry, as dinner is delayed, add a little soy to extend the marinade. Finished chicken should be dark and glossy coated. Serve on a bed of hot rice, with fresh green salad accompaniment. Serves 6.

Chicken Liver and Eggplant Casserole

Lovely to eat, easy to make ahead, this is another winning eggplant dish. (My husband suggested, knowing my proclivity for eggplant specialties, that I title this book *The Eggplant and I*.)

2 *medium eggplants*	½ *lb. fresh mushrooms, sliced*
6 *Tbs. butter*	2 *eggs, beaten*
¾ *lb. chicken livers*	⅓ *cup light cream*
Salt and pepper to taste	¼ *tsp. nutmeg*
1 *tsp. salt*	¾ *cup grated Parmesan cheese*
¼ *tsp. black pepper*	½ *cup bread crumbs*

Peel the eggplants and cut into cubes. Cook in boiling salted water to cover for 10 minutes, or until tender. Drain, cool, and mash the eggplant. Heat 2 tablespoons butter and sauté chicken livers in it until lightly cooked. Season with salt and pepper. Remove livers from skillet and cool. When cool, chop very fine. Sauté sliced mushrooms in 2 tablespoons butter until lightly browned. Set aside. Mix together the beaten eggs, cream, salt, pepper, and nutmeg. Add ½ cup Parmesan

cheese, mushrooms, liver and eggplant. Mix thoroughly. Place in a
large greased casserole. Mix bread crumbs with remaining Parmesan
and sprinkle over the top. Dot with remaining butter, cover and have
ready to go when needed. If dinner threatens to be late, preheat oven
to 350° F., but do not put casserole in. As family assembles, slip casserole into oven, uncover, and let bake 20 minutes, or until fairly firm
and golden brown on top. (This casserole *will* keep in oven a bit
longer than you intended, if you turn oven low and add a few more
sprinklings of bread crumbs mixed with butter to the top.) A splendid
main dish for luncheon as well as dinner. Serves 6.

Chicken and Artichokes

Pollo, poulet, keiniku, however you pronounce it, a chicken is a rose
in any language. And one of its great charms is its flexibility, as for
instance in the way it mingles with so many other ingredients.

¾ *cup olive oil*	3 *cups chicken broth or stock*
1 *fryer chicken, 4 to 5 lbs., cut into 2-inch pieces*	½ *tsp. Worcestershire sauce*
1 *large onion, sliced thin*	10 to 12 *canned artichoke hearts, drained*
½ *lb. fresh mushrooms, sliced*	1 *tsp. salt*
1 *large green pepper, sliced*	½ *tsp. black pepper*
⅓ *cup lemon juice*	¾ *cup toasted almonds*
1½ *cups raw rice, well washed*	

Heat olive oil in large iron skillet. (If artichokes come packed in
olive oil, the oil can be used to make up the amount called for in this
recipe.) Sauté chicken until well browned. Remove from pan. Sauté
onion, mushrooms and green pepper in same skillet until lightly
browned. Add lemon juice and rice. Pour boiling hot chicken broth
over the rice, add Worcestershire sauce, cover and let simmer for approximately 15 minutes—until rice is almost tender. Turn off heat and
add artichoke hearts, salt and pepper to taste. Mix lightly. Place
chicken pieces in a large baking pan. Surround and cover with the
rice mixture. Cover and bake in a preheated 350° F. oven approximately 40 minutes. To keep from drying out if dinner is delayed, add
a little more chicken broth, but add it sparingly. Keep baking dish
covered and reduce heat to 250°. Just before serving, sprinkle toasted
almonds over the top of chicken. Serves 6.

Hungarian-American Paprikash

This do-ahead version of a Hungarian classic is well suited to our modern life on the run. Try it next time you have to play den mother at 4 P.M., with your husband's boss arriving for dinner at 6. Once you have assembled the casserole in the morning, you can forget it until mealtime.

½ cup flour (more if necessary)	½ cup salad oil
2 tsps. salt	1 small onion, chopped
¾ tsp. black pepper	3 cloves garlic, minced
1 Tb. paprika	¾ lb. fresh mushrooms, sliced
5 lbs. frying chicken, cut up	2 cups sour cream

Combine the flour, salt, pepper and paprika. Mix well. Roll chicken pieces in the mixture and brown them briskly in the salad oil in a skillet over medium high heat. When crisply browned, transfer chicken to a casserole. In the same skillet lightly sauté the onion, garlic and mushrooms. Do not cook them thoroughly. Transfer them to casserole too. Pour sour cream over the chicken, sprinkle additional paprika over all, cover and set aside or refrigerate until 1 hour before serving time. Heat in 325° F. oven for 1 hour. Serve with rice or mashed potatoes and a tossed green salad. Serves 6 to 8.

NOTE: you might want to add additional sour cream and paprika about 15 minutes before removing casserole from oven.

Layered Corn and Chicken Casserole

This old New England dish makes a hearty and piquant modern-day do-ahead casserole.

3½ Tbs. butter	½ tsp. dill weed
5 Tbs. flour	2½ cups cooked corn (fresh off-the-cob is best)
2½ cups chicken stock	
1 tsp. salt (more to taste)	3 cups cooked chicken, diced
¾ tsp. black pepper	1½ cups soft bread crumbs
¼ tsp. celery salt	5 Tbs. butter, melted
½ tsp. dry mustard	

In a large heavy skillet, melt the 5 tablespoons butter. Slowly add flour and work into a smooth paste. Add chicken stock little by little. Stir and work until smooth and somewhat thick. Stir until sauce comes to a boil. Add salt, pepper, celery salt, mustard and dill weed. Mix well and remove from fire. Sprinkle half the corn into the bottom of a well-greased wide-mouthed baking dish. Cover with ½ the diced chicken. Pour ½ the sauce over, and repeat layers. Combine bread crumbs with melted butter, toss, and sprinkle over top of baking dish. Set aside until needed. Before dinner, preheat oven to 350° F. and bake casserole, uncovered, for 25 to 30 minutes, until well heated and lightly browned on top. Serves 6.

Sesame Chicken

One of my favorite ways of fixing the ubiquitous chicken, this recipe is popular in my house for Sunday dinner or formal parties. Very easy to prepare, yet most impressive to serve.

5 *lbs. chicken, fryer or broiler*	¼ *tsp. ground cloves*
½ *cup finely chopped onion*	½ to ¾ *tsp. ground cardamom*
3 *cloves garlic, minced*	½ *tsp. ground ginger*
½ to ¾ *cup sesame seeds, untoasted*	2¼ *tsp. salt*
	½ *tsp. freshly ground black*
½ *tsp. dried ground chili peppers*	*pepper*
¼ *tsp. cumin seeds, smashed with pestle*	½ *cup butter or margarine, melted*

Cut frying chickens into servable parts. Remove skin if you prefer. (I keep the skin on, being very fond of crisp skin.) Mix the onion, garlic, sesame seeds, chili peppers and all spices together thoroughly. Pour melted butter over spices and mix well. Spread carefully all over chicken parts in shallow baking pan. Set aside until ready to bake. (Can be prepared in the morning and kept refrigerated until dinnertime.) Bake the chicken in a 350° F. medium oven in the same shallow pan until nicely browned, approximately 40 minutes to 1 hour. You may need to add a little water to the pan to prevent burning. Baste with water occasionally. Delicious served with rice or whipped potatoes. (For company dinners I prefer rice, as it seems a more fitting "Eastern" accompaniment for the spiced chicken, but my children are wild for whipped potatoes with chicken.) Serves 6 to 8.

Spaghetti and Chicken with Mushrooms

Far more succulent than its distant cousin Tetrazzini, this is a natural on rush-rush make-ahead schedules. I usually prepare it the night before, the better to let the flavors blend.

1 *medium onion, chopped fine*	1 *can tomatoes (#2)*
½ *cup diced smoked ham*	1 *Tb. chili powder*
1½ *cups fresh mushrooms, sliced*	½ *tsp. chopped tarragon*
5 *Tbs. butter or olive oil*	¼ *cup dry white wine*
3 *cups diced cooked chicken*	*Salt and pepper to taste*
1 *small green pepper, chopped*	½ *to* ¾ *lb. uncooked spaghetti*
¾ *cup chopped celery*	¾ *cup grated Parmesan cheese*

Lightly sauté the onions, ham and mushrooms in the butter or olive oil. Add the chicken, green pepper and celery. Cook another 5 minutes, then add the tomatoes with their liquid, chili powder, tarragon and white wine. Salt and pepper to taste. Cover skillet and let mixture simmer 20 to 30 minutes. Meanwhile, cook spaghetti in boiling salted water until tender, approximately 10 to 15 minutes. Drain. In a greased baking dish, place a layer of spaghetti, cover it with a layer of the chicken-tomato-mushroom mixture, then another layer of spaghetti, then the chicken, etc. Sprinkle ½ cup grated cheese on top. Cover and refrigerate overnight, allowing time for the flavors to become acquainted. Remove from refrigerator ½ hour before baking time. Bake in a 325° F. oven 45 to 50 minutes. Remove cover, sprinkle remaining cheese over the top, then return to the oven for an additional 5 minutes. Serve with a Caesar salad or tossed greens. Serves 6.

Lazy Sister-in-Law's Chicken

The lazy sister-in-law in question is not mine, I hasten to say for the sake of family harmony, but that of a California friend of mine. This is a variation on a dish that's long been popular out in the sunny clime where people would rather spend time at the beach than in the kitchen.

5 *to 6 lbs. fryer chicken, cut in*	1 *can cream of chicken soup*
parts	1 *can water*
1 *cup raw rice, washed*	½ *tsp. dried thyme*
1 *pkg. Lipton's dry onion soup mix*	1 *tsp. Worcestershire sauce*

Wash chicken, wipe and arrange in a deep baking dish. Sprinkle rice over top. Sprinkle dry soup mix over rice. Combine chicken soup and water. Add thyme and Worcestershire. Mix and pour (unheated) over baking dish. Spread over chicken well. Bake 1 hour in preheated 350° F. oven. Remove, set aside. One hour before serving time, return baking dish to oven, cover, and bake at 225° for 50 to 60 minutes. Serve hot from baking dish with a tossed salad and warm bread or rolls. Serves 6.

Pollo Elegante

Just a fancy way of saying that this is a rich and fancy chicken dish, lovely for a party, and easy to fix and leave, then reheat in the nick of time.

1 *stewing chicken (6 lbs.)*	2 *cloves garlic*
½ *lb. fresh mushrooms, sliced*	1 *can tomatoes with juice (#2½)*
1 *large yellow onion, chopped*	½ *tsp. salt (more to taste)*
½ *green pepper, chopped*	½ *tsp. white pepper*
1 *Tb. olive oil*	2 *needles rosemary, crushed*
1 *cup rice, uncooked*	

Stew chicken in water (or better still, half chicken stock, half water) until tender. Remove, cool, and cut chicken into 2-inch pieces. Discard bones and small pieces (but never throw away—they make great soup). Set aside in a greased deep casserole. Sauté mushrooms, onions and green pepper in olive oil. When onions are golden, add rice to the skillet. Sauté over low fire, stirring constantly, until rice is lightly browned. Add garlic, tomatoes, pepper, salt, and rosemary. Simmer 15 to 20 minutes. Discard garlic buds. Spread the rice-tomato mixture over the chicken in the casserole. Add 1½ inches of the chicken stock. Cover and refrigerate until baking time. When needed, bake at 350° F. for 40 to 50 minutes, adding more stock if needed. Add sparingly, for this dish should not be mushy. Superb with a big green salad and hot Italian bread. Serves 6.

Doomsday Chicken with Wild Rice

One of the horrors of entertaining is the belated guest, i.e., he who is invited for dinner at 7:30 and manages to arrive ready for cocktails at 9 P.M. No soufflé or exquisitely timed conceit for him! Serve him

Doomsday Chicken—it's far better than he deserves. Aside from the flavor, which is special, the joy of this dish is that it can stay in the oven practically forever (would you believe Doomsday?) without being ruined. P.S. It is also a good dish for commuting husbands when winter train schedules are erratic.

¼ lb. butter or margarine	1 medium onion, minced
1 tsp. salt	2 cups wild rice, uncooked
½ tsp. black pepper	2 cups whole mushrooms
6 broiler chicken halves	

Melt butter in large skillet. Add salt and pepper and stir. Quickly brown the chicken halves over quite high fire. When lightly browned (but barely cooked), set aside. Sauté onions in the remaining butter. Cook wild rice according to directions on package. Place cooked rice in large roasting pan. Toss mushrooms with rice lightly. Stir in the onion and remaining butter from skillet. Place broiler halves on top of rice. Cover roaster and place in a slow oven (300° F.). Now relax and forget all about the late-arriving guests or spouse. Dinner will be moist and succulent no matter *when* you serve it. (Well, within limits.) Serves 6.

Spicy Chicken

Was there ever a creature created as versatile and delicious as chicken? The best paean of praise to this funny-looking but beautiful-tasting bird is a dish such as this, one of my favorite chicken delights.

½ cup butter or margarine	2 tsp. dried thyme
1 roasting chicken, 5 to 6 lbs.	3 Tbs. chopped parsley
2 large onions, sliced thin	1½ tsps. white pepper
4 cloves garlic, chopped	2 Tbs. curry powder
1 large green pepper, sliced	2½ tsps. salt
¼ cup currants	½ cup blanched almonds, sliv-
2 cans tomatoes (#2) with liquid	ered and toasted

Melt ¼ cup butter in a large deep skillet. Cut the chicken into serving-sized pieces and brown well in the butter. Set aside in deep casserole. Next, sauté onions, garlic and green pepper in remaining ¼ cup butter. Add the tomatoes, currants, and liquid and all the seasonings. Simmer for 15 minutes. Pour over the chicken, cover and set aside.

Thirty minutes before serving, bake the chicken, covered, in a preheated 350° F. oven. Sprinkle almonds over the chicken and serve.
Rice, hot bread and a green salad are congenial companions to this
dish. Serves 6.

Chicken, Wine and Leeks

A rich and exotic cousin of the humble onion, the leek is a joy in
gourmet cooking. I use it whenever I want to give a dish a "little extra
something."

1 *roasting chicken, 5 to 6 lbs.*	2 *medium onions, sliced*
1½ *lemons*	6 *whole cloves*
3 *cups water*	1 *large bay leaf*
⅓ *cup butter*	1 *tsp. salt*
6 *leeks, cut in 1-inch pieces (use*	⅛ *tsp. dried thyme*
only white part)	¼ *tsp. nutmeg*
6 *small carrots, peeled and sliced*	½ *tsp. black pepper*
thin	4 *cups dry Chablis or sauterne*
5 *stalks celery, cut into 2-inch*	1 *Tb. fresh chives, chopped*
pieces	

Clean chicken and rub ½ lemon over it inside and out. Place in
large kettle or Dutch oven with 3 cups water. Cover tightly and bring
to slow boil over low heat. While chicken simmers, melt butter in
skillet and sauté leeks, carrots, celery and onions. Remove from heat
when leeks begin turning yellow. When chicken comes to a boil, transfer it to large casserole and pour the leek mixture over it. Add all
seasonings except chives. Pour 3 cups wine over top. Cover and bake
approximately 2 hours in a 350° F. oven. If dinner is delayed, keep
adding remaining wine little by little, to keep chicken moist. If delay
turns into desperation, turn oven off and let tightly covered casserole
keep warm inside. Serve chicken on heated platter with sauce poured
over top. Garnish with chives and remaining lemon, sliced. Serves 6.

Catalán Chicken

Although my Castillian friends would call it heresy, I do feel that
the best cuisine in Spain is the Catalán. The marinated chicken is an
example.

5 to 6 *lbs. fryer or broiler chicken*
¾ *tsp. salt*
½ *tsp. black pepper*
2 *sprigs fresh thyme (or ½ tsp.*
    dried)
3 *cloves garlic, minced*
1 *lb. prunes, pitted*
1 *Tb. butter*

1 *large onion, chopped*
2 *Tbs. flour*
¼ *cup butter or margarine*
1 *cup water*
1 *cup dry red table wine*
2 *Tbs. chopped fresh chives*
¾ *cup pine nuts*

Cut chickens into serving-sized pieces. Save any fat included. Mix together the salt, pepper, thyme and half the garlic. Rub mixture over the chickens. Place chickens in a deep bowl, cover and refrigerate 4 to 5 hours, preferably overnight. Soak prunes at least 1 hour, until soft. Remove pits. Render the chicken fat in a large iron skillet. Add 1 tablespoon butter and sauté onions until golden. Remove onions to a Dutch oven. Then dredge the chicken pieces in flour. Add remaining butter to skillet and brown the chicken. When browned, place chicken pieces in Dutch oven. Then add water, wine, chives, remaining garlic, and additional salt and pepper to taste. Simmer in skillet for 30 minutes. Sauce may be poured over chicken in Dutch oven or may be stored in refrigerator until needed. Thirty minutes before serving, pour sauce over chicken, add pine nuts, and heat thoroughly. Serve with hot rice or buttered noodles, salad and warm Italian bread. Serves 6 to 8.

Chicken and Macaroni Casserole

This recipe has it all over Tetrazzini for me. It's moister and the almonds give it extra pizazz.

3 *cups elbow macaroni*
5 *cups diced cooked chicken*
2½ *cups mayonnaise*
1 *tsp. celery salt*
⅛ *tsp. Tabasco sauce*
1 *tsp. garlic salt*

1½ *Tbs. lemon juice*
1 *tsp. salt (more to taste)*
½ *tsp. black pepper*
2 *tsps. grated lemon rind*
2¼ *cups grated Swiss cheese*
2 *Tbs. chopped parsley*

Cook macaroni in boiling salted water until barely tender. Drain, rinse well, drain again. Mix with chicken and mayonnaise, stir and mix well. Combine all ingredients except parsley and add to macaroni.

Mix well. Place mixture in a greased deep baking dish. Set aside until needed. Thirty minutes before serving, place casserole in 350° F. oven and heat. Sprinkle parsley over the top and serve hot. (Leftovers taste delicious served cold.) Serves 6.

Transplanted Tandoori Chicken

This make-it-well-ahead chicken dish is not quite as hot-hot-hot as its Indian cousin, but sufficiently spicy for most American palates.

5 to 6 *lbs. fryer or broiler chicken*
2 *cups yogurt*
3 *cloves garlic, minced*
1 *Tb. coriander, ground*
1 *tsp. ground cardamom*
1 *tsp. black pepper, freshly*
   ground
½ *cup cider vinegar*

1 *tsp. crushed red chili pepper*
1 *tsp. dry mustard*
¾ *tsp. ground ginger*
¾ *tsp. cumin*
4 *tsps. salt*
3 *Tbs. lemon or lime juice*
½ *cup salad or peanut oil*

Cut chicken into serving-sized pieces. Mix all other ingredients except oil. Be sure to mix well. (I usually use a blender.) Pour mixture over the chicken in a shallow pan, so that all the chicken parts are coated with the mixture. Cover with foil and refrigerate at least 8 hours, preferably overnight. (A great party dish for working wives to prepare in advance!) Turn the chicken over from time to time. At dinnertime, remove chicken pieces from marinade and place on a rack over a shallow baking pan. Bake in a medium 350° F. oven for approximately 1½ hours. Baste with the marinade for the first hour. Then, if the chicken becomes dry use the salad oil for basting during the last ½ hour or so. Serve with rice and a fresh tossed salad. Serves 6.

Ivy Chicken Epicure

I owe thanks to my good friend and gourmet cook Cathleen Schurr, who served me this dish when she was suffering from a bad case of poison ivy and prepared the entire dinner for six wearing gloves! Later, in giving me the recipe, she noted: "Poison ivy hands, though not essential, add considerably to the flavor." I have to disagree—it was as delicious when I served it, *sans* ivy, as the first time. It is a great favorite at our house, but we always call it Ivy Chicken.

1 *roasting chicken (6 lbs.)*	¾ *tsp. dried thyme*
⅓ *cup flour*	3¾ *tsps. salt*
⅓ *cup shortening, melted*	1½ *Tbs. hot paprika*
3 *medium onions, chopped*	¾ *tsp. black pepper*
3 *green peppers, chopped*	*Pinch each of rosemary, basil,*
6 to 8 *cloves garlic, chopped*	*oregano*
1 *6-oz. can Italian tomato paste*	1¼ *cups dry beer*
4 *fresh tomatoes, chopped*	

Cut chicken into serving-size pieces, then dust with flour. Brown pieces in the melted shortening over medium heat. When nicely browned, set aside in large casserole. Brown onions, peppers, and garlic in skillet. Remove from heat and add tomato paste and tomatoes and seasonings. Mix well, then add beer. Pour mixture over chicken in the casserole. Set aside. An hour and a half before serving, place casserole in slow 200° F. oven. Bake covered in this low oven for ½ hour, then turn oven up to 350° and continue baking for last hour. Serve with rice, green salad and hot rolls or Italian bread. Serves 4.

Chicken and Pork Adobo

This is the national favorite dish of the Philippines, and well it might be! It is flexible too. You may prepare it ahead and finish it off in the last half hour. Or you may let it simmer on until Friend Husband arrives for dinner, then do the finishing off.

3 *lbs. pork butt*	3 *Tbs. salt*
6 or 7 *cloves garlic, chopped*	3 *cups water*
1½ *cups white vinegar*	1 *large frying chicken*
1½ *Tbs. whole peppercorns*	

Cut the pork into 2-inch cubes and trim off excess fat. (Some fat should be left on for cooking.) Mix together the garlic, vinegar, peppercorns, salt and ½ cup water. Cut chicken into small pieces, approximately 2 or 3 inches in size. Mix pork and chicken together. Pour spicy mixture over the meat and chicken and marinate *at least* 2 hours, preferably 5 or 6. (Overnight is even better.) Add 1 cup water and place pork, chicken and marinade in a large deep skillet. Cook slowly the first hour, adding water little by little if mixture threatens to get dry.

Continue cooking over very low heat. After everyone arrives, ready for dinner with bated breath, let mixture cook relatively dry. When water-vinegar mixture has evaporated, serve at once. Hot rice is the classic accompaniment. Serve also a sparsely cooked green vegetable and a crisp salad. Serves 6 amply.

Chicken in Coconut

Unless you are a descendant of Queen Liliuokalani, the Hawaiian name for this marvelous dish is virtually unpronounceable, (and equally hard to remember I might add, hedging wildly). But the dish itself is memorable indeed, and will firm up your title as Hostess with the Mostest (and Bestest).

6 *small tomatoes*	2 *large onions, chopped*
2½ *tsps. brown sugar*	1 *green pepper, chopped*
3 *cloves garlic, chopped*	6 *whole coconuts (brown)*
Salt and pepper to taste	3 *ears fresh corn (or fresh frozen)*
½ *tsp. Tabasco sauce*	6 *bay leaves*
3 *tsps. Worcestershire sauce*	6 *Tbs. white wine*
3 *to 4 lbs. chicken*	1½ *Tbs. flour*
6 *slices bacon*	

Wash and halve the tomatoes. Place in saucepan with 1 tablespoon brown sugar, garlic, salt and pepper to taste, and a healthy dash of Tabasco and Worcestershire sauces. Cook over a low fire, stirring often, until tomatoes are soft. Set aside. Cut the chicken into sections and remove the skin. Fry the bacon slices lightly and remove from the heat to drain. Brown the chicken parts in the bacon fat, adding salt and pepper as needed. When lightly cooked, remove chicken from skillet, cool, and remove meat from bones. Cut chicken meat into cubes. Meanwhile, brown the onion and green pepper in the bacon fat. Remove the stewed tomatoes from the saucepan and add them to the onion-pepper mixture in the skillet. Simmer slowly until thick. Saw off the coconuts about ¼ inch from the top (maybe you can talk your husband or Boy Scout son into tackling this chore the night before your gala) and remove the coconut meat carefully from the inside. Work with care to prevent cracking the coconuts. Shred the coconut meat and mix it with 1 tablespoon of the coconut milk. Shave the fresh corn and add the kernels to the coconut mixture. Then stir into onion-pepper-tomato mixture. Add chicken pieces. Taste and add more salt and pepper if desired, along with another drop or two of Worcester-shire sauce. Mix well and scoop mixture into the six coconuts, filling almost to the top. Set aside or refrigerate several hours until needed. Put one bay leaf in each coconut, along with 1 tablespoon white wine per coconut. Make a flour and water paste and seal the tops. Place coconuts in a cake pan with 1 inch of water on the bottom to prevent scorching. Bake in a 325–350° F. oven for 45 minutes to one hour. Baste now and then to prevent scorching. Serve on platter trimmed with watercress or parsley. Serve with tossed green salad and warm rolls or Italian bread. Serves 6.

NOTE: Once the job of sawing off the coconut tops has been done, you may use and reuse your coconut "bowls," taking care to scour and wash them carefully after each use. They also make very effective cups for fancy tropical drinks, *à la* Trader Vic. I sometimes use mine for soup, if I am serving a slightly Oriental dinner.

F.N.H.B. Company Noodles

The old expression "Family Hold Back—F.H.B.," when there isn't quite enough food to go round, can now be altered to "F.N.H.B.—Family *Needn't* Hold Back." This is a lovely stretchable main course for family or company dinner, particularly when someone drops in un-expectedly and stays and stays and stays.

1/4 *cup butter or margarine*	1 *Tb. chopped parsley*
1/4 *cup flour*	1/4 *cup butter or margarine*
2 *cups chicken broth, heated*	6 *large fresh mushrooms*
3/4 *cup light cream*	1 1/2 *cups diced cooked chicken*
3/4 *cup sauterne or other white*	1 *cup cubed cooked ham*
wine	*Pkg. noodles (8 ozs.), cooked and*
1 1/2 *tsps. salt (more to taste)*	*drained*
3/4 *tsp. white pepper*	1/2 *cup grated Parmesan cheese*
1/8 *tsp. dried tarragon*	

In a deep heavy skillet heat 1/4 cup butter or margarine. Add flour and blend well. Slowly stir in *heated* chicken broth. Stir until smooth. Add cream and continue stirring until sauce is slightly thickened and smooth. Add wine slowly, stir again, and add salt, pepper, tarragon and parsley. Stir well and remove from heat. Set aside. In another skillet, melt 1/4 cup butter or margarine and sauté sliced mushroom *stems* and whole mushroom caps. Remove caps and set aside. Add chicken and ham to mushroom stems and mix well. Remove from heat. Now, add cream sauce to cooked noodles and toss lightly. Place in deep greased casserole. Add chicken and ham mixture to noodles and mix lightly. Place mushroom caps over top of casserole. Sprinkle Parmesan over top. If dinner threatens to be later than you'd planned, set casserole aside, covered. When the moment finally arrives, remove cover, and place casserole in preheated 350° F. oven for 20 minutes—or until heated thoroughly and Parmesan browns lightly. Serve hot with a chilled vegetable salad and hot rolls. Serves 6 more than amply.

Cairo Kabobs

Throughout the Middle East, cooking with skewers is as old as the Nile. Part of the tourist game in wandering through the souks and casbahs watching the sidewalk skewer specialists (like our hot chestnut and bagel vendors) is to guess what type of meat is being grilled and what spices have been used in the marinating. The only sure way of knowing is to spend a few pennies for a sample. Even sampling doesn't *always* provide an answer. The mysterious spices and seasonings of the Middle East elude one. As they might your guests when you serve them this well-seasoned delicacy.

6 *whole chicken breasts*	¼ *tsp. dry mustard*
1½ *Tbs. yogurt*	½ *tsp. turmeric*
1½ *tsps. vinegar*	¼ *tsp. ground cardamom*
1½ *tsps. lemon juice*	12 *cherry tomatoes*
½ *tsp. salt*	12 *onion slices*
1 *tsp. hot curry powder*	2 *green peppers, cut into squares*

Wash and skin the chicken breasts. Cut each breast into 16 fairly even-sized squares. Place in large flat cake pan. Mix together the yogurt, vinegar, lemon juice, salt, curry powder, mustard, turmeric, and cardamom. Mix well and pour over the chicken. Allow to marinate at least 3 hours, turning from time to time. At dinnertime, thread the chicken on skewers, alternating with the tomatoes, onion slices and green pepper squares. Broil outside over hot coals, *à la* Cairo, or in a kitchen broiler, turning and basting from time to time with the marinade. Takes about 15 to 20 minutes. Serve on a large platter, garnished with fresh tomato slices sprinkled with fresh basil and (optional) the good black Greek or Italian olives that come packed in oil not water. Rice is a *must* as accompaniment. Serves 6.

Chicken Curry (Kureéchikeé)

The home of curry is India, but it is popular throughout the Orient. When I had been living in Manila just a few months, a Filipino friend was describing some typical Filipino dishes to me. "And of course," she added, "You have tried our kureéchikeé." I confessed I hadn't. She was horrified that I did not know this local delicacy. And as she described it, I realized she was talking about my old favorite curried chicken. Of all the curry recipes I have sampled over the years, I think I'm fondest of this one. It's the white raisins that make it special. I always make it a day ahead to let the flavors melt together.

5 to 6-*lb. roasting chicken*	½ *lemon*
2 *Tbs. celery leaves*	1 *cup light cream*
2 *Tbs. parsley*	4 to 6 *Tbs. curry powder*
1½ *tsps. salt*	¼ *tsp. chili peppers*
5 *medium onions*	¼ *tsp. powdered mace*
1 *large* or 2 *small tart apples*	¼ *tsp. dried cumin*
¼ *cup butter or margarine*	1 *Tb. salt*
¼ *cup flour*	½ *tsp. grated lemon rind*
1½ *cups seedless white raisins*	

Place chicken (whole) in large kettle with 1 quart water. Add celery leaves, parsley, 1½ teaspoon salt and 1 onion, quartered. Cover and simmer gently until chicken is tender (1 hour or more). Remove chicken and cool. Strain stock and discard onion, etc. Save stock. When chicken cools, remove skin and separate from bones in large pieces. Add skin and bones to stock, along with additional 1 or 2 cups water, and simmer stock over lowest heat for 40 minutes to 1 hour. Strain stock again and set aside. Peel and chop coarsely onions and apples. Melt butter in large heavy skillet and sauté onions and apples until golden. Remove for the moment, and add flour to the butter, smoothing into a paste. Sauté until golden brown. Slowly add 1 quart chicken stock, stirring all the while. Cook over low fire, and keep stirring until sauce is smooth and thickens. Return onion and apples to sauce. Blend, and add raisins, juice from ½ lemon. Simmer 10 minutes slowly. Then add cream and keep stirring. Mix together curry powder, chili peppers, mace, cumin, remaining salt and lemon rind. Add just enough water to make a paste and add to the sauce. Stir until blended. Pour sauce over chicken and set aside until needed. Refrigerate overnight if possible. At serving time, place chicken and sauce in large skillet and reheat slowly for 20 minutes. Serve with condiments. (I consider a curry incomplete without at least 4, preferably 6, "sprinklies," extras to sprinkle over the top.) Chutney is essential; also good are chopped almonds or peanuts, grated coconut, chopped hard-boiled eggs, broiled bacon chopped in small bits, fried bananas diced. Serves 8.

Chicken à la Bourgeoise

Don't let the title put you off, this is a most elegant and special chicken dish. A French chef may wince at preparing it in advance, but I have experimented with it both ways and can report that it weathers the wait very well indeed, provided you don't keep it waiting too long. Two to three hours is par.

2 *broiler or fryer chickens*	2 *carrots, cut in thin strips*
½ *cup salad oil*	3 *Tbs. chopped parsley*
Salt and pepper to taste	6 *anchovy fillets, minced*
¼ *cup butter, melted*	3½ *Tbs. lemon juice (white wine*
3 *scallions, sliced thin*	*may be substituted)*

Wash and quarter the chickens. Brown them lightly in heated oil. Sprinkle with salt and pepper (go easy on the salt, for the anchovies are salty) and transfer the chicken to an earthenware casserole. In a skillet melt the butter and add to it the scallions, carrots, parsley, anchovies and lemon juice. Mix well and quickly add to the chicken. Cover and set aside. When ready to bake, put the casserole, covered, in a 350° F. preheated oven for 30 to 40 minutes. While the chicken is in the oven, check occasionally to be sure it is moist. Pour a little more melted butter over it if it seems to require it. Serve hot on a hot platter, garnished with watercress and thin slices of lemon. Serves 6.

Baked Chicken Moroccan Style

You don't have to commute from Tangiers to enjoy this North African treatment of chicken. It is so delicious though, you may *feel* you're living in Morocco when you eat it. (No belly dancers included in the recipe however.)

1 *cup butter*	1 *tsp. cinnamon*
2 *medium-to-large frying chickens*	¾ *cup almonds, toasted*
1½ *cups raw rice*	½ *cup raisins*
1 *tsp. ground ginger*	½ *tsp. saffron*
1 *tsp. black pepper*	1½ *tsps. salt*

Melt the butter in a skillet, add the whole chickens and brown on all sides. Set aside and make stuffing. *To make stuffing:* cook rice in 2¾ cups boiling salted water. When the water is absorbed, remove from heat and add ½ teaspoon ginger, ½ teaspoon pepper, ½ teaspoon cinnamon and the almonds. Soak the raisins in 1 cup boiling water for a few minutes. Drain and add to the rice, along with ¼ teaspoon saffron. Toss lightly with a fork until well mixed. Stuff the chickens with this mixture and skewer the openings closed. Place the chickens in a baking dish with a cover. Mix together ½ teaspoon each of pepper, ginger and cinnamon, ¼ teaspoon saffron and 1½ teaspoons salt. Pour over the mixture 1 cup boiling water. Mix well and add to the chickens. Heat in a medium (350° F.) oven for 45 minutes. Remove and set aside until dinnertime. Then, ½ hour before serving time, reheat in oven, adding a bit more water if needed to keep the birds from becoming dry. Serve hot. Serves 6.

Curried Chicken en Casserole

Basically a curry, this dish can be prepared well ahead, then reheated at the last fatal moment. It is possible to add all the accoutrements to the rice as part of the casserole or serve them on a separate divided tray at the table. I opt for serving them separately myself, but the mixture is different and interesting to try.

6 *lbs. fryer chickens*
¼ *cup melted butter or cooking oil*
1½ *tsps. salt*
¼ *tsp. white pepper*
1 *large onion, chopped*
3 *cups uncooked rice*

¾ *cup white raisins*
½ *cup flaky coconut*
½ *cup salted peanuts or almonds*
2 to 3 *tsps. hot curry powder*
3 *bananas, fried*
4 *strips fried bacon, crumbled*
¼ *cup chutney*

Cut chickens into pieces. Fry in butter or oil until lightly crisp. Salt and pepper and remove from skillet. Gently sauté onion in the skillet until golden. Set aside. Cook rice. Then, if you wish to mix the accoutrements, add first the raisins to the onions in the skillet, sautéing them until they puff up. Then add the cooked rice. Mix well, then stir in the coconut and nuts. Add curry, stirring thoroughly. Place the rice mixture in an ungreased casserole. Put the chicken pieces on top of the rice. Cover and set aside until needed. (Can be refrigerated if made early in the day.) Bake approximately 45 minutes in a 350° F. oven. Serve with sliced fried bananas and bacon (fried separately) and chutney. If you prefer to serve the raisins, nuts and coconut at the table, simply omit them from the onion, rice and curry mixture in the skillet. Both ways are appetizing. It's all a matter of tradition. Serves 6 to 8.

Barbecued Chicken Casserole

I had always considered Barbecued Anything demanding until I found this do-it-ahead recipe.

½ cup flour	1 pkg. frozen cut corn, barely
2½ tsps. salt	thawed
¼ tsp. black pepper	3 Tbs. brown sugar
3½ lbs. chicken, cut into parts	1 cup catsup
½ cup salad oil	3 Tbs. Worcestershire sauce
2 small onions, sliced	1 cup water
½ cup chopped celery	1 tsp. Tabasco sauce
½ cup minced green peppers	¼ tsp. chili peppers

Mix the flour with salt and pepper. Dip the chicken pieces in the flour and sauté in salad oil until crisply brown. Remove, drain and place in the bottom of a 3-quart casserole. Sauté the onion in the remaining oil in skillet. Then add celery, green pepper and all the remaining ingredients. Mix well and pour over the chicken. Cover and refrigerate 4 to 6 hours or more. Remove from refrigerator one hour before baking. Heat oven to 350° F., bake 30 to 40 minutes. Serves 6.

Chicken Limey

This has nothing to do with Cockney London, luv, but it is a piquant way to serve baked or broiled or barbecued chicken—easy, effortless and early-in-the-day started.

3 chickens, broilers or fryers	½ to ¾ cup lime juice
3 tsps. MSG	½ cup corn oil
1½ tsps. salt	3 Tbs. onion, chopped coarse
Freshly ground black pepper to	3 tsps. dried tarragon
taste	¾ tsp. Tabasco sauce

Wash and quarter each chicken. Sprinkle each one with 1 teaspoon MSG (monosodium glutamate), and ½ teaspoon salt, and pepper. Place in a flat cake pan to marinate. *Marinade:* Add the lime juice to the corn oil. Mix with the onions, tarragon, Tabasco and 1 teaspoon salt. Whip until frothy, then pour the mixture over the chicken. Set aside or refrigerate at least 2 hours. Turn chicken pieces occasionally. Delicious if broiled on outdoor grill or on a rack in the oven. Baste with the marinade as you cook the chicken. Broil 15 to 25 minutes, turning often. Keep moist with marinade. Serve with buttered rice, green beans and tossed salad. Serves 6 to 8.

Chicken Lemonade

Lemonaded instead of marinated is a simple but tartly delicious way to serve chicken at cookout time. In fact it is so tasty I use this recipe even indoors—under the broiler, or in a skillet.

5 *lbs. chicken, broiler or fryer*	½ to ¾ *tsp. marjoram or* ½ *tsp.*
½ *cup coarsely chopped onion*	*dill weed*
⅓ *cup fresh parsley*	½ *cup olive or salad oil*
½ *cup lemon juice*	

Cut the chickens into large pieces. Combine all the other ingredients except oil and mix well together. Set aside. Brown the chicken pieces in hot oil lightly. Remove from skillet. Place in bowl and pour lemon juice-herb mixture over the pieces. Allow to lemonate for several hours. At cookout time, remove chicken from marinade, place on grill and cook over low coals, basting with the marinade. Add more lemon juice if chicken requires it. Serves 6.

Frying method: using the same ingredients, this dish is equally good if sautéed in skillet. If prepared this way, cover chicken with the lemon-herb mixture, add ¼ cup water and cook slowly in covered pan, approximately 30 minutes.

Chilled Chicken in a Blanket

This is a truly superb summer party dish—make it a full day ahead.

1 *5-lb. roasting chicken*	1 *Tb. lemon rind*
2 or 3 *cans* (10½ *ozs. each*)	3 *Tbs. butter or margarine*
chicken consommé	3 *Tbs. flour*
6 *tiny new carrots*	¼ *tsp. powdered mace*
3 *white onions, peeled*	1½ *Tbs. lemon juice*
2 *large stalks celery, halved*	1 *tsp. salt*
1 *bay leaf*	½ *tsp. black pepper*
½ *pint light cream*	

Clean the chicken and place it in a large pan or kettle, with enough stock, broth or consommé to cover it. Add whole carrots, onions and halved celery to the kettle. Add bay leaf, cover, and let simmer until chicken is tender—approximately 1 hour. When tender, remove from heat and cool in kettle. When cool, chicken should be skinned. Remove the meat from the bones in as large pieces as possible. Arrange the chicken pieces on a large platter, with the white meat in the center. Press chicken into a mold-form. Set aside while you prepare the sauce. Warm the cream in the top of a double boiler. Add lemon rind. In a separate pan, melt the butter, add the flour and make a smooth paste. Add the hot cream to the paste, stirring to prevent lumps. Cook the sauce in double boiler for 15 minutes, thinning a little with chicken stock or broth if necessary. Before removing from fire, add mace, lemon juice, salt and pepper to the sauce. Stir well. Sauce should be substantial (fairly thick) when ready. Pour it over the chicken evenly, so that all the chicken is covered. Refrigerate overnight. Trim chicken with parsley curls, fresh radishes and the whole carrots from the stewing kettle. Serves 6.

Chicken-Almond Mousse

Another warm weather delight Chez Brooks is this easy-does-it chilled mousse. The beauty of a mousse is that nobody but the cook knows how simple it is to prepare. Dazzlement is in the eye of the beholder!

½ cup cold water
2 envelopes plain gelatin
1½ cups boiling water
¼ tsp. salt
¼ tsp. white pepper
1½ Tbs. chopped onion
2 eggs

½ cup blanched almonds
1½ cups diced cooked chicken
1 cup chicken broth
¼ cup peeled and diced cucumbers
¼ tsp. basil
1 cup heavy cream

Dissolve gelatin in cold water. Then combine softened gelatin with boiling water, salt and pepper. Add onion and put into blender. Cover, and blend at high speed for 35 seconds. Add eggs and almonds. Cover and blend again for 20 seconds at high speed. Add chicken, broth, cucumbers and basil. (If blender is too full, remove already-blended ingredients.) Cover and blend again at high for 10 seconds. Remove cover, but keep motor running as you add cream. Combine all ingredients and mix thoroughly. Pour mixture into a mold or loaf pan and chill. At serving time, unmold and garnish mousse with slivers of raw carrot, cucumbers and radishes. Serves 6.

Yesterday's Turkey Casserole

Actually, this adaptable dish can be made with leftover chicken, ham or even shrimp or other seafood. It is also good just as a rice casserole accompanying a main course.

1½ *cups diced celery*
6 *scallions, cut into* ¼*-inch*
    pieces
3 *Tbs. olive oil*
Salt to taste

3 *cups cooked rice*
2 *cups diced leftover turkey*
3 *Tbs. soy sauce* *
½ *cup chopped blanched*
    almonds

Sauté celery and scallions in the oil until golden, then add rice, turkey, soy sauce and a pinch of salt. Mix well. Put mixture in casserole and set aside. At baking time, heat oven to 350° F. and bake for 45 minutes, covered. Brown almonds in butter, and sprinkle them over the casserole at serving time. Serves 6.

Spanish Duck Montaña

Cooked mountain style (montaña), this treatment is a marvelous introduction to duck for anyone who *thinks* duck is too greasy. Duck, like goose and lamb, seems to arouse more unwarranted animosity than most other foods. I suspect it is because all three *can* be badly prepared, and once bitten twice shy. But don't be shy of *this* duck dish. It is proof, I feel, that well-prepared duck can proudly take its place among *la cuisine glorieuse*.

1 6 to 7-*lb. duck*
⅓ *cup olive oil*
2 *Tbs. hot paprika*
2 *large onions, chopped coarse*
¼ *to* ⅓ *cup flour, sifted*
⅔ *cup sherry*
2½ *cups bouillon or chicken stock*

2 *medium tomatoes, sliced*
½ *cup ripe black olives, sliced*
¼ *cup chopped canned pimiento*
½ *tsp. salt*
¼ *tsp. black pepper, freshly*
    ground

* If you live anywhere near a Chinese or Japanese food store, I strongly recommend Japanese soy sauce. It has infinitely more body and flavor than the American-produced facsimile.

Wash and quarter the duck. Brown it in oil mixed with paprika and heated in a Dutch oven or large heavy roasting pan. When duck is nicely browned, set it aside. Pour off half the grease. Then add the onions and sauté until light brown, about 5 minutes. Slowly add flour and blend well. Then add sherry and stock, little by little. Stir constantly to prevent lumps. Stir until thickened. Place duck in a baking dish and add tomatoes, olives and pimientos. Pour thickened sauce over all. Taste and add salt and pepper as needed. Cover and bake in a 325° F. preheated oven for approximately 45 minutes. To extend cooking time, lower oven to 275°, add a little bouillon and sherry mixed to prevent drying. Sprinkle more paprika on top. If desperation draws nigh, turn off oven and keep duck covered and warm. Delicious served with rice and a crisp green salad and warm Italian bread. Serves 6.

Duck Española

The strong flavor of duck marries well with garlic and other spices, as in this Spanish adaptation.

1 *large duck, 5 to 7 lbs.*	1½ *cups celery, chopped*
1 *tsp. salt*	1½ *cups raw carrots, diced*
½ *tsp. black pepper*	2½ *cups tomato juice*
3 *Tbs. salad oil*	3 *Tbs. tomato paste*
2 *large onions, chopped*	1 *large bay leaf*
3 *cloves garlic, minced*	¼ *tsp. dried chili peppers*
¾ *lb. fresh mushrooms, whole*	½ *tsp. dried thyme*
1 *green pepper, chopped coarse*	⅓ *cup stuffed olives, sliced*

Cut duck into serving pieces and rub with salt and pepper mixed. Sauté in heated oil in skillet until nicely brown all over. Transfer to large casserole. Discard all fat except 3 tablespoons. In remaining fat, sauté onion, garlic, and mushrooms. When golden brown, push to side of skillet and add green pepper, celery and carrots. Sauté a minute or two and add tomato juice, tomato paste, bay leaf, chili peppers and thyme. Mix well, simmer 5 minutes and pour over duck. Cover casserole and bake in 350° F. oven 45 minutes. Remove and set aside till needed. Fifteen minutes before dinner, add olives and return duck to oven and reheat. Serve with side dish of buttered noodles or hot rice and a green salad. Serves 6.

Long Island Duckling with Sour Cream

Serve this to your gourmet friends. Skip it and stick to a more conventional treatment for the finicky folks. The taste is superb, but the sour cream makes a foamy design over the bird, giving it the appearance of an abstract work of art, sort of a "Found Construction" or assemblage. Picky eaters might object. (Don't tell them what they're missing.)

6 to 7-lb. duck, cut into serving pieces	Duck giblets, chopped fine
¼ cup flour	⅛ tsp. rosemary, crushed
½ tsp. salt	¼ tsp. dried thyme
½ tsp. black pepper	3 Tbs. chopped parsley
5 Tbs. lard	⅛ tsp. dried tarragon
2 large onions, minced	1½ cups claret wine
2 cloves garlic, minced	1 pint sour cream

Dredge the serving-sized pieces of duck with flour mixed with salt and pepper. Brown quickly in the lard. When brown on all sides, place duck in a large casserole. Lightly brown the onions and garlic in the same lard. Add them to casserole, along with chopped giblets, and all the herbs. Pour claret over the top and cover casserole. Bake in a 350° F. oven for 1½ hours. Remove and set aside until needed for dinner. Thirty minutes before serving time, stir sour cream into casserole. Turn duck, so sour cream gets well mixed. Return covered casserole to oven, and reheat for 30 minutes. Serve with hot rice, seasoned with Soy Butter (p. 161). Serves 6.

Cassoulet

No relation to Chevrolet, but both drop the T at the end. There are fads in foods, as in fashion, and a dish will achieve Instant Acclaim. Every dinner party for months will feature the same main course. Then the fever subsides, and the dish is dropped or forgotten for years. Cassoulet had its "Season" several years ago, but it is far too good and too improvisationable to be banished so summarily.

3 *cups dried small pea beans*
2 *qts. water*
2½ *tsps. salt*
⅓ *cup diced salt pork*
1 *bouquet garni* *
3 *carrots, peeled and quartered*
2 *medium onions, quartered*
¼ *tsp. black pepper*
3 *cloves garlic, minced*
3 *Tbs. drippings from roasted*
  duck
½ *lb. lean pork, cubed*

½ *lb. link pork sausages, halved*
½ *Polish sausage, cut in pieces*
½ *lb. beef or lamb, boned and*
  cubed
1 *Bermuda onion, chopped*
¾ *cup chopped shallots*
¾ *cup chopped celery*
1 *can tomato sauce (8 ozs.)*
⅛ *tsp. cayenne pepper*
¾ *cup dry white wine*
1 *small duck, roasted, boned and*
  cut into 2-inch pieces

Soak the beans overnight in a large kettle with the water and salt. (To expedite: boil for 5 minutes, then soak a mere hour—but it's far better with longer soaking time.) Skim top. Add salt pork, *bouquet garni,* carrots, quartered onions, black pepper, and garlic. Bring to quick boil, then reduce heat and simmer slowly for 1 hour. Skim foam from top from time to time. In a large skillet, heat duck drippings and brown the pork, sausage and beef (or lamb). Transfer meats to the kettle and cook with beans. Sauté the Bermuda onion, shallots and celery in remaining oil or drippings. When lightly brown, add tomato sauce, cayenne pepper, and wine. Simmer 10 minutes, and then add to the kettle. Continue cooking over lowest heat until meats are tender (60 to 70 minutes). Add water if necessary. Skim off excess fat and discard *bouquet garni.* Pour contents of kettle into a large casserole and add the cooked pieces of duck. Cover and set aside. Thirty minutes before serving, bake the casserole, uncovered, in a 350° F. oven. Virtually a meal in itself—with a large tangy salad. Serves 6 to 8.

Conejos Mexicano

Which is pidgin for hare. Pidgin Spanish that is. The hare is pure American and can be bought frozen at most supermarkets. "How do you prepare a rabbit?" friends have asked. In truth, nothing could be simpler, particularly these days when rabbits come all cleaned and

---

* For your *bouquet garni,* tie together in a piece of cheesecloth: ¼ teaspoon each chopped parsley, thyme and celery seed, 4 whole cloves, 4 whole peppercorns, 1 bay leaf and 3 rosemary needles.

ready to cook. Most recipes for chicken adapt easily to rabbit, though cooking time is usually a bit longer (a hare's breath longer perhaps?)

¼ *cup salad oil*	1 *bay leaf*
2 *cloves garlic, minced*	2¼ *tsps. salt*
1 *large onion, sliced thin*	¼ *tsp. black pepper*
1 *medium green pepper, sliced*	¾ *tsp. MSG*
2 *slices bacon, uncooked*	1½ *cups raw rice, washed*
3 *lbs. rabbit, cut into serving*	3 *cups boiling water*
pieces	12 *ripe olives, whole*
3 *Tbs. chopped parsley*	½ *cup sherry wine*
4 *whole cloves*	4 *Tbs. finely chopped pimientos*

Heat the oil in a large skillet. Add garlic, onion, and green pepper and sauté until lightly browned. Add bacon and rabbit pieces. Brown thoroughly, turning often. Drain bacon and crumble. Mix together parsley, cloves, bay leaf, salt, pepper, bacon, and MSG. Sprinkle over rabbit in skillet. Add rice and cook 3 minutes, stirring constantly. Pour boiling water over all, cover skillet, and simmer until rice is cooked, approximately 35 to 45 minutes. Add olives, sherry and pimientos. Keep covered and set aside until mealtime. Fifteen minutes before serving, reheat skillet, stirring to prevent sticking. Delicious with a tossed greens, spinach-onion salad and hot Italian bread. Serves 6.

Rabbit in Red Wine

My mother had a prejudice against rabbits—on the dining table. Consequently I never tasted this succulent beastie until I was in post-World War II, tightly rationed London. I was beginning to eat my roast chicken dinner one evening when I suddenly noticed its huge hind quarter, quite unlike any chicken of my acquaintance. The meat was delicious, and I have been a confirmed hare-ophile ever since. Particularly when the rabbit is laced with wine and herbs.

½ *cup flour*	½ *cup olive oil*
1 *tsp. salt*	3 *cloves garlic, chopped*
½ *tsp. black pepper*	2 *cups dry red wine*
2 *rabbits, cut into serving-sized*	½ *tsp. dried basil*
pieces	½ *tsp. dried thyme*

Combine flour, salt and pepper in flat bowl. Dip rabbit pieces in this mixture and cover well. Heat oil in large iron skillet, and brown the garlic in oil. Add rabbit pieces and brown well. Place rabbit in a deep baking dish. When all the pieces are browned, pour remaining oil and garlic over the rabbit in baking dish. Add the wine, basil, thyme. Cover, and bake in a hot (375° F.) oven for 1 hour—or until quite tender. Remove from oven, set aside. Reheat in 350° for 30 minutes before serving. (Add a little more wine if needed when you reheat.) Serves 6.

Hasenpfeffer

This Austrian classic requires marinating for 3 or 4 days, welcome news for the make-it-aheadites.

1 *cleaned rabbit (frozen rabbit is very satisfactory—thaw first)*	6 *peppercorns, crushed*
	3 *bay leaves*
2 *large onions, sliced thin*	½ *cup wine vinegar*
3 *cloves garlic, minced*	¼ *cup dry white wine*
1 *tsp. celery seeds*	2 *or more cups water*
½ *cup celery leaves*	3 *Tbs. butter*
8 *whole cloves*	2 *Tbs. flour*
1 *tsp. salt (more to taste)*	1½ *cups sour cream*

Wipe rabbit with damp cloth and place in a deep glass bowl. Combine onions, garlic, celery seeds and leaves, cloves, salt, pepper, bay leaf, vinegar and wine. Add 2 cups water (or more to cover) and mix thoroughly. Pour over rabbit. Cover tightly and refrigerate at least 3 days. (There's always a tendency to walk away and forget about it forever—if you have this problem, write a note on your calendar. Beware the hare!) Turn now and then to be sure marinade is covering all sides. The day you are serving the rabbit, brown it in butter in a hot deep skillet. (Reserve marinade.) Turn to brown on all sides. Lower heat and simmer 30 minutes. Set aside. Later, just before serving time, strain the marinade and add it, little by little, to the rabbit, as you heat it over a medium fire. When rabbit is well heated, remove to a platter. Add flour to sauce to thicken it. When thick and smooth, add sour cream, stir well and pour over rabbit. Trim with parsley and a sprinkling of paprika and serve at once. Serves 6.

CHAPTER IV

From the Garden

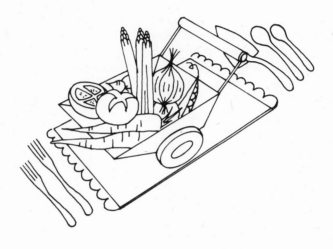

There is something a trifle grim about the phrase "meatless meals" that brings into instant focus ration cards, elderly writers with beards and knickers nibbling grasses, and dietetically approved squares of jellied asparagus on a single lettuce leaf.

Actually, most of the recipes in this "meatless" chapter can easily be served as accompaniment to a roast, chops or skewered meats. But in themselves, they also offer a bit of variety as luncheon main courses or on those nights when a lighter menu is requested.

For instance, you can afford to be flexible with a smile when your husband walks in the door with the comment "I took a client to lunch today—five courses, ugh! I'm still stuffed. Can't we just have soup for dinner?" if you have a vegetable casserole in the oven. The chops you were planning to broil as soon as he arrived can be poked back in the refrigerator and saved until tomorrow. The vegetable casserole that was to have *accompanied* the chops can now be *the* dinner. Presto!

105

With a salad, there's a light dinner in a twinkling. And no recriminations necessary about "I slaved over a hot ham all afternoon and, sob, you won't even eat it." Marriages have fallen over less.

Eggplant Américaine

Eggplant has undergone a revival, a glamourizing in recent years, thanks largely to the many delicious Middle Eastern recipes available now. Yet eggplant was long a staple in pioneer American cooking. This recipe is a compromise: it is home-grown, yet relies on interesting seasonings to enliven it.

2 *large eggplant (or 3 small)*	¼ *tsp. dried thyme*
2 *Tbs. butter or olive oil*	¼ *tsp. oregano*
3 *fresh medium tomatoes*	½ *tsp. salt*
1 *large onion, chopped*	¼ *tsp. black pepper, freshly*
1 *cup rice, uncooked*	*ground*
¼ *tsp. celery salt*	¼ *cup sherry wine*
2 or 3 *needles rosemary*	½ *cup water*
¼ *tsp. dried basil*	

Prick eggplant with fork in several places. Place in flat round cake-pan and heat quickly in hot (425° F.) oven until soft. Remove, cool, then carefully scoop out interiors, leaving the shell as complete as possible. Set aside. Sauté in butter tomatoes (cut into thick slices), the eggplant filling, and chopped onion until lightly browned. Add rice, stir constantly, and sauté until rice is golden. Add herbs, and salt and pepper to taste. Mix all well. Set aside in container until needed for dinner.

Dinner preparation: stuff hollowed out eggplants with the tomato-rice-eggplant mixture. In saucepan, heat the sherry and water. Meanwhile, place stuffed eggplants in baking pan that fits snugly. Pour the hot liquids over the eggplants, cover, and bake at 350° F. until heated through, about 30 minutes. Serves 6.

Baked Squash with Pecans

You can, in a pinch, short-cut this delicious dish, by using frozen squash, but at the risk of sounding like a purist, I must admit it's not *quite* as special.

2 *lbs. yellow squash*
1 *large onion, chopped coarse*
1 *cup water*
1½ *tsps. salt*
4½ *Tbs. butter, melted*
2 *Tbs. flour*
1 *cup light cream*

1 *egg, beaten slightly*
¾ *cup pecans, chopped coarse*
¼ *tsp. nutmeg*
Salt to taste
2 *Tbs. orange juice*
1 *Tb. grated orange rind*
⅓ *cup cracker crumbs, crushed*

Peel and slice (thin) squash and place in saucepan with onion, 1 cup water and salt. Bring to a fast boil, cover, lower heat and continue cooking for 10 minutes—or until squash is tender. Remove from heat, drain and mash with potato masher. Set aside. Then melt butter in saucepan and blend in flour until smooth. Slowly add cream, stir constantly, and cook over low fire for 4 or 5 minutes. Beat egg. Stir a spoonful of the hot cream mixture into the egg and whisk it vigorously. Add another spoonful, then slowly pour egg mixture into saucepan of thickened cream. Keep stirring to prevent curdling and lumping. Cook over lowest fire 5 minutes or so, until mixture thickens. Pour over squash and mix well. Add pecans, nutmeg, orange juice and rind little by little. Mix thoroughly. Pour into well-greased baking dish. Sprinkle cracker crumbs over top. Dot with a little butter and bake in 325° F. preheated oven 20 minutes. Remove from oven until needed. Before serving, reheat baking dish in 325° F. oven for 15 minutes, or until thoroughly heated and lightly browned on top. Serves 6.

NEGLECTED ZUCCHINI

Unless you come from an Italian background, chances are you overlook the adaptability of that delicious, if innocuous, vegetable zucchini, a type of squash which lends itself (perhaps because of its very blandness) to endless culinary improvisations. Here are a couple of zucchini dishes I like because of their make-ahead aspects.

Zucchini Marinara

3 *large zucchini*
¾ *cup olive oil*
2 *cloves garlic, chopped*
1 *Tb. chopped basil leaves*

½ *tsp. salt*
½ *tsp. black pepper*
1 *Tb. chopped parsley*
¾ *cup wine vinegar*

Peel the zucchini and cut into 1-inch cubes. Sauté the cubes in olive oil until lightly browned. Remove from heat and drain on paper toweling. Grease a medium-sized casserole and place a layer of zucchini in it. Mix together all the herbs and spices and sprinkle lightly over the zucchini. Then place a second layer of zucchini in the casserole, sprinkle again with the herb mixture, and continue this until the zucchini are all added to the casserole, ending with the herbs on top. Bring wine vinegar to a fast boil and pour it over the casserole. Cover the casserole and refrigerate. Allow marinade to stand at least 12 hours. When ready to serve, drain the liquid from the casserole and serve at room temperature. (This marinade may be kept at least a week.) Serves 6.

Zucchini Pie

6 *large zucchini*   ¾ *pound mozarella cheese, sliced*
3 *Tbs. flour*   *very thin*
1½ *cups olive oil*   1½ *cups tomato sauce* *
4½ *Tbs. freshly grated Parmesan*
   cheese

Peel the zucchini and slice into 1-inch pieces. Sprinkle pieces with flour and sauté them in olive oil until lightly browned. Grease a medium-large casserole and place a layer of zucchini on the bottom. Cover with a sprinkling of Parmesan, a layer of tomato sauce, then a layer of mozarella slices. Add another layer of zucchini and repeat the process until all ingredients are used up. Be sure mozarella ends up on top. Cover casserole and set aside (or refrigerate) until ready to heat and serve. At serving time, preheat oven to 375°F. and bake for 25 to 35 minutes. (Be sure to remove casserole from refrigerator ½ hour before putting it in the oven, to allow it to warm up to room temperature.) Serves 6.

Sweet Potato and Orange Casserole

If you, like me, have always found the Southern sweet potato-marshmallow combination incomprehensible, you'll probably like this slightly tarter treatment of that lovely yam.

---

* See page 117 for tomato sauce, or use canned sauce with basil added.

6 *large sweet potatoes, boiled and skinned*
¼ *cup butter, melted*
⅓ *cup molasses*
¼ *cup orange juice*
3 *eggs, separated*

¼ *tsp. salt*
½ *cup sugar*
1 *tsp. ground ginger*
1 *tsp. ground nutmeg*
2 *Tbs. grated orange rind*

Mash the sweet potatoes and combine with butter, molasses and orange juice. Mix well. Beat egg yolks briefly and add to sweet potatoes. Combine salt, sugar, ginger, nutmeg and orange rind. Mix well and add to potatoes. Mix well and spoon into a greased casserole. Set aside. Just before dinnertime, beat egg whites until very stiff. Fold them into the casserole and bake in a preheated 350° F. oven for approximately 25 minutes. Serve hot. Good with a baked ham. Serves 6.

Spicy Beets and Onions

This serves a dual function: delicious cold as a relish or served hot with meat. Best news of all: it improves with age and can be kept refrigerated for weeks.

4 *large onions, sliced thin*
4 *large beets, parboiled, peeled and sliced*
1 *cup water*
½ *tsp. garlic salt*
6 *whole cloves*
¾ *cup white vinegar*

⅛ *tsp. dry mustard*
1½ *Tbs. sugar*
¾ *tsp. salt*
¼ *tsp. black pepper*
2 *whole sticks cinnamon*
⅛ *tsp. celery salt*

Combine onions, beets and water in large saucepan. Add remaining ingredients and mix well. Bring mixture to a boil, and simmer over low heat for 10 to 12 minutes. Mix well and set aside. Refrigerate. To serve hot, add 1½ tablespoons butter and reheat at serving time. Serves 6.

Onion-Celery-Green Peppers Supreme

Who says a vegetable casserole can't be exciting? Well, anyhow, delicious. Here's one to refute all the antivegetarian arguments.

1½ *cups celery, lightly cooked*
   and drained
1 *medium green pepper, par-*
   boiled and drained
12 *small onions, cooked and*
   drained
¾ *cup blanched almonds, halved*
¼ *cup butter*
¼ *cup flour*
½ *tsp. MSG*
⅛ *tsp. dry mustard*

1½ *tsps. salt*
¼ *tsp. black pepper, freshly*
   ground
⅛ *tsp. nutmeg*
1 *cup milk*
½ *cup light cream*
⅓ *cup grated Parmesan cheese*
¼ *cup buttered bread crumbs*
   (use 2 tsps. butter to butter
   crumbs)
1 *Tb. paprika*

Dice celery and green peppers. In a greased casserole, place alternate layers of whole onions, almonds, celery and green peppers until used up. In a medium skillet, melt butter over low heat. Blend in flour until smooth. Add MSG, mustard, salt, pepper and nutmeg. Blend. Slowly stir in milk and cream. Stir and cook until sauce is creamy and thickened. Pour sauce over casserole. Mix together Parmesan, buttered crumbs and paprika. Mix well and sprinkle over the top of casserole. Cover and set aside. At dinnertime, bake in a preheated 350° F. oven until warmed through, bubbly and lightly browned. An inspired accompaniment to a baked ham or pork roast. Serves 6.

Honeyed Onions

The honey glaze on this dish is not cloying and turns onions into a company-casserole vegetable.

30 *tiny white onions, peeled*
6 *cups hot water*
3 *Tbs. ketchup*
3½ *Tbs. honey*
4½ *Tbs. butter, soft*

½ *tsp. salt*
⅛ *tsp. white pepper*
¼ *tsp. cayenne pepper*
½ *tsp. Worcestershire sauce*

Boil onions in salted boiling water for 15 to 20 minutes or until barely tender. Drain and arrange them in a fairly shallow greased baking dish. Combine ketchup, honey and butter and mix well. Add seasonings and mix again. Spread mixture over onions and cover. Bake in preheated 350° F. oven for 30 minutes. Baste once or twice. Remove from oven and set aside until needed. At mealtime, reheat in 350° oven for 30 additional minutes—baste once to be sure glaze covers onions. Nice accompaniment for a pork roast. Serves 6.

Cheddar Cheese and Asparagus Casserole

The phrase "meatless meal" always sounds to me like Starvation Sal. But it needn't *be* that way, not with an elegant vegetable casserole such as this.

1 *lb. fresh asparagus (or 1 large can cooked)*
1 *Tb. butter*
1 *Tb. flour*
½ *cup light cream*
½ *tsp. salt*
¼ *tsp. black pepper*

¼ *tsp. chili pepper*
1 *Tb. paprika*
½ *lb. sharp Cheddar cheese, cubed*
1 *small can mushrooms*
1 *hard-boiled egg*
½ *cup slivered blanched almonds*

Trim ends and cook asparagus completely (but not overmuch) in boiling salted water. (If you use canned asparagus, drain it, but save 1 tablespoon liquid for the cheese sauce.) Melt butter in a saucepan, add flour and mix into a smooth paste. Add asparagus juice and, slowly, the cream. Cook over low fire, stirring constantly. Add salt, pepper, chili pepper and paprika. Mix well and add cheese. Stir mixture until cheese is dissolved. When sauce is fairly thick, but still pourable, add mushrooms, drained. Mix well. Line a greased casserole with half the asparagus. Cover with half the cheese sauce, then a layer of sliced hard-boiled egg. Repeat. Top with a sprinkling of almonds. Cover and set aside. Reheat for 15 to 20 minutes at mealtime in a 350° F. oven. Serves 6.

Potato-Tomato Special

These two rhyming words actually go well together on the table too. For a slightly different potato dish, give this combination a whirl.

9 *large potatoes, peeled and quartered*
3 *Tbs. tomato purée*
1 *large onion, sliced thin*

2 *cups water*
½ *tsp. salt*
¼ *tsp. black pepper*
¼ *tsp. dill weed*

Put all the ingredients into a large saucepan and simmer over a

slow, slow fire for 30 minutes. Add water if mixture seems to be getting
dry. Set aside and reheat for 10 minutes when dinnertime approaches.
Serve with roast lamb, pork or beef. Serves 6.

Monarchal Potato Salad

Many people have at least one food or dish that they dislike and
rarely eat. With my husband it is potato salad, that basic staple in many
homes, consisting of cooked diced potatoes mixed with mayonnaise,
celery, onions and pickles, and usually served cold. After years of trying
to find one potato salad recipe which would entice him, I discovered
this, which usually elicits ecstatic comments and second helpings.

6 *large potatoes, boiled in their*
   skins
½ *tsp. salt (more to taste)*
½ *tsp. black pepper, freshly*
   ground
¼ *cup olive oil*
2½ *Tbs. wine vinegar*
1 *large green pepper, chopped*
   fine
1 *Tb. pimiento, cut in pieces*
⅛ *tsp. garlic salt*
1 *Tb. capers*

6 *small stuffed olives, sliced*
4 *large green onions, finely*
   chopped
2 *slices bacon, cooked and*
   chopped
1½ *Tbs. white wine*
3 *Tbs. chopped parsley*
15 *blanched almonds, cut fine*
⅓ *cup mayonnaise (more if*
   necessary)
½ *tsp. dill weed*
3 *eggs, hard-boiled and sliced*

Peel the boiled potatoes and cut into cubes. Add salt to taste, pepper,
olive oil and wine vinegar. Set aside to marinate for an hour or more.
Then combine other ingredients, except for mayonnaise, dill weed and
eggs. Mix well and add to potatoes. Add enough mayonnaise to hold
the salad together. Refrigerate until needed. About ½ hour before
dinner, allow salad to stand at room temperature. Garnish with dill
weed and slices of hard-boiled eggs. Standing awhile longer won't dam-
age it. Serve with cold cuts or cold roast beef for a family or company
buffet. Serves 6 generously.

Curried Green Bean and Almond Casserole

There are times when the vegetable makes the meal. This is one to
serve with a simple roast or even hamburgers. *It* takes star billing.

1 to 1½ lbs. fresh string beans
1 cup water
1 tsp. salt
¼ cup butter

1 Tb. flour
1 tsp. curry powder
½ cup milk
¾ cup toasted almonds, slivered

Wash the fresh beans and trim the ends. Cut beans into thirds. Boil water with salt added, then add beans. Cook at medium heat 4 minutes. (Beans should be undercooked, merely wilted.) Drain immediately and put beans in medium-sized casserole. Melt butter, add flour and curry powder mixed, and stir well. Slowly pour in milk, and keep stirring until sauce thickens smoothly. Add a little more flour if necessary. When smooth, but not too thick, set aside. Add almonds to beans and toss lightly. Pour sauce over beans, cover and keep as is until dinner is more or less ready. When the meal is imminent, put casserole in a preheated 325° F. oven for 10 to 20 minutes. Serve hot with a simple meat dish. Serves 6.

Mushroom and Green Bean Casserole

One needn't slave all day over a hot stove to produce perfection. *Voilá!* Make this a full day ahead for *real* perfection.

3 cans whole green beans
1 can consommé, undiluted
¼ lb. butter or margarine
½ lb. fresh mushrooms, sliced

½ tsp. Maggi
¼ tsp. salt
½ tsp. caraway seeds

Place the drained beans in a large bowl. Pour the consommé over beans and marinate 2 hours. Melt butter in skillet, add mushrooms and sauté until lightly browned. Add to the beans, along with seasonings. Mix well and pour into a greased casserole. Cover and set aside. Keep overnight if possible. To serve: bake 30 minutes in a medium-low oven (325° F.). How easy can cooking get? Serves 6.

Green Bean and Sour Cream Casserole

Another bean dream, this. It too thrives on being made a day ahead.

3 *Tbs. margarine, melted*   1¼ *cups sour cream*
1 *onion, sliced thin*   6 *cups canned or frozen green*
1½ *tsps. salt*   *beans*
½ *tsp. black pepper*   ¾ *cup grated Cheddar cheese*
1 *tsp. grated lemon rind*   3 *Tbs. margarine*
3 *Tbs. flour*   ¾ *cup bread or cracker crumbs*

Melt 3 tablespoons margarine in a skillet and sauté onion slices in
it until golden. Add salt, pepper, lemon rind, parsley and flour. Mix
well and add sour cream. Gently stir in the drained beans. Place mixture in greased casserole. Sprinkle Cheddar cheese over the top. Melt
remaining 3 tablespoons margarine and mix with the bread crumbs.
Sprinkle over the top of the casserole. Set aside, covered, until needed.
At that time, bake casserole in 350° F. oven for 25 minutes. Serves 6.

Glazed Carrot and Apple Casserole

This makes a tangy side dish for a ham or pork roast.

4 *Tbs. butter or margarine*   ¼ *cup sugar*
1 *large onion, sliced*   ⅛ *tsp. nutmeg*
6 *carrots, peeled and cut into 4* ¼ *tsp. salt*
    pieces   ¼ *tsp. dried sage leaves*
2 *large tart apples, unpeeled but* ⅛ *tsp. cinnamon*
    cored and sliced into ½-inch ¼ *tsp. black pepper, freshly*
    slices   *ground*

Melt butter or margarine in a large skillet. Add onion and sauté
until golden. Add carrots and cook 5 minutes longer. Add apples, sugar
and remaining ingredients. Mix well, cover skillet and simmer over
lowest heat for 40 minutes. Stir occasionally to keep from sticking. If
dinner is delayed, set aside covered. Just before eating, reheat for 10
to 15 minutes, stirring frequently. Serve hot as accompaniment to meat.
Serves 6.

Brussels Sprouts in Cheese-Almond Sauce

As a child I called Brussels sprouts Green Death. I consider it a mark
of some maturity that I have learned to tolerate, yes, even like them
under certain circumstances. The following is one of the circumstances.

2 lbs. fresh Brussels sprouts,
    washed and trimmed
1 tsp. salt
1½ Tbs. caraway seeds
½ tsp. black pepper, freshly
    ground
3 Tbs. butter

3 Tbs. flour
¾ cup light cream
½ cup condensed beef bouillon
2 Tbs. blanched almonds, slivered
    and lightly browned in butter
⅓ cup grated Cheddar cheese

Soak Brussels sprouts in cold salted water for 15 minutes. Drain and cook with caraway seeds in boiling salted water for 10 to 12 minutes, or until lightly tender. Do not overcook. (They should still be bright green in color.) Drain and place in medium casserole. Add caraway seeds as well. Grind pepper over sprouts. Meanwhile, melt butter and stir in flour until blended and smooth. Slowly add cream and bouillon and cook, stirring, until smooth and slightly thickened. Add the almonds and half the cheese. Mix well and pour sauce over sprouts. Sprinkle remaining Cheddar over the top. Cover and set aside until family or guests arrive. Then uncover and place in a preheated 350° F. oven for 10 minutes or so. Serve piping hot as a side dish for beef, seafood or ham. Serves 6.

Sweet and Sour Kidney Bean Casserole

This dish is not only piquant to the taste—but to the eye as well. Red and yellow, but not mellow. Somewhat spicy.

1 cup salad oil
2 large onions, chopped coarse
2 large green peppers, chopped
    coarse
2 cups canned tomatoes, drained
1½ Tbs. sweet pickle relish
2½ Tbs. chili sauce
¾ tsp. salt
½ tsp. black pepper
¼ tsp. dried basil

1 Tb. chopped fresh chives or
    parsley
½ tsp. dried oregano
⅛ tsp. dried thyme
3 Tbs. brown sugar
4½ cups cooked red kidney beans,
    drained
1 can kernel corn (12 ozs.),
    drained
2½ Tbs. lemon juice

Heat oil in a large heavy skillet. Sauté onions and green peppers until lightly browned. Add tomatoes, sweet pickle relish, chili sauce, salt, pepper, basil, chives (or parsley), oregano, thyme and brown sugar. Mix well and simmer 5 minutes over low heat. Then add beans and corn. Mix well and spoon into a large deep casserole. Keep covered until needed. This dish loves to be kept waiting. When the Hungries have assembled, place casserole in preheated 350° F. oven and heat thoroughly for 10 minutes—or until hot clear through. Sprinkle lemon juice over the top and serve at once. A delicious hot dish to serve with cold cuts or a cold buffet. So easy but somewhat more festive than the ubiquitous baked beans. Serves 6 generously.

Spicy Garbanzos

Chick peas or garbanzos lend themselves to various treatments and especially love to be spiced up, as in this make-it-ahead recipe.

2 *cups dried chick peas*
2 *quarts water*
2½ *tsps. salt*
4 *Tbs. butter or margarine*
2 *large onions, chopped coarse*
3 *small fresh tomatoes*
⅛ *tsp. powdered cumin*
¾ *tsp. dried chili peppers*
Pinch of mace

¼ *tsp. black pepper, freshly ground*
¼ *tsp. powdered ginger*
⅛ *tsp. Worcestershire sauce*
1 *tsp. powdered turmeric*
6 *leaves fresh mint (or ½ tsp. dried)*
1 *can beef bouillon, undiluted*

Soak peas in salted water in a large kettle overnight. Bring to a boil in same water they were soaked in. Simmer peas 30 minutes or so—until tender. Drain, but reserve water. Melt butter in skillet and add onions, cooking till golden. Add tomatoes and all seasonings. Simmer over low fire for 15 minutes. Add bouillon, peas and enough pea liquid to cover. Simmer covered for 15 minutes. Remove to casserole, cover and set aside until needed. Reheat for 15 minutes in preheated 325° F. oven at dinnertime. Excellent adornment for baked ham. Serves 6.

Limas Alone

Limas alone make a delicious casserole accompanying a roast or simple meat main course. They are also an attractive supplement to a cold buffet.

2¼ *cups lima beans (canned)*
1 *large onion, chopped fine*
1 *clove garlic, minced*
½ *cup celery, diced*
¼ *cup chopped parsley*

1 *can tomato soup, undiluted*
½ *tsp. dried thyme*
Salt and pepper to taste
1½ *cups crisp bread crumbs*
6 *slices bacon, uncooked*

Drain the beans and mix them with the onion, garlic, celery and parsley. Pour into a greased casserole and add tomato soup, thyme, and salt and pepper to taste. Stir well. Sprinkle with bread crumbs. Cut bacon slices into squares and place them on top of the bread crumbs. Cover and set aside until dinnertime. Thirty minutes before serving time uncover casserole and bake in medium (350° F.) oven until crumbs are lightly browned and bacon is crispy. Serves 6.

All-Purpose Tomato Sauce

Tomato sauce is the Italian equivalent of Chinese fried rice—in other words anything goes! Make it with hamburger, or hot sausage or no sausage, mushrooms, no mushrooms, whatever is on hand. Of course there are a few basics. Such as tomatoes. The key word is improvise. Here is one improvisation. Now it's your turn.

1½ *lbs. lean ground beef (or ½*
   lb. ground pork and 1 lb.
   ground beef)
3 *Tbs. olive oil*
1 *large onion, chopped*
3 *or 4 cloves garlic, minced*
1 *green pepper, chopped fine*
1 *large can tomatoes (2 lbs.*
   12 ozs.)
2 *cans tomato sauce (8 ozs. each)*
1 *can tomato paste (6 ozs.)*

1 *tsp. salt (more to taste)*
½ *tsp. black pepper, freshly*
   ground
½ *cup Burgundy or other red*
   wine
3 *or 4 needles rosemary*
¼ *tsp. fennel seeds*
¼ *tsp. dried marjoram*
¾ *tsp. dried basil**
½ *tsp. dried oregano*

Sauté the meat in half the olive oil until browned and cooked

---

* Fresh basil leaves are infinitely better, but harder to come by. If you find them, use more, maybe 1 tablespoon.

through. Drain excess fat, crumble the meat and set aside. In remaining olive oil, in the same skillet, sauté onion, garlic, green pepper. When lightly browned, return the meat to the skillet. Add tomatoes, tomato sauce and tomato paste, salt and pepper to taste. Simmer approximately 30 minutes. Then add the wine, rosemary, fennel seeds and remaining seasonings. Simmer over slowest of fires for another 30 minutes. Set aside or refrigerate until needed. Yield: 3 cups.

Marinara Sauce—Basic

The beauty of this classic is that it can be made ahead and frozen for use at any time. The longer the ingredients live together the happier they are. Further, like a good goulash or Chinese fried rice, the ingredients of a marinara sauce may vary with what's on hand.

¼ *cup olive oil*
2 *large onions, chopped coarse*
4 *cloves garlic, minced*
1 *medium green pepper, chopped*
　fine
1 *small carrot, sliced and*
　chopped fine
4 *cups canned tomatoes with*
　liquid

½ *cup Chianti or other red wine*
1 *tsp. salt (more to taste)*
¾ *tsp. black pepper, freshly*
　ground
2 *Tbs. fresh basil (or 1 tsp. dried)*
½ *tsp. dried thyme*
½ *tsp. dried oregano*
½ *cup parsley, chopped*
¼ *tsp. ground fennel*

Heat the oil in a large iron skillet. Add the onion, garlic, green pepper and carrot. Sauté until all are translucent. Stir and add tomatoes and red wine. Simmer over low fire for 30 minutes. Then add salt and pepper to taste and remaining herbs. Simmer over lowest fire 30 to 45 minutes. Set aside to cool. Store and use as needed. Makes approximately 4 cups.

NOTE: mushrooms, hamburger or chopped hot or sweet Italian sausage may be used in this expandable sauce. If used, add and brown before adding tomatoes and wine.

CHAPTER V

Pastas and Rice
Are Very Nice

If you want to be practical about it (and who doesn't?) there is probably no better way to economize on your food budget than by serving pasta or rice dishes frequently.

But practicality aside, pasta (all those marvelous shapes and sizes of spaghetti, noodles, macaroni, *et al*) especially lends itself to so many different types of recipes—like a great actor wearing many disguises, assuming a new identity with each new role. Marco Polo, that indefatigable traveler (no commuter he!), may have brought the first pasta back from China, but the Chinese would not recognize its Italian metamorphosis. Whatever the original debt to the Chinese, many European cultures have now made pasta part of their own cuisines and adapted the original to their own national dishes. Hungarian, Russian, Jewish, and Mexican cuisines have now claimed pasta as their own.

119

Even in diet-conscious America, the popularity of pasta has accelerated in recent years. Rice, too, shows promise of replacing our ubiquitous potato as the national carbohydrate. And no wonder! Like pasta, rice offers limitless possibilities of combinations with other foods, making it a gourmet's delight.

And, if you really insist on being practical, both pasta and rice are great menu stretchers when that unexpected guest drops by and stays and stays and stays.

A Lazy Lasagne

Of all the meals that can wait, is there any that waits more graciously than lasagne? Some dishes, as I seem to be repeating broken-record style, improve with a waiting period. Lasagne actually *demands* a wait. Oh, you can serve a perfectly edible whipped-up-on-the-spot lasagne, but it isn't half the lasagne it would have been if you'd made it yesterday or even two days ago.

12 *ozs. lasagne*	1 *lb. ricotta cheese*
4 *cups tomato sauce (recipe*	½ *lb. mozarella cheese*
page 117)	½ *cup grated Parmesan cheese*

Cook the lasagne in boiling salted water (enough water to cover and then some). Drain and rinse well in cold water. In a deep oblong greased baking dish, spoon some of the sauce on the bottom, cover with a layer of lasagne, more sauce, spoonfuls of ricotta, topped with thinly sliced layer of mozarella. Repeat in that sequence until used up. End up with sauce on top to keep the dish moist while baking. Sprinkle Parmesan over the top. Cover and refrigerate until needed. When ready to heat up, preheat oven to 375° F. Bake for 25 to 30 minutes or until piping hot through and through. Serve with an additional dish of Parmesan for sprinkling. If dinner is late, turn oven to 300° F., add more Parmesan to the top, and keep well covered. Serves 6 to 8.

Noodles Supreme

Marco Polo introduced, so legend has it, the Chinese noodle to Europeans. From it evolved various pastas, for which I am eternally grateful. Not the least of these was the Italian-style noodle, which is at its best in this make-ahead casserole.

8-oz. *package noodles (½ inch wide)*
1 *cup cottage cheese*
1½ *Tbs. Worcestershire sauce*
2 *cloves garlic, minced*
¼ *tsp. white pepper*

1 *cup sour cream*
1 *large onion, chopped fine*
¼ *tsp. Tabasco sauce*
2 *Tbs. chopped green pepper*
½ *tsp. salt (more if needed)*
¼ *cup Parmesan cheese, grated*

Undercook the noodles in a big kettle of boiling salted water for 6 to 8 minutes. Drain well and combine them with all the other ingredients except the Parmesan. Mix well and place in a greased casserole. Top with the Parmesan sprinkled evenly over all. Set aside until time to bake. This can be made a day ahead and refrigerated until needed. Bake in a medium (350° F.) oven for 30 minutes or so—until top is lightly browned. Serve with a side dish of Parmesan and one of sour cream. Marvelous dish to accompany roast beef. Serves 6 to 8.

Noodles and Mushrooms Supreme

A variation of the above, this is slightly richer and more substantial. To the above recipe simply add 1 cup sliced mushrooms sautéed briefly in 2 tablespoons butter. Add the butter from the skillet to the casserole mixture and stir well. If mixture needs loosening, add additional ¼ cup each of sour cream and cottage cheese.

Spinach-Macaroni Marinara

This traditional Italian tomato sauce is a happy wedding of ingredients that improve with the cooking and simmering together, like partners in a good marriage. It can be made a day ahead.

1½ *lbs. raw spinach*
¾ *lb. elbow macaroni*
1 *lb. ricotta cheese*
3 *eggs, lightly beaten*
⅓ *cup parsley, chopped*
2 *Tbs. fresh basil, chopped*

1 *cup grated Parmesan cheese*
2 *tsps. salt*
½ *tsp. black pepper, freshly ground*
3½ *cups marinara sauce (recipe page 118)*

Rinse spinach well and discard stems. Drain and cook quickly over high flame with minimum water, until leaves are barely wilted. Drain well and chop coarsely. Set aside. Place macaroni in a large kettle filled with boiling salted water. Cook briefly for 5 minutes, stirring to prevent sticking. Do *not* cook thoroughly. Drain pasta well and add it to spinach. Toss lightly, and add ricotta, beaten eggs, parsley, basil, all the Parmesan except 2 tablespoons, salt and pepper. Mix loosely. Add marinara sauce, mix well and place in a good-sized greased casserole. Sprinkle 2 tablespoons Parmesan over the top. Cover and set aside until family appears on the threshold. Then bake, uncovered, in a preheated 375° F. oven for 20 to 30 minutes. Do not overcook. Serve with a side dish of Parmesan and, if desired, sour cream. Delicious! Serves 6.

Herb-Cheese Noodle Casserole

Marco Polo might not recognize these noodles, but that's evolution for you!

1 *package (8 ozs.) wide noodles*	2 *Tbs. dehydrated onion,*
6 *cups water*	*chopped*
½ *cup butter*	½ *tsp. dried thyme*
¼ *cup flour, sifted*	1 *tsp. fresh parsley, chopped*
½ *tsp. Worcestershire sauce*	1 *tsp. salt*
½ *tsp. dried basil*	½ *tsp. savory*
½ *tsp. dried oregano*	1 *tsp. paprika*
½ *tsp. black pepper, freshly*	2 *cups milk*
ground	2 *cups grated sharpest Cheddar*
	½ *cup grated Parmesan cheese*

Cook noodles in 6 cups boiling salted water for 5 minutes. Cover tightly and remove from heat. Let stand 10 minutes covered. Drain, rinse with warm water, drain again. When thoroughly drained, place in mixing bowl and dot noodles with ¼ cup of butter. In saucepan, melt remaining butter over a low fire. Stir in flour until blended into a smooth paste. Add Worcestershire sauce and all seasonings. Mix well, and cook 2 or 3 minutes, stirring constantly. Slowly stir in milk, little by little, until well blended and smooth. Keep stirring as mixture thickens slightly. Add Cheddar, stir until melted and smooth, and remove sauce from heat. Add sauce to noodles, toss well, and turn mixture into a greased deepish casserole. Set aside until needed. Before serving, sprinkle Parmesan cheese over the top and reheat in medium 350° F. oven for 10 to 15 minutes. Serves 6.

Green Rice Casserole

This treatment of staple old rice makes a regal accompaniment to boiled lobster or fresh crab or any simply prepared main dish.

2 *cups rice, cooked*
1¼ *cups grated Cheddar cheese*
1 *medium onion, chopped fine*
2 *small cloves garlic, minced*
1 *tsp. salt (more to taste)*

½ *tsp. black pepper, freshly ground*
1 *cup chopped parsley*
3 *egg yolks, beaten*
¼ *cup butter, melted*
3 *egg whites*

Mix the rice and Cheddar together. Add onion, garlic, salt, pepper and parsley. Mix well, then add beaten egg yolks. Place mixture in a greased deep casserole. Pour melted butter over the top. Cover and set aside for at least 2 hours (can be refrigerated). At dinnertime, beat egg whites until stiff. When the hour looms, fold egg whites carefully into casserole mixture. Preheat oven to 350° F. Wait until everyone is assembled before popping casserole in oven. Then bake it for 15 to 20 minutes. Light and fluffy, it makes a splendid side dish for seafood or a roast. Serves 6.

Modified Chinese Fried Rice

This easy and stretchable dish makes a sassy accompaniment to a roast or meat loaf. Or, if you add meat, shrimp or chicken to it, it becomes the main course itself. Very flexible. Like the original fried rice, anything left over can go into it with palatable results.

2 *cups green onions, chopped*
1½ *cups diced celery*
½ *cup diced green pepper*
3 *Tbs. salad oil*
3 *cups cooked rice*

3 *Tbs. soy sauce*
Salt to taste (careful—soy is salty!)
1 *egg, slightly beaten*
1 *cup blanched almonds, chopped*

Sauté onions, celery, green pepper in salad oil lightly. Do not brown. Stir frequently. Add the rice and soy sauce. Mix well. Taste, then add salt if needed. Add slightly beaten egg and stir again. Remove from fire and spoon into a baking dish. Refrigerate until ready to bake. Preheat oven to 350° F. and place casserole in to heat—35 to 50 minutes. Brown almonds lightly in butter and sprinkle over the top of casserole just before you serve it. Serves 6.

NOTE: if you make this a main course, add the meat or seafood (cooked) before adding the egg.

Almond-Raisin Rice

No, this isn't a dessert, it's a pleasing variation on plain hot rice, but baked and spiced up a bit. An easy way to dress up a boiled beef or simple dinner.

1/4 cup butter	1 can beef bouillon
1/4 cup onions, chopped	1/4 tsp. dried thyme
1 1/2 cups raw rice, washed	1/2 tsp. salt
1/4 cup raisins	1/4 tsp. black pepper, freshly
1/2 cup blanched almonds,	ground
chopped	1 tsp. dried parsley
2 cups water	

Melt butter in heavy skillet. Add onions and sauté until golden. Add rice, stir and brown lightly for 5 to 8 minutes. Remove to a medium casserole. Add raisins and almonds. Heat water and bouillon to a boil, add thyme, salt, pepper and parsley and pour over rice. Cover and bake in preheated 350° F. oven for 20 minutes. Remove and set aside until serving time. Reheat 10 to 15 minutes. If dry, when you return rice to oven, add just a *little* boiling water to moisten. Serves 6.

Curried Eggs

This meatless wonder makes a fine weekend or ladies' lunch dish. Assemble it in the morning, then simply "finish it off" after the sherry is served.

2 Tbs. butter	1/8 tsp. Tabasco sauce
2 Tbs. flour	9 eggs, hard-boiled
1 cup hot milk	1 stalk celery, diced fine
1 1/2 Tbs. curry powder (more to	1 1/2 Tbs. diced green pepper
taste)	1/4 cup bread crumbs
1/4 tsp. onion salt	1/2 cup blanched almonds,
1/4 tsp. salt	chopped

Make a cream sauce in top of double boiler over hot water. Melt butter and add flour, blending smooth. Stir with wire whisk as you add the hot milk slowly. Keep stirring and cook for 10 to 12 minutes. Add curry powder and other seasonings, and mix well. Remove from heat. Place eggs, halved or sliced in ½-inch slices, in a deep casserole. First place one layer of eggs, then sprinkle a little of the celery and green pepper over them, then pour some of the curry sauce over, and repeat process. Mix bread crumbs and almonds and sprinkle over the top. Set aside until time to heat. Fifteen minutes before serving, place casserole in a pan with 1 inch of hot water in a preheated 325° F. oven. When topping is nicely browned, remove casserole and serve. Serves 6.

Creole Eggs

Another meatless wonder, this. I serve it sometimes for Sunday brunch but it is equally pleasant for the Tuesday Bridge Club *and* you can prepare it early, right after the kidlets leave for school.

¾ *stick margarine*
2 *large onions, chopped fine*
1 *stalk celery, diced fine*
1 *green pepper, diced fine*
1 *medium carrot, pared and diced*
2 *cloves garlic, minced fine*
1 *large can (1 lb. 12 ozs.) tomatoes*
¼ *tsp. black pepper, freshly ground*

½ *tsp. salt (more to taste)*
¼ *tsp. Tabasco sauce*
¼ *tsp. dried tarragon*
¼ *tsp. Creole seasoning*
1½ *cups your favorite white sauce*
8 to 10 *hard-boiled eggs*
½ *cup dry bread crumbs*
½ *cup almonds or peanuts, chopped*

Melt the margarine in a deep skillet. Add onions, celery, green pepper, carrot and garlic and sauté until brown but not *too* brown. Add tomatoes with liquid and continue cooking until mixture thickens. Then add seasonings. In a separate pan heat the white sauce. Place a layer of eggs, sliced ½ inch thick, in a medium casserole. Cover with a layer of the white, spread thin, then a layer of the Creole sauce. Repeat layers. Top with the bread crumbs mixed with the nuts. Set aside until needed. Then place in a pan of hot water (1 inch deep) and set into a preheated oven of 350° F. Heat thoroughly for 10 to 18 minutes, or until hot throughout. Serve with a fruit-and-gelatin salad or a tossed green salad. Easy but attractive! Serves 6.

CHAPTER VI

Salads for All Seasons.
Dressings too

Whether you serve your salad before, during or after the main course, nothing serves so well as punctuation, an exclamation mark really, to a good dinner.

An ample salad can also be a counterpoint to an elaborate meal, or, on certain occasions, a meal in itself. (When it is too hot to cook or too late to cook, for instance.) Assorted greens and vegetables, tartly seasoned, make their own crisp statement. Summer or winter, spring or fall, salad has become virtually a mainstay of our modern dinner menu.

The following recipes mostly emphasize greenery, reflecting, I fear, my own special interests. I have genuflected briefly in the direction of gelatin salads, though you'll find more fruit-and-Jell-o salads on every other page of the women's magazines than you'll have time to shake a fork at. A book reflects its creator, as a kitchen reflects its cook. For that reason, Gentle Reader, you'll have to turn elsewhere to enlarge your collection of Jell-o salad recipes.

126

Mushroom and Zucchini Salad

This unusual combination really works! Chill it long enough to marry the flavors.

1 *lb. zucchini, cut into 1-inch slices*
½ *lb. raw mushrooms, sliced*
1½ *Tbs. lemon juice*
5 *Tbs. olive oil*
1 *Tb. tarragon vinegar*
2 *cloves garlic, minced*
½ *tsp. dried oregano, crushed*

2 *tsps. fresh basil leaves*
½ *tsp. black pepper, freshly ground*
1 *tsp. salt*
½ *head lettuce*
6 *leaves romaine*
3 *Tbs. freshly grated Parmesan cheese*

Cover and steam zucchini on a rack over boiling water for 5 minutes. Chill in refrigerator for 2 to 3 hours. Meanwhile sprinkle sliced mushrooms with lemon juice and chill too. When both are thoroughly chilled, combine in mixing bowl. Toss. Mix together olive oil, vinegar, garlic, oregano, basil, pepper and salt. Pour over mushrooms and zucchini. Toss again and chill at least 2 hours. At serving time, wash lettuce and other greens. Pour mushroom mixture over, toss, and sprinkle with Parmesan. Serves 6.

Spinach-Onion and Blue Cheese Salad

This is a real conversation stopper—and delicious! Serve it with a simple main course, as it gathers all the attention to itself.

1 *lb. fresh spinach*
½ *cup blue cheese, crumbled*

1 *large onion, sliced thin*
2 *scallions, chopped coarse*

Wash the spinach leaves thoroughly several times. Trim away stems and damaged leaves with kitchen shears. Drain well. Combine with well-crumbled blue cheese, onions and scallions. Toss lightly but well. Chill 1 or 2 hours minimum. Serve lightly dressed with an oil-vinegar Italian dressing. Serves 6.

Rice and Bacon Salad

This highly unusual combination makes a delicious chilled salad.

1½ cups raw rice
8 strips bacon, cooked crisp
⅓ lb. Cheddar cheese, diced fine
⅓ cup mayonnaise
5 green onions, chopped
2 tsps. salt
2½ Tbs. bacon fat
1 green pepper, chopped fine

½ cup sweet pickles, chopped
6 to 8 radishes, sliced thin
¼ tsp. black pepper
¼ tsp. dill weed
¼ cup fresh parsley, chopped
    fine
½ tsp. paprika

Place rice in large saucepan with 2¾ cups salted water. Bring to a quick boil, then turn heat low, cover pan, and continue cooking until rice is tender, about 15 minutes. Add loosely crumbled bacon and Cheddar cheese while rice is warm. Place in large bowl, add remaining ingredients except parsley and paprika and toss lightly to mix well. Refrigerate, covered, until well chilled. To serve, mound rice salad on lettuce leaves. Sprinkle lightly with parsley and paprika. Serves 6.

Ham and Green Bean Salad

On a balmy summer day this salad makes a substantial enough main dish, served with hot rolls, or, if you *really* want to cope with the oven's heat, a rice or vegetable casserole.

1½ lbs. fresh green beans
½ cup water chestnuts, sliced
2 cups diced cooked ham
2 medium onions, sliced thin
¾ cup radishes, sliced thin
¾ cup celery, diced
½ cup salad oil
¼ cup wine vinegar

1½ Tbs. prepared horseradish
1 Tb. dry mustard
½ tsp. black pepper (more to
    taste)
⅛ tsp. dried thyme
Salt to taste (depends on saltiness
    of the ham)

Trim beans and cut in half. Cook in boiling salted water until barely tender. Do not overcook. Drain and cool slightly. Add water chestnuts, ham, onion, radishes, and celery. Combine oil, vinegar, horseradish, mustard, pepper and thyme. Mix well. Pour dressing over bean mixture. Taste and add salt if needed. Refrigerate until well chilled (several hours at least). Serve cold, sprinkled with fresh parsley or toasted sesame seeds on top. Serves 6.

Salmagundi Salad

This may sound like a cold stew, but it is really a delicious summer main course in its own right, perfect for those days when it is much too hot to turn the oven on.

2½ *cups diced cooked lamb*
¾ *cup diced cooked potatoes*
¾ *cup diced cooked carrots*
3 *sweet pickles, chopped*
1 *Tb. caraway seeds*
1 *Tb. parsley, chopped*
½ *tsp. salt (more to taste)*

½ *tsp. black pepper*
2 *eggs, hard-boiled and chopped*
½ *cup barely cooked peas*
½ *cup French dressing (home-made)*
¾ *cup mayonnaise*

Combine meat, potatoes, carrots, pickles and mix well. Add caraway, parsley and season to taste with salt and pepper. Lightly mix in eggs and peas so they do not mush up. Pour French dressing over all and chill 2 to 3 hours. At serving time, add mayonnaise and mix lightly. Serve on lettuce leaves. Serves 6.

Turkish Salad

Pronouncing the Turkish name for this takes longer than making it —*Patlican Salatasi.*

1 *lb. eggplant*
1 *lemon*
½ *cup olive oil*
¼ *tsp. dried tarragon*
½ *tsp. salt (more if needed)*
¼ *tsp. black pepper, freshly ground*

1 *Tb. wine vinegar*
3 *medium tomatoes, fresh, cubed*
3 *large green peppers, chopped*
1 *large onion, chopped fine*
6 *large green olives*
6 *black olives*

Bake the eggplant in a cake pan in hot oven (450° F.) very quickly. Punch fork in the skin to prevent bursting. When soft but not tender, remove from oven and cool. Peel off skin with knife and cut eggplant into 1-inch cubes. Place in a big bowl and sprinkle with lemon juice. Let stand 10 minutes. Pour olive oil over eggplant, then tarragon, salt and pepper. Mash the eggplant with a fork. Add vinegar and mash again. Stir to be sure liquids cover, and refrigerate until needed. At serving time, add tomatoes, green peppers, onion and olives. Toss lightly and serve. Serves 6.

Makaroni Salat

Which translates easily into macaroni salad (surprise!), Danish style. It's refreshing chilled on a summer day. Good for picnics and cookouts too. (After all, everything at a cookout needn't be cooked *out,* or even cooked.)

1½ *cups heavy cream, whipped*	1½ *tsps. white vinegar*
1½ *tsps. sugar*	2 *Tbs. horseradish*
¾ *tsp. salt*	1¾ *cups elbow macaroni, drained*
½ *tsp. white pepper*	*and chilled*
¼ *tsp. lemon juice*	3 *Tbs. fresh parsley, chopped*

Whip cream until very stiff. Fold in sugar, salt, pepper, lemon juice and vinegar. Add horseradish last. Mix lightly with macaroni and chill again. Serve garnished with parsley. Serves 6.

Modern Macaroni and Cheese Salad

This is a welcome new twist on a simple old favorite.

1½ *cups elbow macaroni*	*Dash of Tabasco sauce*
1½ *cups diced celery*	¾ *tsp. dry mustard*
½ *cup peeled and diced cu-*	3 *Tbs. chopped parsley*
cumber	¾ *tsp. salt*
3 *cups cubed Swiss cheese*	½ *tsp. black pepper, freshly*
½ *cup coarsely chopped walnuts*	*ground*
1½ *cups mayonnaise*	3 or 4 *large lettuce leaves*
1 *tsp. Worcestershire sauce*	

Boil macaroni in salted water until tender. Drain, rinse, and drain again. Set aside to cool. Mix together celery, cucumbers, cheese and nuts. Add to cooled macaroni along with mayonnaise. Mix Worcestershire, Tabasco, mustard, parsley, salt and pepper together. Stir into macaroni mixture. Mix well. Refrigerate until needed (at least 2 hours). Serve on bed of lettuce or use as filling for hollowed-out fresh whole tomatoes. Makes a refreshing summer luncheon salad. Serves 6.

Lentil Salad

If gazpacho is a soup that's really a salad, then perhaps this is a salad that's really a soup. It's a wonderful change as a party salad and, joy of joys, it *must be* prepared a day ahead.

2 *cups dried lentils*
1 *medium onion, studded with*
    4 *cloves*
½ *tsp. salt*
1 *large bay leaf*
¼ *cup finely chopped green*
    pepper
⅛ *cup finely chopped shallots*

⅛ *tsp. dried marjoram*
1½ *Tbs. chopped parsley*
2½ *Tbs. olive oil*
3½ *Tbs. peanut oil*
2 *Tbs. tarragon vinegar*
¼ *tsp. black pepper, freshly*
    ground

Rinse the lentils in cold water, then soak them overnight in enough cold water to cover. Drain and put them in a kettle with onion, salt and bay leaf. Cover with water and bring to a boil. Simmer until lentils are soft but not mushy (1 hour or so). Drain lentils and allow to cool. Discard bay leaf and onion. Mix together green pepper, shallots, marjoram and parsley. Toss with lentils in deep bowl. Mix oils and vinegar and toss with vegetables. Sprinkle pepper over top and refrigerate overnight. Turn before serving, and sprinkle with additional pepper and parsley. Serves 6.

White Bean and Scallion Salad

A nice bitey salad to be served with any somewhat bland main course. Crusty Italian bread heated is good with it, too.

¾ *lb. dried white beans*
3 *Tbs. lemon juice*
2 *cloves garlic, minced fine*
6 *Tbs. olive oil*
3 *scallions, trimmed and chopped*

½ *tsp. salt (more to taste)*
¼ *tsp. black pepper, freshly*
    ground
1 *Tb. chopped fresh parsley*

Soak the beans at least 12 hours, preferably overnight. Drain and simmer in a large kettle in enough water to cover. Should take approximately 2 hours. When tender, drain and cool. Combine lemon juice, garlic, oil, scallions, salt and pepper. Mix well and pour over beans. Chill at least 2 hours. Serve with parsley sprinkled over top. Serves 6.

Sour Cream Potato Salad

This potato salad is so different that my husband doesn't even think of it as potato salad. It's more a vegetable salad that just happens to have a few potatoes, too.

3 *hard-boiled eggs*
2 *lbs. potatoes, cooked and diced*
½ *cup peeled and diced*
  cucumber
2 *medium onions, minced*
⅓ *cup thinly sliced radishes*
½ *cup finely chopped celery*
2½ *tsps. chopped chives*
3 *Tbs. cider vinegar*
1 *tsp. hot prepared mustard*

1 *tsp. salt*
½ *tsp. garlic salt*
¼ *tsp. black pepper, freshly*
  ground
¼ *tsp. cayenne pepper*
½ *tsp. caraway seeds*
2 *cups sour cream*
½ *cup mayonnaise*
1 *Tb. chopped parsley*

Chop hard-cooked egg whites fine. Mix with potatoes, cucumber, onions, radishes, celery and chives. Mix well. Mash the egg yolks with a fork and combine with vinegar, mustard, salt, garlic salt, pepper, cayenne, and caraway seeds. Mix well. Blend in sour cream and mayonnaise. Combine with vegetables and toss lightly. Refrigerate 3 to 4 hours. Serve on a bed of lettuce, with parsley sprinkled over the top. Nice for a picnic or cookout. Serves 6 to 8.

Luau Special

It is undoubtedly a weakness on my part, but I do not generally share the all-American love of Jell-o and Jell-o salads. The following is an exception—and I am sure it is the sour cream that makes it so.

2 *pkgs. lime Jell-o*
2 *cups hot water*
2 *cups ice water*

½ *pint sour cream*
1 *large (1 lb. 4 oz.) can crushed*
  pineapple, drained

Dissolve the Jell-o in hot water. Stir thoroughly and add ice water. Set in refrigerator to thicken. Keep watch. When Jell-o begins to thicken, whip it with a rotary beater until fluffy. Combine the sour cream with pineapple. Carefully fold in the Jell-o. Pour into a mold and chill 5 to 6 hours. Garnish with fresh or fresh-frozen fruits and serve. It makes a pleasant family dessert as well with a whipped cream topping. Serves 6.

Tuna Salad in Sour Cream

These pleasing and slightly different flavors go well together.

3 *cans (6½ oz.) tuna fish*	10 *whole black peppercorns,*
1½ *cups sour cream*	*crushed well*
¼ *cup lemon juice*	¾ *tsp. salt*
1 *Tb. finely chopped celery*	½ *tsp. dried rosemary*
1 *medium onion, minced fine*	⅛ *tsp. ground cloves*
1½ *Tbs. chopped fresh chives*	¼ *tsp. dill weed*

Drain the tuna and break it apart, keeping it in bite-sized chunks. Combine sour cream with lemon juice. Mix well. Add celery, onion, chives and seasonings. Mix thoroughly. Pour mixture over the tuna, covering lightly. Chill 1 hour. Toss with fork, to be sure all tuna is covered well. Return to refrigerator for at least 1 additional hour. Serve on bed of lettuce. Good for lunch on warm days. Serves 6 to 8.

Spanish Tuna Salad

So what's new about tuna fish salad? Not much—unless you're a Spaniard with a flair. Basically, this is a tossed green salad with tuna added.

½ *large head leaf lettuce*	12 *ripe olives*
3 *stalks celery, cut in 1-inch*	3 *fresh tomatoes, cut in wedges*
pieces	1 *can (6½ oz.) tuna, chunk style*
2 *Tbs. finely chopped onion*	1 *hard-boiled egg, sliced*

Wash lettuce and drain on paper toweling. Pull lettuce leaves apart as you would for regular tossed salad. Place in large salad bowl. Add celery, onion, olives and tomato wedges. Toss well. Break tuna into bite-sized chunks and add to salad, along with egg slices. Toss carefully, not overmuch. Refrigerate 1 hour at least. Just before serving, pour an oil-vinegar-tarragon dressing over the salad. Toss very lightly to coat. Serves 6.

Tarragon Dressing

Same as the usual oil-vinegar dressing, but add 1 teaspoon dried tarragon to complement the tuna.

Mushroom, Roquefort and Spinach Salad

This is a happy change from the popular tossed greens. It can be readied well ahead of schedule, too.

10 to 12-oz. *package of fresh raw*
 spinach, washed and
 trimmed
¼ *cup Roquefort or blue cheese,*
 crumbled fine

1 *bunch scallions, washed, pared*
 and sliced thin
¼ *lb. raw mushrooms, washed*
 and sliced not-too-thin
5 to 6 *strips bacon, broiled crisp*
 and crumbled

After washing spinach, be sure to dry it well in toweling or paper towels. Place in large salad bowl. Crumble cheese over and toss well. Add scallions and mushrooms and mix well again. Sprinkle crumbled bacon over top. Cover with wax paper and chill until needed. Serve tossed with Italian dressing or, for a delicious change, try the Lemon-Mustard Dressing below. Serves 6.

Lemon-Mustard Salad Dressing

This is a marvel on spinach salads or any tossed greens. Make it ahead and chill well.

2 *Tbs. lemon juice*
6 *Tbs. olive oil*
⅔ *tsp. salt*
3 *cloves garlic, minced fine*
¼ *tsp. dry mustard*
⅛ *tsp. dried thyme*

¼ *tsp. freshly ground black*
 pepper
¼ *tsp. sugar*
1 *egg yolk*
⅛ *tsp. grated lemon rind*

Combine lemon juice and olive oil and blend. Add all ingredients and mix in electric blender or blend well with hand beater. Chill well before tossing with green salad. Shake before adding to salad. Yield: approximately 1½ cups.

SOUR CREAM DRESSINGS FOR SALADS

A refreshing dressing for salad greens or chilled vegetable salads is one containing sour cream. The following are all variations on a sour cream theme. And all good.

Sour Cream and Dill Dressing

1½ cups sour cream
½ tsp. onion salt
1½ Tbs. dill weed

½ tsp. freshly ground black
    pepper

Combine and mix thoroughly all ingredients. Chill in a jar 2 to 3 hours. Before serving, mix well and pour over salad greens, coating the leaves well. Yield: 1½ cups.

Sour Cream and Caper Dressing

1½ cups sour cream
3 Tbs. capers
½ tsp. onion salt
4 Tbs. wine vinegar

1 tsp. garlic salt
½ tsp. freshly ground black
    pepper

Combine all ingredients in blender. Blend over high speed for 20 seconds. Remove to refrigerator. Chill for 1 or more hours. Yield: 2 cups.

Sour Cream-Mint Dressing

This is a good one for fruit salads.

⅛ tsp. salt
3 Tbs. finely chopped fresh mint

¼ tsp. grated lemon peel
2 cups sour cream

Mix together salt, mint and lemon peel. Add to sour cream and blend thoroughly. Refrigerate until needed. Yield: 2½ cups.

Sour Cream-Caraway Dressing

2 *cups sour cream*   2 *Tbs. caraway seeds*
½ *cup finely chopped cucumber*   ½ *tsp. salt (more to taste)*
½ *tsp. freshly ground black*   ½ *tsp. onion salt*
   pepper

Combine all ingredients and blend well. Chill until needed. Especially good as dressing for leafy vegetables—try it on a raw spinach salad. Yield: 3 cups.

Sour Cream-Blue Cheese Dressing

This is delicious served on crisp romaine or other salad greens. It is also good as a dressing for a chilled cooked vegetable salad.

⅓ *lb. blue cheese, crumbled*   ½ *tsp. celery salt*
¾ *pint sour cream*   ½ *tsp. onion salt*
¼ *cup mayonnaise*   ½ *tsp. black pepper, fresh*
1⅔ *Tbs. wine vinegar*   *ground*
¾ *tsp. salt*   ½ *tsp. paprika*
½ *tsp. garlic salt*

Mash the blue cheese and mix it with sour cream and mayonnaise. Slowly stir in wine vinegar. Combine all the salts, pepper and paprika and add them to the sour cream mixture. Mix well. Dressing should be lumpy but well mixed. Refrigerate until needed. Stir before pouring over greens. Toss lightly. Yield: approximately 2 cups.

Green Goddess Salad Dressing

A wonderful variant on the usual Italian dressing for greens, this also may be kept refrigerated for at least two weeks. It is an equally happy choice on a vegetable salad.

1 *cup mayonnaise*   3 *Tbs. chopped dried parsley*
2 *Tbs. eschalot vinegar*   2 *Tbs. finely chopped onions*
2 *Tbs. garlic vinegar*   1 *Tb. lemon juice*
2 *Tbs. tarragon vinegar*   ½ *cup heavy cream*
1 *Tb. anchovy paste*

Combine mayonnaise with all the vinegars, anchovy paste and herbs. Mix well. Combine lemon juice with cream slowly, and add to the mayonnaise mixture. Put in electric blender and blend at high speed for 15 seconds. Store in refrigerator and use as needed. Yield: approximately 2½ cups.

Wine and Mustard Dressing

This make-ahead dressing is a pleasant change from oil-*cum*-vinegar as a covering for a tossed green salad. This recipe makes enough dressing for a salad for six. Double the recipe if you want to keep it a day or two.

3½ *Tbs. dry white wine*
1 *Tb. dry mustard*
1 *egg yolk*
⅔ *cup salad oil*
1¼ *Tbs. lemon juice*

⅓ *tsp. salt*
2 *tsps. finely chopped chives*
¼ *tsp. dried basil*
2 *tsps. finely chopped fresh*
   parsley

Combine wine and mustard, mix well, and let stand (not refrigerated) 10 minutes or so. Beat egg yolk into the mixture with wire whisk or electric mixer (mixer is really better for the next step). Slowly add oil, then lemon juice, beating vigorously all the while. Mix together salt, chives, basil and parsley. Fold carefully into the wine-oil mixture. Chill, covered, until needed. Yield: 1½ cups.

Cousin Molly's Old-Fashioned Dressing

Good on greens, but also on fruit salads, this will keep refrigerated for months. Cousin Molly was so thrifty of her time, I suspect she made her jug of it once a year.

2 *eggs, slightly beaten*
1 *tsp. salt*
½ *cup white vinegar*
½ *cup sugar*

2 *Tbs. flour*
1 *cup sour cream*
2 *Tbs. prepared mustard*

Combine all ingredients except mustard. Mix well and place in the top of a double boiler over boiling water. Cook until mixture is thick —but keep stirring as it cooks. Add mustard after you remove thickened dressing from stove. Mix well. (Mustard gives it a golden color.)

May be stored. When serving, thin slightly with sweet or sour cream.
Yield: 2 cups.

Lemon-Pineapple Dressing

Generally I lean to simplicity when it comes to salad dressings and
avoid like the plague the icky-gooey whipped-cream type dressings.
But this rich dressing for fruit salads is really exceptionally good *and*
it's neither icky nor gooey, though it does have whipped cream in it.

½ cup sugar   ⅛ tsp. nutmeg
2 eggs, beaten   ¼ cup lemon juice
2½ tsps. flour   1 cup canned pineapple juice
Pinch of salt   ½ cup light cream, whipped

Combine the sugar and eggs and beat well. Add flour, salt, nutmeg
and lemon juice and beat again. Pour mixture into the top of a double
boiler. Add pineapple juice and cook over boiling water until mixture
thickens. Keep stirring to prevent burning. When slightly thick, remove and cool. Chill at least 3 hours before serving. When ready to
serve, fold in whipped cream. Pour dressing over any fruit salad.
Really special. Yield: 2½ cups.

CHAPTER VII

Soups

Seasonal Strong Suits

My husband thought this chapter should be combined with the one on breakfasts, but I decided to play a conventional game. Be daring, though, and try a soup or two at seven A.M. on a bleak, blurred December. Watch out—you may become a morning soup addict. At least in winter.

Virtually any of the hot soups included here are as delicious at seven A.M. as seven P.M. Another lovely thing about soup is that most of those included here age well (within reason of course) and are as good the third day as the first. And many of the chilled ones taste equally good heated.

Soups lend themselves to improvisation and flexible schedules. Soup, a tossed salad and bread or rolls make as light a dinner as a nonhungry man could desire. But a nourishing one at the same time. And filling for the youngsters, too.

To make a good soup, you need a good stock. If you become a soup-happy family, you'll find yourself coveting every leftover bone. Chicken

139

bones, beef bones, lamb bones, but best of all ham bones add flavor to most soups. In Spain they eat Quarter Hour Soup, which is quite thin and watery. And therein lies another secret of good soup: time. No decent, savory soup can be made in 15 minutes. But once made, soup *can* be kept. Chances are, you won't be saying a *soupçon*, but "Soup's on!"

Paloc Leves

Leves is Hungarian for soup. The origin of Paloc is a mystery. But there is no mystery about this hearty Hungarian soup, which doubles as a stew for cold winter evenings. A meal unto itself, it calls for a crisp tossed salad as its only necessary accompaniment.

¼ cup lard	1 bay leaf
4 small onions, chopped coarse	Salt to taste
2 lbs. lamb shoulder, whole	½ lb. green beans, sliced length-
2 tsps. sweet Hungarian paprika	wise
1 can condensed beef bouillon (or	½ lb. potatoes, peeled and cubed
1½ cups beef stock)	1 Tb. flour
6 cups water	⅔ cup sour cream

Melt lard in large kettle. Add onions and brown lightly over a low fire. Set aside. Cut lamb into 1-inch cubes, trimming off fat. Add lamb to onions and brown for 15 minutes. Add paprika, stir constantly for 2 minutes. Then add stock or bouillon, water and bay leaf. Cook 30 to 45 minutes, or until lamb is almost tender. Salt to taste, then add beans. Cook 10 minutes. Add potatoes and cook until tender, about 15 minutes. Add more salt to taste. Skim fat from liquid. Put kettle aside, covered, ready to heat up and serve when required. Like many another delicious dish, this improves with waiting.

At serving time, blend flour with sour cream, and then stir into the simmering soup. Remove immediately from the heat and allow to stand for five minutes. Serve with a flourish. A balanced peasant dish fit for an Emperor! Serves 6 to 8.

Cream of Lentil Soup

This is a pleasing variation of a wondrously hearty soup, plain lentil soup. Like its relative, it makes a good luncheon meal-in-itself, accompanied by crusty sourdough bread and a green salad.

1 *lb. dried lentils, washed*
1 *ham bone with ham still on it*
3 *qts. water*
2 *medium carrots, diced*
3 *cloves garlic, minced*
2 *medium onions, chopped*
1 *large stalk celery, chopped*
2 *bouillon cubes*
1 *bay leaf*

2 *ozs. salt pork, chopped*
¼ *tsp. dry mustard*
¼ *tsp. Worcestershire sauce*
½ *tsp. black pepper*
Salt to taste (ham is salty—so go easy)
1 *cup light cream*
2 *Tbs. chopped fresh chives*

Soak the lentils and ham bone in large kettle with 3 quarts water. Be sure to have a good meaty ham bone. Soak overnight. Use same water for cooking. Add carrots, garlic, onions, and celery, bouillon cubes; bay leaf, salt pork and mustard. Bring to a boil, cover and simmer for 1½ to 2 hours, or until lentils are mushy. Remove ham bone and cut off meat in tiny pieces. Return meat to soup. You may force mixture through sieve if you like, but soup is equally good without being strained. Remove bay leaf. Add Worcestershire sauce and pepper. Taste, and add salt if needed. Simmer 10 minutes longer and set aside. Refrigerate if you are keeping it overnight. Before serving, simmer 10 minutes to reheat, add cream and serve piping hot. Garnish each bowl with a sprinkling of fresh chives. Makes approximately 2 quarts.

Spanish Sausage and Chick Pea Soup

This liquid meal-in-itself may be prepared several days ahead and may even be frozen if you like. It's substantial winter fare.

2 *cups dried chick peas*
4½ *cups water*
2 *large onions, chopped*
¼ *cup diced celery*
3 *cloves garlic, minced*
1½ *Tbs. olive oil*
4 *cups ham broth*
½ *cup cooked and diced smoked ham*

½ *lb. Spanish sausage, sliced*
⅛ *tsp. dried thyme*
¼ *tsp. cayenne pepper*
1 *large raw potato, peeled and diced*
1 *tsp. salt*
½ *tsp. black pepper*
2 *Tbs. chopped parsley*

Put chick peas and water in large kettle. Bring to fast boil and keep boiling 2 to 3 minutes. Set aside to stand 1 hour. Meanwhile, sauté onion, celery and garlic in heated olive oil until golden. Add to chick peas in kettle, along with ham broth. Bring to boil, lower heat and simmer, covered, approximately 2 hours, or until chick peas are soft. Add ham, sausage, thyme, cayenne and potato to kettle. Continue simmering until potato is tender, about 15 minutes. Add salt and pepper to taste. Set aside or freeze until needed. Reheat for 10 to 15 minutes before serving. Sprinkle parsley over top of each bowl. Serve piping hot. Serves 6.

U.S. Senate Bean Soup

This is a version of a classic American soup, much loved by many of our Presidents and legislators. I make it a bit more garlicky than the Washington original, but you may suit yourself. A meal in itself, it keeps for several days. (It can also be frozen.)

1/2 lb. dried beans (navy, marrow, great northern or pea beans)	2 ozs. salt pork, diced
1 large smoked ham hock	2 medium onions, chopped coarse
3/4 cup diced celery	2 medium potatoes, cooked mushy
1/2 cup diced carrots	3/4 tsp. black pepper
4 cloves garlic, minced	1 tsp. salt (more to taste)

Wash beans and cover with water in large kettle. Bring to fast boil, then lower heat and boil 5 minutes. Remove kettle from heat and let stand 1 to 1½ hours. Add ham hock. Skim, and bring to boil again. Simmer, covered, 2½ hours or until beans become mushy. Add celery, carrots, garlic, salt pork, onions and potatoes. Simmer gently for 1 hour more. Stir occasionally. Remove bone, dice meat and add meat to kettle. Test for saltiness. Add pepper and salt to taste. Set aside until needed. Reheat 10 to 15 minutes over low fire. Serve with big green salad, crusty rolls or bread, and, to be festive, a chilled white wine. Serves 6 to 8.

Hungarian Tomato Soup With Ham

Soups are a Hungarian specialty, and this one is a delight. It loves to be reheated as needed.

1 *ham bone with meat on it*
3 *large onions, sliced thin*
1 *bay leaf*
3 *large carrots, peeled and sliced*
   into thin strips
1 *white turnip, peeled and sliced*
   thin

10 *medium ripe tomatoes (canned*
   ones may be used)
1 *Tb. caraway seeds*
12 *whole peppercorns*
½ *tsp. salt*
¾ *cup sour cream*
1 *cup croutons*

In large kettle combine ham bone and water to cover. Bring to a boil and simmer 1 hour. With a spoon, strain off fat, add onions, bay leaf, carrots and turnips. Add additional water to cover. Simmer for 1 hour longer. Remove bay leaf. Add tomatoes, caraway seeds, peppercorns and salt, also a little more water if needed. Simmer 2 hours. Set aside. When ready to serve, strain out peppercorns and reheat soup for 15 minutes. In each bowl, place a spoonful of sour cream, pour hot soup over the top and sprinkle croutons over soup. Serve piping hot with crackers or, Hungarian style, with crusty bread. Serves 6 to 8.

Macaroni Soup

Read on, this is far better than it sounds. In fact, it makes a very substantial main course on a chill winter's evening.

½ *lb. dried navy or pinto beans,*
   washed
1 *ham bone*
1 *bay leaf*
2 *Tbs. margarine*
2 *cloves garlic, minced*
1 *large onion, minced*
½ *cup minced celery*
4 *Tbs. diced salt pork*
⅓ *cup diced cooked ham*

Dash of Tabasco sauce
¼ *tsp. dried red pepper, crushed*
⅛ *tsp. ground fennel*
½ *tsp. salt (more to taste)*
½ *tsp. black pepper*
½ *lb. macaroni, cooked and*
   drained
½ *cup chopped parsley*
½ *cup grated Parmesan cheese*

Soak the beans overnight in 1½ quarts water. Skim and cook beans in same water, with ham bone and bay leaf added. Simmer over low fire until beans are tender, approximately 1½ hours. Melt margarine in skillet and sauté garlic and onions. When golden, add celery and cook 3 minutes. Add salt pork and ham and continue cooking 5 minutes. Add Tabasco, red pepper, fennel, salt and pepper to taste, and mix well. Put mixture into kettle with beans. Continue simmering 15 minutes. Set aside. Fifteen minutes before serving, add drained macaroni and parsley and heat. Serve in bowls, sprinkled with grated cheese, and serve with hot crusty bread. Serves 8.

Winter-Hearty Black Bean Soup

This is delicious, may be kept several days and really improves with the keeping.

4 *cups dried black beans*	2 *medium carrots, diced*
1 *ham bone*	3 *medium onions, chopped*
3½ *qts. water*	½ *cup sherry wine*
1 *bay leaf*	2 *tsps. salt (more to taste)*
¼ *tsp. dried thyme*	½ *tsp. black pepper*
¼ *tsp. dried marjoram*	1 *lemon, sliced thin*
2 *cloves garlic, minced*	1 *hard-boiled egg, chopped*
3 *ozs. salt pork, minced*	

Place beans and ham bone in a large kettle and cover with 3½ quarts water. Soak overnight. To cook, add bay leaf, thyme, marjoram, garlic and salt pork, and simmer gently for 1½ to 2 hours. Add carrots and onion and simmer 1 hour longer. Discard bone and put soup mixture through blender, little by little. When smooth, return soup to kettle. Heat over low fire and add sherry and salt and pepper to taste. Simmer 10 minutes. Set aside until needed. Reheat and serve in bowls garnished with lemon slices and a sprinkling of egg. Serves 6 to 8.

Scottish Cock-a-Leekie Soup

This hearty soup is a veritable meal-in-itself. Like many good things, it improves with age—well, a day or two.

1 *fowl*, 5 to 6 *lbs., cut up*
3 *large onions, sliced thick*
1 *clove garlic, minced*
1 *tsp. salt (more to taste)*
2 *stalks celery, cut in thin strips*
Celery leaves, cut from stalks
2½ *qts. cold water*
1 *bay leaf*

⅛ *tsp. cayenne pepper*
¾ *tsp. poultry seasoning*
¾ *tsp. black pepper*
4 *large raw potatoes, peeled and diced*
3 *Tbs. barley (optional)*
12 *leeks, cleaned and sliced*
4 *Tbs. chopped parsley*

Place chicken in large kettle, along with onions, garlic, salt, celery, celery leaves, and cold water. Bring to a boil, add bay leaf, cayenne pepper, poultry seasoning and pepper, and cook gently for 1½ hours, or until chicken is tender. Remove chicken, cool, remove skin and bones and cut into thin slices. Skim fat from chicken broth, remove bay leaf, and add chicken, potatoes, barley, and leeks. Simmer 30 minutes longer. Remove from heat and let stand (or refrigerate) until needed. Reheat 10 minutes at serving time. Sprinkle with parsley and serve with a tossed salad and good crusty bread. Serves 6 to 8.

Avgolemono Soup

You may call this delicious soup Egg and Lemon Soup, if the authentic Greek name is too tongue-twisting. By any name, the taste is the same: superb. It is simple to make partially ahead of time, with just a few flourishes before serving.

8 *cups chicken broth, strained*
4 *eggs*

½ *cup raw rice, well washed*
2 *lemons*

Heat the chicken broth, bringing it to a slow broil. Add rice and simmer over low fire until rice is cooked, approximately 15 minutes. Set broth aside until mealtime. When ready to serve, whip the eggs until light and frothy. Slowly beat in the juice of two lemons. Dilute the mixture with 2 cups of the warmed soup, beating continuously so that mixture does not curdle. Slowly add this to the rest of the soup, beating as you add. Bring soup almost to a boil, but not quite. Serve immediately. Really refreshing. (I often serve it in the living room, before summoning guests to the table, in good-sized, handleless Japanese teacups. It makes a pleasant transition from cocktails to dinner.) Serves 8.

Herbed Cream of Chicken Soup

This is another day-ahead soup, which improves with time. The herbs and chicken need time to get acquainted.

1 *fryer chicken, cut up*	1 *tsp. salt*
3 *chicken bouillon cubes*	½ *tsp. dried thyme*
4 *cups water*	⅛ *tsp. turmeric*
1 *large onion, whole*	¼ *tsp. dried tarragon*
1 *large bay leaf*	⅛ *tsp. nutmeg*
2 *stalks celery, trimmed and halved*	½ *tsp. dried marjoram*
2 *carrots, peeled*	½ *tsp. black pepper*
½ *cup butter*	1 *tsp. chopped chives*
½ *cup flour*	⅛ *tsp. summer savory*
2 *cups milk*	1 *Tb. sesame seeds, toasted*
2 *cups light cream*	1 *tsp. chopped parsley*

Place cut up chicken in large kettle. Add bouillon cubes, water, onion (whole), bay leaf, celery and carrots. Bring to fast boil, lower heat and simmer, covered, until chicken is tender, approximately 1½ hours. Remove from heat, cool, and remove chicken from kettle. Strain liquid and save. Bone chicken and cut meat into tiny pieces. Rinse out the same kettle and melt butter in it. Stir in flour until smooth paste. Over low heat, slowly add milk and then cream, keep stirring, and cook until thick. Add salt. Mix all herbs together and add to milk-flour mixture. Slowly stir in the reserved chicken liquid and keep cooking until mixture is smooth and not too thick. Add chicken, mix well, and remove from heat. Taste and add more salt and pepper if needed. Set aside until needed. At serving time, sprinkle mixture of parsley and sesame seeds over each bowl. Makes approximately 2 quarts. Serve with thick crusty bread.

Ukranian Vegetable Soup

Good and hearty, this nourishing soup may be made a day ahead and reheated with impunity.

¼ *tsp. dried basil*	¼ *cup chopped celery*
2 *bay leaves*	3 *medium onions, chopped*
½ *tsp. black pepper*	*coarse*
½ *tsp. dried marjoram*	2 *white turnips, peeled and diced*
1 *tsp. salt (more to taste)*	1 *large can tomatoes, with liquid*
3 *qts. water*	1 *Tb. lemon juice*
1 *ham bone*	1¼ *Tbs. brown sugar*
1 *beef soup bone*	3 *Tbs. flour*
1½ *cups slivered raw cabbage*	1 *cup sour cream*

Mix all seasonings together and put in large kettle, along with water and bones. Bring to quick boil, cover kettle, and simmer over low heat for 1½ hours. Remove from heat, strain through cheesecloth and keep broth. Return broth to kettle and add cabbage, celery, onion and turnips. Simmer over low fire for 30 minutes. Add tomatoes, lemon juice and brown sugar and simmer an additional 30 minutes. Blend flour into a tiny bit of cold water. When smooth, add to soup. Stir until thickened slightly. Add more salt and pepper if needed. Remove from heat. Reheat over low fire for 10 to 15 minutes before serving. Serve with sour cream as side dish to ladle into soup at table. Serves 8 to 10.

Senegalese Cream Soup

This lightly curried soup is a culinary delight. You will even curry favor with the antispice brigade when you serve it.

2 *Tbs. butter or margarine*	⅛ *tsp. ground cumin*
1 *large stalk celery, chopped fine*	¼ *tsp. salt (more to taste)*
1 *large onion, minced*	1 *Tb. flour*
1 *large apple, peeled and*	1 *qt. chicken stock or broth*
chopped	½ *pint light cream*
4 *Tbs. curry powder*	1½ *cups diced cooked chicken*

Melt the butter in a deep skillet. Lightly brown the celery, onion and apples, stirring often to prevent burning. Add the curry powder, cumin and salt. Mix well and simmer 15 minutes over the lowest heat. Stir and add flour. Slowly add the broth or stock, and cream, stirring to thicken smoothly. Simmer and stir for 25 minutes or so, until you have a smooth curry sauce. Strain and add the chicken. Mix well and set aside or refrigerate until needed. Age improves a curry, so make this a day ahead if you like. Reheat at serving time for 10 minutes. Or, for a summer menu, serve chilled with a sprinkling of parsley or chopped chives on top. Serves 8 to 10.

Black Bean Soup with Red Wine

A hearty, nourishing soup can be a meal unto itself—as a sampling of this substantial dish proves.

½ *tsp. baking soda*	1 *Tb. wine vinegar*
1 *lb. dried black beans*	1 *cup Burgundy or other red wine*
½ *cup salad oil*	½ *tsp. salt*
2 *large onions, chopped*	2 *bay leaves*
4 *cloves garlic, minced*	¼ *tsp. black pepper, freshly*
1 *green pepper, chopped fine*	*ground*
6 *strips cooked bacon, crumbled*	¾ *cup sour cream*

Add baking soda to a kettle of cold water and soak the beans overnight. When soaked, drain and wash the beans, and add to large kettle with 2 quarts fresh water. Simmer over a low fire at least 1 hour. Meanwhile, heat the oil in a skillet, and sauté the onions, garlic and green pepper until golden brown. Add to the beans, along with the bacon, wine vinegar, wine, and seasonings. Simmer gently until beans are tender. Pour soup through a sieve. Add salt and pepper if needed and set aside. Reheat and serve hot with a dab of sour cream in the center of each bowl. (This soup improves with age, and can actually be prepared 2 to 3 days ahead, refrigerated and reheated when needed.) Serves 8.

Country Corn and Potato Soup

The key to success with this hearty soup is a generous ham bone. As in so many soups, a ham bone adds extra flavor.

1 *large ham bone with meat on it*
6 *cups raw potatoes, peeled and diced*
2 *medium onions, chopped*
1½ *cans cream-style corn*
3 *cups milk*
⅛ *tsp. dried thyme*
⅛ *tsp. celery seeds*

1 *tsp. caraway seeds*
6 *Tbs. minced parsley*
½ *tsp. salt (more to taste)*
½ *tsp. black pepper*
2 *cloves garlic, peeled*
¼ *cup butter*
2 *cups croutons*

Crack ham bone, cover with water and simmer approximately 1½ hours. Add water if needed. Remove bone and cut off meat. Place ham bone, potato and onion in large kettle. Add ham stock and additional water to make 8 cups. Simmer over low heat ½ hour, or until potato is tender. Add corn, milk, thyme, celery seed, caraway, parsley, and salt and pepper as demanded. Simmer all together 30 minutes longer. Set aside until needed. Sauté garlic cloves in melted butter. When golden brown, add croutons, stir and mix well. Remove from heat, and remove garlic. Drain croutons. When soup is reheated at serving time (for 10 minutes), top each bowl of soup with a sprinkling of garlic croutons. Serves 6 to 8.

Hungarian Blueberry Soup

Many Europeans are fond of chilled fruit soups. I think you'll find them refreshing on a hot day.

1½ *pints blueberries, well washed*
3 *cups water*
¾ *cup sugar*
½ *tsp. grated lemon rind*
2 *thin lemon slices*

⅛ *tsp. nutmeg*
2 *sticks cinnamon*
¾ *cup Burgundy or other red wine, chilled*
3 *cups sour cream*

Combine blueberries and water in saucepan. Add sugar, lemon peel and slices, nutmeg and cinnamon. Bring to a rapid boil, turn heat low immediately and simmer 15 minutes, uncovered. Strain and save liquid. Discard pulp. Refrigerate liquid at least 3 hours, preferably longer. At serving time, mix together the chilled wine and sour cream, add to chilled soup, mix and serve immediately. Serves 6.

Russian Gazpacho

This mestizo version of the classic Andalusian cold soup contains beets and beet juice, which is why I call it Russian. I suppose it *could* be called Spanish borscht, but no, it really is gazpacho, a refreshing liquid salad that *should* be made ahead and chilled.

1 *raw egg*
1 *very small onion, sliced*
3 *medium-sized tomatoes, in quarters*
1 *small cucumber, peeled and sliced*
1 *tsp. salt*
¼ *tsp. chopped basil*
3 *Tbs. wine vinegar*
½ *10½-oz. can undiluted beef bouillon*

½ *green pepper, sliced and seeded*
¾ *small (8¼ ozs.) can beets with juice*
2 *small cloves garlic, peeled*
½ *tsp. freshly ground black pepper*
2 *Tbs. olive oil*
½ *cup ice water*

Put all ingredients into blender, cover and blend at high speed for 2 to 4 seconds, or until all ingredients are mixed together. (Some people like the mixture more puréed. I prefer it less so, with more body.) Chill in refrigerator until needed. Serve with a few toasted croutons and a sprinkling of fresh parsley on top. A great summer soup. Serves 8.

Chilled Avocado Soup

This elegant soup is worthy of a really special party or company dinner. Save it for the boss's arrival if you choose.

3 *Tbs. butter*
1½ *cups leeks, chopped coarse*
1 *clove garlic, minced*
1 *large onion, chopped fine*
2½ *tsps. mild curry powder*
2 *cups diced raw potatoes*

3 *cups chicken broth*
2 *medium avocados, diced*
1½ *cups heavy cream*
½ *tsp. lemon juice*
⅛ *tsp. Tabasco sauce*
⅛ *tsp. white pepper*

In a large kettle, melt butter, then add leeks, garlic and onion and sauté until barely limp. Stir in curry powder, then potatoes. Cook 5 minutes longer, stirring all the while. Add chicken broth and increase heat. When broth comes to a boil, lower heat and simmer 15 minutes—

or until potatoes are cooked. Remove kettle from heat and cool. Put half the diced avocados into blender with half the soup. Blend one minute until smooth. Pour into large bowl. Then put remaining avocado and soup into blender and repeat. Add to soup already in bowl. Add heavy cream and stir well. Then add lemon juice, Tabasco, pepper and salt as needed. Refrigerate at least 2 hours. Serve cold. Makes 6 generous servings.

Swedish Plum Soup

Cold fruit soups are a Scandinavian specialty. This is especially cooling and should be made hours ahead to develop a good "chill."

1 *can (17 ozs.) purple plums,*
    drained
2½ *Tbs. lemon juice*
½ *tsp. grated lemon rind*
¼ *tsp. salt*

½ *tsp. cinnamon*
2 *cups sour cream*
1 *large lemon, sliced*
18 *whole cloves*

Remove plum pits. Force plums through coarse sieve. Add enough water to plums to make 5 cups. Stir in lemon juice and grated rind. Add salt and cinnamon and mix well. Add sour cream and put mixture into blender. Blend at high speed for 2 minutes. Refrigerate at least 2 hours. At serving time, place in bowls or cups. Top each with a lemon slice stuck with cloves. Serves 6.

Easy Vichyssoise

Some dishes have been so gourmetized that timid cooks are afraid to tackle them. Like a soufflé, vichyssoise is often feared as being "too difficult," yet nothing could be easier to make. It's at its best if chilled overnight, and its reputation makes it a sure-fire way to impress company. (Maybe we should *keep* its easiness a secret.)

4 *Tbs. butter*
1 *large onion, chopped fine*
    fine
4 *large leeks, washed and chopped*
4 *cups chicken stock, seasoned*
4 *medium raw potatoes, sliced*
    thin

6 *whole cloves*
1 *large bay leaf*
2 *cups cream*
3 *cups milk*
¾ *tsp. salt*
½ *tsp. white pepper*
3 *Tbs. chopped fresh chives*

Heat butter in large kettle. Add onions and leeks and sauté for 5 minutes until golden, *not* brown. Add chicken stock, potatoes, cloves and bay leaf and bring to a boil. Cover and simmer gently for ¾ hour. Put mixture through a fine sieve and return to kettle. Add cream and milk and bring to scalding boil. Season with salt and pepper. Refrigerate overnight. Chill soup bowls 2 to 3 hours before serving. Pour soup and garnish with sprinkling of fresh chives. Almost as good served hot on a wintry day. Makes approximately 2 quarts.

High Humidity Special

Save this salady soup for the hottest day of the year! It's a chiller-diller.

1 *pint light cream*	⅛ *tsp. black pepper*
1½ *tsps. lemon juice*	½ *cup small curd creamed*
1 *tsp. horseradish*	*cottage cheese*
Dash of Tabasco sauce	3 *Tbs. chopped green onions*
1 *can condensed tomato soup*	½ *cup sour cream*
½ *tsp. salt*	2 *Tbs. chopped parsley*

Mix together the cream, lemon juice, horseradish, Tabasco, tomato soup, salt and pepper. Beat with an electric mixer until fairly smooth. Add the cottage cheese and onion and mix well. Chill at least 4 hours. Also chill the bowls to be used in serving the soup. At serving time, pour mixture into bowls, top each bowl with a spoonful of sour cream, topped with a sprinkling of parsley, and presto!—instant air conditioning. Serves 6.

Quickie Curried Chicken Soup

This is better if made a day ahead and chilled. Serve it on the hottest day of the year, but don't limit it to that. It's delicious even on *warm* days.

3 *cans cream of chicken soup* 1 *Tb. curry powder*
3 *cups cold milk* 1 *tsp. paprika*
¼ *cup finely chopped green* 1 *egg, hard-boiled and chopped*
   onions *Rind of fresh lemon*

Combine soup, milk and onions. Mix well. Slowly add curry powder and blend well until smooth. Refrigerate overnight. At serving time, pour soup into slightly chilled bowls and sprinkle over the top paprika, egg and thinly slivered lemon rind. Serves 6 to 8.

CHAPTER VIII

Breads That Can Wait

Many of the recipes for meats and main courses in this book are complemented by the serving of hot Italian or French bread. It is a bonus perhaps that such bread, spread with butter and herbs, may be cut, wrapped well in aluminum foil and set aside hours ahead of time. Then, still wrapped in foil, it may be heated in nothing flat, a perfect *foil* if you will for the food it accompanies.

Garlic bread, which spread across the land with such furor after World War II, has become almost an entertaining cliché, yet it is still delicious as embellishment to an Italian dinner. But there are many other herbs in the garden, and the following are a few examples of how herbs and butter heated on crusty loaves can turn the *staff* into the *hot stuff* of life.

Impromptu Scallion Rolls

Easy to prepare ahead, these rolls enliven a routine dinner.

¾ *cup butter*	1 *tsp. salt*
¾ *cup chopped scallions*	12 *prepared dinner rolls*
2 *Tbs. chopped parsley*	

Let butter stand at room temperature until soft and spreadable. Blend scallions and parsley into it. Add salt to taste. Mix well. Slit the top of each dinner roll in the form of an X. Spread the scallion butter into the slits. Place rolls in a baking pan (round cake pans work fine), cover with aluminum foil and set aside until needed. Before serving, heat rolls for 5 to 8 minutes in a hot (375° F.) oven.

Anchovy-Garlic Bread

You don't have to serve an Italian dinner to serve this bread—but it helps!

¾ *cup butter*	2 *cloves garlic, minced*
1 *tsp. anchovy paste*	1 *loaf French or Italian bread*

Let butter stand until soft enough to blend easily. Add anchovy paste to it and mix well. Add minced garlic cloves and blend thoroughly. Split loaf of bread lengthwise. Spread each side with butter mixture. (Be generous.) Wrap bread in foil and set aside. At serving time, remove foil and heat bread under broiler until lightly browned. Serve at once.

Banana-Walnut Bread

This is a pleasant bread to serve with curried foods. Or toast it for breakfast.

3 *ripe bananas, mashed*	2 *cups flour, sifted*
½ *cup butter or margarine*	1¼ *tsps. baking soda*
1 *cup sugar*	⅛ *tsp. grated lemon rind*
2 *eggs, beaten slightly*	¾ *cup walnuts, chopped fine*

With electric mixer, beat mashed bananas until light and fluffy.

Set aside. Cream butter until light, then add sugar and cream them together. Add eggs and beat well. Sift flour, baking soda and lemon rind together. Add to egg mixture, mix well, and fold in chopped nuts. Carefully fold in bananas. With a rubber-tipped spatula, pour mixture into a greased loaf pan. Bake in 350° F. oven for 50 to 60 minutes. Top should be lightly browned. Cool slightly in pan, then turn out on to rack to cool completely. Do not slice until thoroughly cooled. Loaf may be foil-wrapped, saved several days. Slice fairly thin, but not paper thin.

Cranberry-Walnut Bread

This is a tart and delightful bread that *should* be made ahead and left to stand *at least* 4 hours. Serve it with poultry, or try it sliced thin and toasted and buttered as a lovely breakfast bread.

2 *cups flour, sifted*	1 *cup whole cranberry sauce*
¼ *tsp. cinnamon*	1¼ *cups walnuts, chopped coarse*
1 *tsp. salt*	1 *egg, beaten slightly*
1¼ *tsps. baking soda*	⅔ *cup milk*
½ *tsp. grated orange rind*	¼ *cup butter, melted and cooled*
¾ *cup sugar*	

Sift together the flour, cinnamon, salt, baking soda, grated orange rind and sugar. Mix together the cranberry sauce and walnuts. In another bowl, combine the slightly beaten egg with milk and the cooled melted butter. Mix and add to the cranberry-nut mixture. Blend into the flour mixture lightly. Do not beat—simply stir until dry ingredients are moistened. Pour batter into a well-greased loaf pan. Bake in 375° F. preheated oven 50 to 60 minutes. When you remove loaf from oven, let it stand 5 minutes before turning out on to a rack. Leave on rack until loaf is completely cooled. Leave, uncovered, at least 4 hours, or overnight if you wish. (The bread cuts more easily if really firm and cold.)

Apple-Nut Bread

Served for dinner with a pork roast or for afternoon tea or for breakfast, this is a delicious and versatile bread. Make it a day ahead if you like.

¼ cup vegetable shortening
⅔ cup sugar
2 eggs, well beaten
2 cups flour, sifted
1 tsp. salt
1 tsp. baking soda

1¼ tsps. baking powder
1¼ Tbs. grated lemon rind
2¼ cups raw apples, peeled and
    loosely grated
1 cup walnuts, chopped coarse

Cream together shortening and sugar until light and fluffy. Slowly beat in the eggs. Keep beating until well mixed. Sift together flour, salt, baking soda, baking powder and lemon rind. Mix well and add alternately with apples to the egg mixture. Add nuts last and blend all together. Pour into greased and floured loaf pan and bake in a preheated 350° F. oven approximately 1 hour. Remove to rack and cool thoroughly before slicing.

Austrian Honey Bread

Prepare this light honey bread the day before and heat it briefly as a breakfast bread. Delicious! And no kneading!

2 cups flour
½ tsp. salt
1 tsp. cinnamon
½ tsp. grated lemon peel
¼ tsp. nutmeg

½ cup sugar
1 cup milk
½ cup good quality honey
1 Tb. butter or margarine
1¼ tsps. baking powder

Sift together the flour, salt, cinnamon, lemon peel and nutmeg. Mix well and add sugar. Combine milk, honey and butter in a saucepan over a low heat. Mix constantly as butter melts and blends with other ingredients. Slowly add baking powder. Stir well. Add milk-honey mixture to dry ingredients. Stir well with a wooden spoon. Pour mixture into a greased and floured bread pan (or meat loaf pan) and bake in a preheated 350° F. oven for approximately 50 minutes. Caution: This delicate bread burns easily, so be vigilant while it is baking. Check often. When golden brown and done, let stand on rack for 15 minutes before removing from pan. Good served warm with butter.

Spicy Cheese Bread

Make this a day ahead, then serve it sliced thin as breakfast toast or as a toasted base for scrambled eggs. It is also delicious toasted and buttered as sandwiches, with ham, turkey or corned beef filling.

1 *package yeast*	⅛ *tsp. powdered mace*
¼ *cup warm water*	⅛ *tsp. powdered ginger*
½ *cup milk*	2 *Tbs. butter, melted*
½ *cup cold water*	¾ *cup grated sharpest Cheddar*
1 *Tb. sugar*	*cheese*
½ *tsp. salt*	3¼ *cups flour, sifted (more if*
⅛ *tsp. dry mustard*	*needed)*

In a large mixing bowl, dissolve yeast in warm water. Set aside. Scald milk in saucepan. When scalded, quickly remove from heat and add cold water. Set aside to cool slightly. Blend into the yeast the sugar, salt, mustard, mace, and ginger. Mix well, then slowly add the cooled milk. Mix slightly, and add melted butter, the cheese, and 1 cup of the sifted flour. Beat by hand until mixture is smooth. Set bowl aside in a warm room or alcove and let rise, covered, for 30 minutes. Return bowl to kitchen, add remaining flour and knead with hands until dough is stiff. (Add a little more flour if needed.) Cover bowl and set aside in warm place again. Allow to rise until dough is doubled in size—usually takes approximately 1 hour. (Warm place should have temperature of approximately 85 to 90°—I use my furnace room.) When dough is doubled, return it to kitchen and continue kneading by hand, very gently this time, until dough becomes shiny smooth. Form it into loaf and place in large greased loaf pan. Cover pan and set aside to rise further for 45 minutes. Bake in a 375° F. preheated oven about 45 minutes, or until a golden, glowing brown. Remove from oven, cool, then cool on rack until completely cooled. Keep 4 to 5 hours before slicing.

Apricot Nut Bread

Easy to make ahead, this delicious bread will keep in foil for a week or more in the refrigerator or freezer. It is nice at teatime or as a supplement to a simple roast dinner.

1 *cup hot water*
1 *cup dried apricots, cut fine*
1 *cup sugar*
2 *eggs, beaten slightly*
2¾ *cups flour, sifted*
1 *Tb. baking powder*

½ *tsp. baking soda*
1 *tsp. salt*
½ *tsp. cinnamon*
½ to ⅔ *cup walnuts, chopped*
   coarse

Pour very hot water over the cut apricots. Set aside to cool. Mix sugar with the eggs until well creamed. Sift flour, baking powder, soda, salt and cinnamon together. Mix well and add to the egg-sugar mixture. Add apricot-water mixture, then walnuts. Blend carefully and allow to stand 15 minutes. Preheat oven to 350° F. Pour mixture into a loaf pan. Sprinkle a mixture of sugar and cinnamon over the top. Bake approximately 1 hour. Set aside to cool. When cooled, remove from pan and wrap in foil until ready to slice. Delicious warm too. Can be reheated briefly when ready to serve.

Applesauce-Raisin-Nut Bread

This light delight is great at teatime, but also, if reheated, makes a lovely breakfasty *kuchen*. Serve it also as accompaniment to baked ham.

½ *cup margarine*
⅔ *cup light brown sugar*
2 *eggs*
1 *cup applesauce (light, not*
   dense)
1¼ *tsps. baking powder*
2 *cups flour, sifted*

½ *tsp. cinnamon*
¼ *tsp. nutmeg*
¾ *tsp. baking soda*
½ *tsp. salt*
¾ *cup walnuts, chopped coarse*
½ *cup raisins, softened in hot*
   water and drained

Cream margarine until smooth, then add brown sugar slowly, creaming well as you add. (Use electric mixer if possible.) Beat eggs in, one at a time. Add applesauce and mix thoroughly. Sift together all dry ingredients, including spices. Mix well, and add little by little to the applesauce batter. Keep a cup of dry mixture aside and add nuts and raisins to it. Stir to cover, and slowly add to batter. Mix well. Pour into a well-greased loaf pan. Bake in a preheated 350° F. oven for 45 to 55 minutes. Remove from oven and allow to stand 8 to 10 minutes before turning carefully on to a rack to finish cooling. When thoroughly cooled, place in airtight container and store overnight. (This isn't necessary, of course, if you plan to serve the bread later in the day you bake it.)

Orange Nut Bread

Light and cake-textured, this bread is good toasted for breakfast or served plain for tea or dessert. Versatile and easy.

⅓ cup margarine	3 cups flour, sifted
1 cup sugar	¾ tsp. salt
1 egg, beaten slightly	5 tsps. baking powder
1 cup orange juice	¾ cup walnuts, chopped
3 Tbs. grated orange rind	

Cream margarine and beat sugar in slowly. When mixture is light and fluffy, add egg. Keep beating and add juice and rind. Sift together flour, salt, baking powder and add to the sugar-egg mixture. Stir just enough to moisten dry ingredients, but do *not* beat. Fold in nuts carefully. Pour mixture into greased meat loaf pan. Bake in preheated 350° F. oven for 50 to 60 minutes. When done, remove from oven and let stand on rack a few minutes to cool.

Basil Butter

The following makes ½ cup, which should be enough to serve 6.

½ cup butter, soft	1½ Tbs. fresh basil, chopped, or
2 tsps. lemon juice	1 tsp. dried basil
¼ tsp. grated lemon rind	⅛ tsp. salt

Cream together the butter, lemon juice and lemon rind. Mix well. Add basil and salt and continue mixing until well blended. Can be made several days ahead and stored, covered, in refrigerator. Basil butter is delicious as a topping for fish, melted and served with steamed artichokes, in the skillet when scrambling eggs, in fact in numerous improvised ways where melted butter is used. Yield: approximately ½ cup.

Dill Butter

½ cup soft butter
¼ tsp. salt

¾ tsp. dill weed

Cream together or put in electric blender for 10 seconds. Spread on sliced Italian bread before heating. Also good for egg or fish dishes. Yield: approximately ¾ cup.

Curry Spread

½ cup mayonnaise
2 Tbs. soft butter
⅛ tsp. white pepper

1 Tb. curry powder
⅛ tsp. salt

Mix all ingredients together. Add more or less curry powder to taste. Spread over French or Italian bread before heating. A dab on poached eggs is very nice too. Or as a spread for meat sandwiches. Yield: approximately ¾ cup.

Sesame Butter

½ cup butter, softened
¼ tsp. salt

3 Tbs. sesame seeds
¼ tsp. dried parsley

Combine all ingredients. Mix well and spread on crusty bread slices before heating. Very good on broiled fish too. Yield: ¾ cup.

Chili-Onion Butter

½ cup soft butter
¼ cup finely minced onion

½ tsp. chili powder

Melt butter and add onion and chili powder. Brush on to bread. Also good on rounds of bread to be toasted as canapés. Try this mix on rye bread, too. Yield: ¾ cup.

Soy Butter

½ cup soft butter

2 tsps. soy sauce

Combine two ingredients. Spread on split hard rolls, to be heated in oven later. Also good on hot cooked rice or for frying scrambled eggs. Yield: ½ cup.

Savory Butter

½ cup soft butter   ½ tsp. ground sage
¼ tsp. summer savory   ¼ tsp. chopped parsley

Combine all ingredients and mix thoroughly. Spread on sliced crusty bread before heating. Also tangy on sandwich bread with sliced ham or tongue sandwiches. Yield: approximately ⅔ cup.

Watercress Butter

½ cup soft butter   ¼ tsp. salt
1 Tb. mayonnaise   2 Tbs. chopped fresh watercress

Combine all ingredients and mix well. Spread on dinner rolls or Italian bread, and heat. Also good on hot-dog rolls, which should then be heated. Yield: ¾ cup.

Herb Butter

½ cup butter, softened   ¼ tsp. dried basil
¼ tsp. dried thyme   ¼ tsp. paprika
¼ tsp. mace   ¼ tsp. garlic salt
½ tsp. finely chopped parsley   ¼ tsp. seasoning salt
¼ tsp. freshly ground black   ⅛ tsp. marjoram
   pepper

Blend all ingredients thoroughly. Use electric blender if desired. Spread on bread before heating. Use for sautéeing fish, or put a tablespoon in a bowl of fresh, just-cooked peas or green beans. Try it on corn on the cob for a change. Yield: 1 cup.

CHAPTER IX

Dips, Dunks, and Appetizers

Dips and appetizers serve a different function for the family and for company.

For the family, a dip is a pre-dinner snack, a stopgap for appetites on the rampage. For you, on days when you've had the Brownies or Cub Scouts or nurse's aiding or anything else that might have kept you away from home, hearth and kitchen range, a dip prepared in the morning and refrigerated all day can be a cooksaver at 6 P.M. when all appetites break loose.

And when your husband arrives, no matter what chaos may be prevailing in the kitchen, you can shove a cocktail into one of his hands, a cracker-*cum*-dunk into the other and lead him to his newspaper in a quiet corner of the living room. Then it's back to the kitchen onion peeling for you. But he won't mind the wait half so much with both hands full of goodies.

For company entertaining, the dip is *your* chance to relax (I'm assuming of course that you have a pop-it-into-the-oven dinner baking merrily in the kitchen) and have a little get-guests-acquainted-with-one-another conversation before drifting off to the kitchen to apply the finishing touches to the meal. No matter how well organized a dinner party is in advance, there always seems to be *something* to do at the last minute. But if the dip or appetizer is prepared ahead, that's one point for your team. (Sad to say, no matter how immaculate I think the house looks, nor how smoothly every course may be served, nor how gloriously natural the centerpiece I have fussed over for 50 minutes looks, it is always a bit of a blow at the end of the evening, after all guests have departed, to discover one rolled-up child's sock lying under the couch or a baseball in the seat of a chair!)

DIG THESE DIPS

Cocktail time is supposed to be relaxed—and I'm all for that—and to help make it so for the hostess dips whipped up earlier in the day do their bit. Or, in the language of the under-thirty crowd, here are a few hip dips that really do their thing.

Garbanzos* Arabesque

⅓ cup sesame oil (available in
    Chinese groceries)
½ cup lemon juice
¼ cup water
½ tsp. salt
3 cloves garlic, crushed

1 cup cooked garbanzos (chick
    peas) (canned ones may be
    used if drained)
½ tsp. olive oil
1 tsp. minced parsley

Combine the sesame oil, lemon juice, water, salt and garlic in a blender. Blend on low speed for 15 seconds. Slowly add garbanzos and blend till smooth. Refrigerate at least 2 hours. When ready to serve, pour olive oil over the top in quick drops and garnish with parsley. Serve with crackers or crusty bread.

Middle Eastern Dip

1 large eggplant
1 tsp. salad oil
⅓ cup sesame oil
½ cup lemon juice

3 cloves garlic, crushed
½ tsp. salt
½ tsp. olive oil
¾ tsp. chopped parsley

   * Chick peas.

Remove hull and stem from eggplant. Do not peel. Bake eggplant, dotted with salad oil, in a very hot oven (450° F.) until the skin breaks open. Remove from oven and cool. Cut one end off the eggplant and scoop out the insides. Mash well and put into blender, along with the sesame oil, lemon juice, crushed garlic and salt. Blend well, but remove before mixture becomes too smooth. Refrigerate 2 or 3 hours (or longer). At serving time, drip olive oil over the top and trim with parsley. Delicious on crackers or thin toast rounds.

Eggplant Marinara

This is delicious served as a dip or as part of the antipasto tray at an Italian dinner. If you serve it with slices of salami, peppers, artichokes and other cold delights, do not make it in a blender, but keep it in chunkier, more textured form. I usually cube the eggplant and marinate it in the spice-blended vinegar overnight.

1 *large eggplant*	½ *tsp. chopped basil*
½ *cup wine vinegar*	½ *tsp. black pepper*
3 *cloves garlic, chopped*	1 *tsp. oregano*
1 *tsp. salt*	¾ *cup olive oil*
¼ *tsp. thyme*	

Cut eggplant in half and boil in 1 cup water until slightly tender. Add additional water if necessary. It should take about 10 to 15 minutes. Remove from heat and drain on paper toweling. When cool, peel eggplant and cut into large chunks. Combine in blender with wine vinegar, garlic and spices. Refrigerate at least 6 hours. Before serving, add olive oil and blend thoroughly by hand. Good on cheese crackers, melba toast or toasted bread.

Variation on a Garbanzo Theme

2 *cups drained garbanzos (canned ones may be used)*	½ *tsp. black pepper*
3 *anchovy fillets*	2 *Tbs. chopped parsley*
1 *Tb. capers, chopped*	*Dash of lemon juice*
2 *cloves garlic, minced*	⅓ *cup mayonnaise*
1½ *tsps. finely chopped green onions*	

If you use cooked garbanzos (chick peas), you will need a #2 can. Mash lightly. Chop anchovy fillets fine and mix them with capers, garlic, green onions, pepper, parsley, and a dash of lemon juice. Slowly add mayonnaise until mixture is a spreadable consistency. Add to chick peas. Mix well. Pour into a serving bowl and refrigerate for several hours. Serve as dip for celery sticks, cucumbers or crackers.

Quickie Dip

1 *cup sour cream*   1 *tsp. onion juice*
¼ *cup cottage cheese*   ¾ *package dried mushroom soup*
¼ *tsp. Worcestershire sauce*

Mix all ingredients together, blending well. Chill and serve as a dip for crackers or raw cauliflower flowerets or other raw vegetables. Any dried soup may be the base for an inviting dip. Another special favorite of mine is dried split pea soup. The peas give a crunchy flavor to the dip and defy the most penetrating guesses as to "What's in the dip?"

Smoked Herring Dip

An improvisation of my husband's, this has become a favorite party dip at our house. It is easy to make in a blender and keeps for a week or more in the refrigerator.

1 *cup chopped smoked herring*   1 *Tb. finely chopped onion*
½ *cup sour cream*   ¼ *tsp. dried horseradish*

Mix all ingredients together in a blender (or mash up by hand). Spread on crackers or toast at canapé time. Then let your guests guess what the Mystery Dip consists of. Yield: 1¾ cup.

Variation on Middle Eastern Theme

In the Middle East sesame and eggplant go together like ham and eggs. This appetizer is a guaranteed party hit.

1 *medium-sized eggplant*
3 *Tbs. sour cream*
1 *tsp. lemon juice*
3 *Tbs. sesame seeds, toasted*
½ *tsp. onion salt*
3 *cloves garlic, minced*

1¼ *tsps. salt (more to taste)*
½ *tsp. black pepper, freshly*
 ground
¼ *tsp. ground red pepper*
½ *tsp. grated lemon rind*

Poke a fork into the eggplant all over, then bake unpeeled until soft, in a hot (400° F.) preheated oven, approximately 1 hour. Remove from oven and allow to cool. When cool enough to handle, peel eggplant, discard skin, and mash pulp until it is quite smooth. Add all remaining ingredients to eggplant, but reserve 1 tablespoon sesame seeds for later. Beat all ingredients into eggplant well. When thoroughly smashed, mooshed and smooth, refrigerate until well chilled, approximately 3 hours. Serve heaped high in a bowl, with remaining sesame seeds sprinkled over the top. Delicious with toast rounds, toast or crackers. Yield: 3 cups.

Chilled Beef-Sour Cream Appetizer

This is an unusual and delicious appetizer that is easy to make with leftover steak. It should be chilled overnight *at least*.

1½ *cups cooked roast beef or*
 steak (best if rare)
2 *Tbs. lemon juice*
¾ *cup sour cream*
¼ *tsp. Tabasco sauce*
1 *tsp. salt*

½ *tsp. black pepper*
⅓ *cup chopped stuffed olives*
¼ *tsp. garlic salt*
2 *green onions, chopped coarse*
Toast or Melba toast

Cut meat into thin strips 1½ inches long, cut against the grain. Mix lemon juice, sour cream, Tabasco, salt, pepper, olives, garlic salt and onions. Mix thoroughly. Add meat strips and mix lightly. Chill in covered bowl overnight. At serving time, serve in a bowl with spreader and accompanied by strips of buttered toast or plain Melba toast. If you like, sprinkle paprika over top of bowl before serving. Yield: approximately 3 cups.

Crab in Mustard Sauce

This makes an impressive appetizer and impresses the cook most of all with its easiness.

2½ Tbs. dry white wine
2¼ tsps. dry mustard
2 cloves garlic, minced
⅓ cup salad oil
2¼ tsps. lemon juice
¼ tsp. dried tarragon

1 Tb. finely chopped fresh dill
  (or 1 tsp. dill weed)
¼ tsp. salt
⅛ tsp. black pepper
1½ cups crab meat, fresh if
  possible

Combine the wine, mustard and garlic and mix well. Allow to stand at room temperature for 10 or 15 minutes. Use electric mixer to stir salad oil slowly into wine-mustard mixture. Then, little by little, beat in lemon juice and herbs. Be sure everything is well mixed. Stir in crab meat, mix well, and refrigerate for 2 hours. To serve, place marinated crab meat in shells, sprinkle parsley on top and serve as appetizer. Serves 6.

Japanese Shrimp

The seafaring Japanese love shrimp no matter *how* it is prepared. But this treatment is especially popular, and very well suited to American plan-ahead schedules, too.

¾ cup soy sauce
¾ cup fresh lemon juice
1 Tb. grated fresh ginger
  (or 2 tsps. ground ginger)
½ tsp. black pepper, ground
  fresh

Pinch of sugar
36 large shrimp, cooked, shelled
  and deveined
1 large bunch fresh watercress,
  chopped coarse

This dish may be prepared 2 ways. A) Mix together soy sauce, lemon juice, ginger, pepper and sugar. Chill until ready to serve. Chill shrimp separately. At serving time, mix shrimp with watercress on a serving plate. Serve dip separately in a bowl, so shrimp and watercress may be dipped into soy mixture.

B) Combine soy sauce *et al.* Pour over shrimp and chill for 2 or 3 hours at least. Serve marinated shrimp in sauce, garnished with fresh watercress. Serve toothpicks or canapé picks for spearing the shrimp. Serves 6.

Shrimp in Hot Mustard Sauce

This make a piquant appetizer, but it is also delicious as a main course, served with Green Rice or Noodles Supreme. A felicitous summer menu.

36 *raw shrimp, unshelled*	1 *large bay leaf*
½ *tsp. salt*	1½ *Tbs. prepared* hot *mustard*
¾ *tsp. dried thyme*	3½ *Tbs. lemon juice*
2 *slices lemon*	¾ *cup olive oil*
¾ *tsp. dried basil*	1 *tsp. salt*
1 *Tb. whole peppercorns*	1½ *tsps. dried tarragon*
2 *sprigs fresh parsley*	

Place shrimp in a large saucepan with ½ teaspoon salt, thyme, lemon slices, basil, peppercorns, parsley and bay leaf. Pour enough boiling water over to cover shrimp. Bring to a boil and cook 6 minutes. Drain and douse shrimp in cold water. Drain. When shrimp have cooled, peel and devein them. Set aside. Meanwhile, combine mustard and lemon juice and whisk until blended. Slowly add olive oil. Keep whisking until oil is well blended. Stir in salt and tarragon. Whisk again, then pour mixture over the shrimp. Refrigerate in covered bowl at least 2 hours. Stir and turn before serving. Serve on canapé picks as an appetizer. Serves 6.

Shrimp Balls

A holdover from my days as an Old Manila Hand (I always think Virgil Partch would have fun with that old expression), this recipe makes a delicious hot hors d'oeuvre. The balls can be prepared ahead, then popped into the skillet at the last minute.

1 *cup shrimp*	⅛ *tsp. black pepper*
2 *cups mashed soy bean cakes*	¼ *cup finely chopped green*
(available at any Chinese or	*onion*
Japanese food shop)	1 *egg, slightly beaten*
4 *Tbs. flour*	*Salad oil or lard for frying*
1½ *tsps. salt*	¾ *cup soy sauce*

Shell the shrimp and blanch them with boiling water. Drain, then chop them quite fine. Mix with the soy bean cake, flour, salt, pepper and onion. Add egg and mix thoroughly. Form the mixture into small 1-inch balls. Put all the balls on a large plate, cover and refrigerate. When ready to cook, heat the oil or lard in a deep skillet. Drop the balls in and brown quickly, turning once. Drain on absorbent paper and serve hot with canapé picks. As accompaniment, I usually serve a small bowl of soy sauce to dip the balls into. Delicious. Serves 6.

Seviche

Purists will insist on serving an entire Italian menu when they have spaghetti, but I believe strongly in mixing and matching, as the fashion people say. After all, is this country not a melting pot? Well then, where else should a melting pot be found if not in the kitchen? Thus, when I serve this yummy South American appetizer, I never go South of the Border for the main course. Instead, I might have a roast or chicken.

1½ *lbs. cooked shrimp, peeled*	¼ *tsp. black pepper*
¾ *lb. raw scallops, sliced thin*	2 *Tbs. minced green pepper*
Juice of 6 limes (or ¾ cup juice)	¾ *tsp. salt*
½ *tsp. dried oregano*	⅓ *cup olive or salad oil*
Dash of Tabasco sauce	3 *Tbs. chopped parsley*
5 *Tbs. finely chopped red onion*	2 *avocados, peeled*

Cut the shrimp into thirds and mix with the sliced scallops. Place in deep mixing bowl and pour the lime juice over the seafood. Cover and allow to marinate at room temperature at least 3 hours. Stir the mixture every now and then. Approximately 1½ to 2 hours before you plan to serve the appetizer, drain and discard the lime juice. Then add all the other ingredients except the avocados and mix lightly together, as you would toss a salad. Cover again and refrigerate until serving time. To serve, arrange individual portions on small plates. Trim with avocado slices. A refreshingly tart beginning. Serves 6.

Liptauer Cheese Ball

This version of the classic Hungarian *liptoi* may be prepared well ahead of the party. Spread on pumpernickel or other dark bread, it is delicious! It can be refrigerated and kept for days.

8 *ozs. cottage cheese*
1 *cup butter (no substitutes)*
1 *Tb. dry mustard*
1 *Tb. caraway seeds*
1 *Tb. chopped chives*

1 *Tb. capers, chopped fine*
2 *anchovy strips, minced*
1 *Tb. hot paprika*
2 *tsps. chopped parsley*

Cream the cheese and butter together until quite smooth. Add mustard, caraway seeds, chives, capers and anchovies. Blend well (but do not use a blender—you want some texture left). Form into a ball or mound. Sprinkle with paprika and parsley. Chill. Yield: approximately 4 cups.

Chilled Stuffed Grape Leaves

The Greeks have a word for it: *Dolmadakia*. But in any language it makes a festive party hors d'oeuvre.

2 *medium onions, chopped fine*
¼ *cup olive oil*
½ *cup raw rice, washed*
2 *Tbs. pine nuts*
5 *Tbs. raisins or currants*
½ *cup chopped dill*
¼ *cup chopped parsley*
Small bunch scallions, minced

¼ *cup cold water*
Salt and pepper to taste
1 *large lemon*
Pickled grape leaves (can be
  bought canned in specialty
  shops)
¼ *cup olive oil*
1 *cup water*

Sauté onions in ¼ cup olive oil until golden in color. Add rice and cook 10 minutes, stirring constantly to prevent sticking. Add the nuts, raisins, dill, parsley, scallions, ¼ cup water, and salt and pepper. Juice the lemon and add half the juice to the mixture. Cook until liquid is absorbed, about 10 minutes. Set aside to cool.

Unwrap the grape leaves (they usually come tightly rolled in their jar or container) and wash. Drain on absorbent paper. Then place the leaves on a flat table, with the shiny side of the leaf facing down. Put one teaspoon of the cooled rice mixture in the middle of each leaf. Roll each leaf up tightly, starting from the stem, with the ends turned inward toward the center. When all the leaves are rolled, place them in layers in a saucepan so that they fit fairly snugly. Pour the other ¼ cup oil over the leaves, along with the remaining lemon juice and ½ cup water. Place a plate or flat pan cover over the rolled grape leaves to keep them from unrolling. Then boil for five minutes over a high heat. Add ½ cup water and reduce heat. Simmer 15 to 20 minutes longer, or until all water is absorbed and the rice is soft. allow rolls to cool in the saucepan. Remove to a bowl and chill. Delicious serve cold, garnished with lemon wedges. Makes approximately 20 stuffed grape leaves.

Quiche Lorraine

While this lovely dish cannot keep too long, parts of it *can* be readied ahead, so that it is virtually no last-minute trouble. I organize it an hour ahead, for easy assemblage after guests arrive, no matter *when* they finally arrive. It is a great main course for a luncheon, midnight supper, or, as I usually serve it, as an appetizer at a dinner party.

Pastry for a single 9-inch pie	*½ tsp. salt*
6 *slices bacon*	*¼ tsp. nutmeg*
1 *large onion, sliced thin*	*¼ tsp. white pepper*
4 *eggs, lightly beaten*	1 *cup cubed Gruyère cheese*
¾ *cup milk*	*¼ cup freshly grated Parmesan*
1 *cup light cream*	*cheese*

Preliminaries:

Using your favorite pastry recipe, line a pie plate and bake pastry shell in a hot 450° F. preheated oven for 5 minutes, or until shell is just lightly browned. Remove and set aside. Cook bacon until crisp but not dark. Set aside. When cool, crumble it. Pour off bacon fat in skillet, leaving 1 tablespoon for sautéeing the onion slices. Cook them until transparent. Remove from skillet and drain on absorbent toweling. Set aside. Combine eggs with milk, cream and seasonings. Beat vigorously and set aside. Mix the two cheeses together and set aside.

Finale:

Heat oven to 450° F. Sprinkle bacon, onion and cheeses in the bottom of pastry shell. When all guests have assembled, give the eggs a quick beating again and strain them over the pastry shell. Pop pastry into oven. Bake 10 minutes, then reduce heat to 350° and continue baking until *quiche* is firm and light brown on top—about 20 minutes. Serve at once in small wedges. Serves 6.

CHAPTER X

Just Desserts

"Just dessert indeed!" says my eldest son who considers dessert the key to the entire dinner. His favorite query *circa* 4 P.M. is "What's for dessert?" followed by "What's for dinner?" asked in order of importance of course. If the answer is uninspiring, then it's another banana for him or a second piece of cinnamon toast as a midafternoon filler. If the answer is more appealing, then he restrains himself from snacking, to save room for seconds on everything.

But growing boys are not the only people who like something sweet at the end of a meal. Sweet or cool, and sometimes both sweet *and* cool, is often the perfect ending for a rich and highly seasoned meal. Most people look forward to even a light dessert—sometimes *especially* to a light dessert. Chilled and sweetened fruit, or chilled fruit with a sweet liqueur added, can be more refreshing than a heavy, many-layered Viennese splendor of chocolate and whipped cream shaped in Mozart's likeness.

Most desserts can be made ahead and popped on to dessert plates at the last possible moment. There are, however, such heavenly creations as dessert soufflés, which require considerable last-minute whipping and coaxing. These, good as they are, hardly have a place in a make-ahead cookbook.

A dessert that doesn't keep you frazzled in the kitchen whipping, stuffing or stirring before, between and during other courses is the perfect party dessert. Anything too demanding makes you limp and lifeless-of-the-party, and you do, after all, have some responsibility for keeping your guests animated and conversational. A dessert made ahead can make all the difference between a happy and a harassed hostess. Take your choice—and earn your just desserts.

Crème Brulée

This simple but elegant dessert sounds French, is actually Creole, but my recipe comes from a Dutch friend who learned it in the Philippines. Vive la Cuisine Internationale!

½ *quart heavy cream*   6 *egg yolks*
1 *cup powdered sugar*   ¼ *to* ½ *cup brown sugar*

Bring the cream slowly to a boil. Meanwhile beat the egg yolks with the powdered sugar vigorously, until light and pale lemony in color. As cream boils, add it slowly, SLOWLY to the egg mixture, a few drops at a time to prevent curdling the eggs. Pour the mixture into a saucepan and heat over a low fire until the sauce is thickened just enough to coat the mixing spoon. Stir all the time. Do not let the sauce begin to boil. Remove from fire when the spoon is lightly coated, not thick. Beat the sauce lightly once or twice before pouring it into a round baking dish (a ceramic soufflé dish is perfect). Chill at least 2 hours until very cold (the longer the better). Just before serving, sprinkle the top lightly with brown sugar and pop it under the broiler for just a moment, until the sugar melts. Serve at once alone, or as a sauce with fresh strawberries and other fresh fruits. A delight! Serves 6.

CHILLED DESSERTS

The following desserts are summertime magic, so easy to fix ahead and chill, and they crown a rich meal with elegant simplicity. (Or is it simplified elegance? No matter, they *are* good.)

Ambrosia

6 *oranges*
1 *whole fresh pineapple*
1 *whole coconut*
Pinch of salt

⅛ *tsp. nutmeg*
¼ *cup powdered sugar*
3 *Tbs. sherry, Cointreau or rum*

Peel and dice the oranges and pineapple. Crack the coconut and remove the meat, shredding it into slivers. Mix 2 cupsful with the oranges and pineapple. Mix a pinch of salt and nutmeg with the powdered sugar and sprinkle over the fruit. Pour the liqueur over the top and chill 3 to 4 hours. Serve in chilled glass sherbet dishes. Very refreshing. Serves 6.

Spanish Sherried Peaches

6 *ripe peaches, peeled*
3 *tsps. sugar (more if needed)*

2 *cups sweet sherry (more if needed)*

Slice the peaches in a bowl. Sprinkle the sugar over the top. Taste and add additional sugar if required. Pour sherry over all. Sherry should almost cover the peaches. Cover, refrigerate at least 3 hours. Serve with cookies, or as is, or as a topping for vanilla ice cream. Yield: 3 to 4 cups.

Cranberry Mousse

Cranberries are older than our country, but only in recent times have cooks discovered how these tart, delicious berries lend themselves to all kinds of interesting dishes. For instance:

1 *package cream cheese (3 ozs.)*
¼ *cup sugar*
1 *tsp. grated lemon rind*
⅛ *tsp. salt*

1½ *cups whole cranberry sauce (homemade is best)*
1 *cup heavy cream, whipped*
1 *cup sour cream (optional)*

Set refrigerator at coldest point. Cream the cream cheese until light and fluffy. Add sugar, lemon rind and salt to it and keep beating it. Add cranberry sauce and mix *very* lightly. Fold mixture into the cream carefully, making sure it is well (but gently) mixed. Place in freezer tray and put tray in freezing unit of refrigerator. Chill until very firm, at least 3 to 4 hours. Serve ice cold with side dish of whipped cream or sour cream. Or nothing at all if you prefer—the dessert is rich enough heaven knows. Serves 6.

Frozen Cottage Cheese with Raspberries

Just as you can't tell a book by its cover, you shouldn't always judge a dessert by its title. This happens to be delicious. So there!

1½ *cups creamed cottage cheese*	1½ *Tbs. lemon juice*
¾ *cup sugar*	1½ *cups sour cream*
⅛ *tsp. cinnamon*	2 *boxes frozen raspberries,*
½ *tsp. grated lemon rind*	*defrosted*

Set refrigerator at its coldest. Push cottage cheese through a fine sieve or food mill. Add sugar, cinnamon, lemon rind and juice and beat (preferably with electric beater) until smooth. Fold in sour cream and turn frequently until cream is mixed well into cheese. Pour mixture into refrigerator tray and place in freezer unit. Chill thoroughly until mixture becomes firm—at least 2 to 3 hours. Cut into squares to serve. Spread drained raspberries over the top of each serving. Yum. Serves 6.

Chilled Fudge Pudding

In these days of large freezing units in refrigerators, ice cream has become the standard everyday easy dessert in many households. In some families, puddings seem quaintly old-fashioned. Yet they are easy to make, are a good way to increase milk consumption for the youngsters, and offer endless variations on a theme. Take this one for instance. We often do.

1 *cup flour, sifted*	2 *Tbs. margarine, melted*
½ *tsp. salt*	1½ *tsps. vanilla*
½ *cup sugar*	1 *cup walnuts, chopped*
2 *Tbs. cocoa*	¾ *cup brown sugar, packed*
2½ *tsps. baking powder*	¼ *cup cocoa*
½ *cup milk*	1¾ *cups hot water*

Sift together the flour, salt, sugar, 2 tablespoons cocoa, and baking powder in a large mixing bowl. Slowly stir in the milk and mix well. Add the melted margarine and vanilla and mix again. Add nuts, stir well, and spread the batter into a greased shallow 9 x 12 baking pan. Set aside while you prepare the topping: Mix together the brown sugar and remaining cocoa. Stir in the hot (but not boiling) water, mix thoroughly and pour over the top of the pudding mixture in the pan. Bake in a 350° F. oven until pudding sets, about 45 minutes. The batter will rise through the topping as it bakes. Allow to cool slightly before placing in refrigerator. Chill at least 3 hours. Serve with whipped cream or vanilla ice cream topping. (This pudding may be served warm of course, but its real richness seems to come across better if allowed to stand awhile.) Serves 6.

Orange Bread Pudding

I believe in economy—up to a point. Whenever I decide to stretch the household budget, the family usually ends up with bread pudding for dessert. But usually it is orange or lemon bread pudding—a far cry from my *first* bread pudding, which I made with leftover French bread from a dinner party the night before. Thinking that the nicely textured bread would be a marvelous pudding base, I made the loveliest looking and most inedible bread pudding ever devised by woman— I had forgotten that my nice crusty French bread had been spread with aromatic garlic butter!

3 *cups French or Italian bread, broken into pieces (can be stale)*	¼ *tsp. salt*
	2 *tsps. grated orange peel*
3 *cups milk*	¼ *tsp. nutmeg*
3 *eggs, separated*	¼ *tsp. orange extract*
¾ *cup sugar*	¼ *cup sugar*

Break the bread into a large mixing bowl. Pour milk over the top and let stand until bread is softened thoroughly. Beat egg yolks slightly and add to bread. Mix together ¾ cup sugar, salt, orange peel, and nutmeg. Add them to the bread mixture and beat at medium speed in an electric beater. Pour mixture into a greased baking dish. Set the dish in a shallow pan, as you do for baked custard, filled ½ inch deep with hot water. Bake in a preheated 325° F. oven for approximately 1 hour, or until the pudding mixture is light brown on top and begins to separate from the sides of the baking dish. Meanwhile, beat the egg whites with a pinch of salt until very stiff, adding the orange extract and sugar little by little. When pudding is brown, remove it from the oven, spread the eggwhite meringue over it and return to oven. Turn oven up to 350° and continue baking until meringue becomes nicely brown and firm. Remove, cool, and refrigerate. Serve cold. Serves 6.

Cottage Cheese-Sour Cream Pudding

Some like it hot, some like it cold, but I make no promises for it nine days old. (Actually it's so good it wouldn't survive uneaten that long.)

2 *cups cottage cheese*	1 *tsp. salt*
2 *Tbs. sour cream*	*Pinch of white pepper*
4 *Tbs. butter, melted*	⅛ *tsp. nutmeg*
4 *eggs, separated*	2 *Tbs. sour cream*
6 *Tbs. heavy cream*	4 *Tbs. toasted almonds*
¼ *tsp. paprika*	

Mix the cottage cheese, 2 tablespoons sour cream and melted butter together. Beat egg yolks and add them, along with the cream, paprika, salt and pepper and nutmeg to the cheese mixture. Beat egg whites until stiff and fold them in. Pour mixture gently into a well-greased glass baking dish or soufflé dish. Place dish in pan with hot water 1 inch deep. Bake in preheated 350° F. oven. When pudding is firm and beginning to brown, remove from oven (approximately 20 to 25 minutes). Cool, then chill until serving time. Just before serving, spread remaining sour cream evenly over the top and dot with slivered toasted almonds. If you prefer serving it warm, heat it for 10 minutes in a 325° oven before topping with sour cream and almonds. Serves 6.

Rice Pudding Elegante

This bears about the same relationship to a homespun rice pudding as chocolate mousse does to packaged chocolate pudding. As an extra bonus, it *has* to be made well ahead of schedule.

1½ *cups raw long-grain rice*	2 *tsps. grated orange rind*
½ *tsp. salt*	⅔ *cup heavy cream, whipped*
3¼ *cups milk*	2 *large oranges, in sections*
½ *cup orange juice*	⅓ *to* ½ *cup Grand Marnier or*
⅓ *cup sugar*	*Cointreau*
½ *tsp. grated lemon rind*	

Wash rice well, then soak in cold water for ½ hour. Drain and place in a heavy saucepan. Add salt and milk and bring to a boil. Simmer slowly for 25 minutes or so, with cover half on pan. When cooked, remove from heat and cover pan fully. Let stand 15 minutes. Then combine juice, sugar, lemon and orange rind, and mix well. Add to the rice and mix well. Fold in the whipped cream and carefully pour mixture into a well-greased ring mold. Chill at least 5 hours, better still overnight. Before serving, peel and section oranges. Place in bowl and pour liqueur over them. Chill at least 1 hour. To serve, unmold dessert and pile orange sections into the center. Very pretty and refreshing. Serves 6.

Leche Flan

This Spanish dessert, ubiquitous in its homeland, makes a delightful prepared-ahead dessert *anywhere*. I like to serve it especially with rich, spicy dinners, for its simple coolness is refreshing after an especially heavy dinner.

1 *cup brown sugar*	½ *pint milk*
3 *Tbs. water*	½ *pint cream*
6 *eggs*	1 *Tb. vanilla*
1 *cup granulated sugar*	

Place the brown sugar in a skillet with the water. Stir and cook over a low flame until the mixture becomes syrupy and thick enough to spread. Spread over the bottom of a deep (3-inch) cake tin and set aside. Beat eggs until thick and lemony. Add granulated sugar little by little, beating as you add. Add milk and cream and continue beating for 5 minutes. Add vanilla and mix well. Pour mixture into the cake tin over the syrup. Cover the tin with foil and place in a larger pan of hot water 1 inch deep. Place pan in a 350° F. oven on the bottom shelf. Bake 15 minutes, then turn oven low to 250° and bake an additional 45 minutes, or until custard firms. Remove from oven when firm. Cool, and then place in refrigerator for at least 3 hours, until nicely chilled through. To serve, invert pan. The carmelized topping not only looks attractive, it adds piquancy to the dish, which is basically a custard, but a very special one. Serves 6.

A Cool Hollander

This Dutch Rusk dessert is one of those sneaky recipes that has every guest saying "What's in it?" and "Guess I'll have to have seconds to try to figure out how it's made." Smile enigmatically and refrain from telling how easy it is:

¾ *package Holland Rusk*	2 *tsps. cornstarch*
1½ *cups granulated sugar*	¼ *tsp. salt*
½ *cup butter, melted*	3 *eggs, separated*
¼ *tsp. cinnamon*	1½ *tsps. vanilla*
2 *cups milk*	

Grind the Dutch Rusk very fine. Reserve ¾ cup to use as topping. Mix the rest with ¾ cups sugar, melted butter and cinnamon. Mix well, until the crumbs hold together. Press the mixture in the bottom and around the sides of a 9 x 9 baking pan. Heat milk in the top of double boiler. Slowly add to it ½ cup sugar, cornstarch and salt, all mixed together. Cook mixture for 5 minutes over boiling water. Stir to prevent sticking. Cool slightly. Add slightly beaten egg yolks and vanilla. Mix and pour over the crumbs in baking pan. Bake in pre-heated 350° F. oven for 18 to 20 minutes, or until light golden brown on top. Meanwhile, beat egg whites until foamy. Slowly beat in 3 tablespoons sugar. Beat until stiff. Remove baking pan from oven. Ladle meringue on top. Sprinkle remaining crumbs on top of meringue and return pan to oven for 5 minutes or so—until top is golden with a tinge of brown. Cool in pan 3 to 4 hours. Cut into squares and serve. (This recipe is actually supposed to serve 10, but you can *count* on people wanting seconds.)

Mother-in-Law Blueberry Special

This party special was my mother-in-law's inspiration, and it has enlivened more than a few of my own dinner parties. Easy to prepare even the night before, it needs no last minute touches, except a few dabs of whipped cream on top.

1 *package cream cheese (8 ozs.)*	2 *eggs, beaten lightly*
½ *cup butter, softened*	1 *tsp. vanilla*
1 *cup sugar*	1 *can blueberry pie filling*
18 *graham crackers, mashed fine*	1 *cup heavy cream, whipped*

Leave cream cheese and butter at room temperature until soft. Mix together butter and ½ cup of sugar. Add finely crushed graham crackers. Mix well and press into the bottom of a rectangular (9 x 12) baking pan. Set aside. Beat together the remaining ½ cup sugar with cream cheese, eggs and vanilla. Use electric mixer if possible. Mixture should be creamy and runny. Pour over the crust. Bake in preheated 350° F. oven for 15 to 20 minutes—or until cream cheese mixture is lightly browned and loosely formed. Remove from oven and cool. Spread blueberry filling on top, then refrigerate for at least 4 to 5 hours. Cut in squares. Serve cold with whipped cream on top. Serves 12.

Lemon-Angel

This easy-to-make dessert is especially festive for parties, and can be made a day ahead and forgotten. It serves quite a crowd, and is particularly nice in summer.

1 *envelope clear gelatin*
½ *cup sugar*
2 *eggs, well beaten*
½ *tsp. salt*
1 *small can frozen lemonade concentrate, thawed (6 ozs.)*

2 *Tbs. fresh lemon juice*
2 *cups evaporated milk, chilled*
4 *cups angel food cake, in bite-sized pieces (pulled apart)*

In a double boiler mix together the gelatin, sugar, eggs and salt. Add the can of thawed lemonade (do not add any water) concentrate. Cook over a medium heat until the mixture is thick enough to coat a spoon. Takes approximately 5 minutes. Add the fresh lemon juice to chilled evaporated milk and beat with an electric mixer until stiff. Remove the custard from the stove, cool slightly, and then add it to the whipped milk, folding it in carefully. Fold the mixture lightly into the angel food cake pieces. Spoon the concoction into an angel food cake mold and chill. When ready to serve, unmold and slice. Very refreshing. Serves 10.

Almond and Mocha Chiffon Pie

This elegant party dessert is so easy to prepare ahead that you should never admit to guests how *really easy* it is. I promise not to tell.

¾ *cup sugar*
1½ *Tbs. cocoa*
½ *cup strong coffee*
¼ *cup cold water*
4 *eggs, separated*
1 *Tb. plain gelatin*
¼ *cup cold water*

¼ *cup sugar*
1 *graham cracker crust (your own favorite recipe)*
½ *cup blanched almonds, slivered and toasted*
1 *Tb. coconut strands, toasted*
1 *cup heavy cream, whipped*

Combine ¾ cup sugar, cocoa, coffee and ¼ cup water in a saucepan.
Mix and bring to a boil. Lower heat. Add slightly beaten egg yolks,
mix well and cook, stirring, for 2 to 3 minutes. Dissolve gelatin in
¼ cup cold water and add it to egg mixture. Remove from heat and
let cool. While mixture cools, beat egg whites until very stiff. Gradu-
ally add ¼ cup sugar and keep beating. Carefully fold whites into
cooled coffee-egg yolk mixture. Pour into pie tin lined with graham
cracker crust. Chill until needed. At serving time, mix almonds and
coconut together and sprinkle over the top. Top with whipped cream.
Dieters, beware! Serves 6 to 8.

Almond-Apricot Pie

This is one of those party desserts almost guaranteed to result in
vigorous demands for the recipe. The magical part is that it is so easy
to prepare as far as a day ahead.

1 *#2 can apricot halves*	1 *pint vanilla ice cream*
1 *pkg. apricot Jell-o*	1 *graham cracker crust*
1 *Tb. lemon juice*	¾ *cup blanced almonds, slivered*
½ *tsp. grated lemon rind*	*and toasted*

Pour 1 cup apricot juice from can into a pan; bring to a boil. Dissolve Jell-o in it and stir well. Add 1 can of drained, crushed apricots
(minus 6) and lemon juice and rind. Mix thoroughly, then add ice
cream. Mix again and pour mixture into a pie plate lined with a
graham cracker crust. Place pie in freezing unit of refrigerator. Chill
pie for 1 hour, then remove and decorate with the 6 drained apricot
halves. Return to freezer and chill until very cold and firm. Remove
from freezer 1 hour before serving time and place pie on refrigerator
shelf. Sprinkle almonds over the top of the pie just before serving. Pie
is so pretty that I usually cut and serve it at the table. Serves 6.

Almond Praline Soufflé

This is a spectacular, easy to make, yet dazzling to the eye and
palate of the beholder, who will be beholden forever after.

¾ *cup sugar*
¼ *tsp. cream of tartar*
1 *cup blanched almonds*
¼ *cup water*
1 *envelope plain gelatin*
¼ *cup* cold *water*

⅓ *cup boiling water*
2 *eggs, separated*
1½ *Tbs. cognac*
½ *cup milk*
1½ *cups heavy cream, whipped*

Combine sugar, cream of tartar, ¾ cup of almonds and ¼ cup water in a deep saucepan. Cook over medium heat until mixture is dark as molasses. Do *not* stir during cooking process. When very dark, remove from heat and pour quickly on a greased cooky sheet or jelly roll pan. Set aside to cool. When completely cool, remove from pan with a spatula and break praline into 5 or 6 pieces. Put a piece at a time into blender, cover and blend at high speed until praline is powdered—8 to 10 seconds. Continue, piece by piece, until all pieces are powdered. Set aside. (This step may be done days ahead and praline powder kept stored in airtight dry container.) Mix gelatin with ¼ cup cold water. When dissolved, add to boiling water. Blend in blender, covered, 45 to 50 seconds at high speed. Add egg yolks, cognac, milk, and blend 10 seconds longer. Add 1¼ cups powdered praline and blend 5 seconds. Refrigerate mixture for 30 minutes, or until slightly chilled but not firm. Beat egg whites stiff but not dry. Carefully fold them into 1¼ cups whipped cream. Add gelatin mixture carefully. Gently mix and pour into a 1-quart soufflé dish. Chill at least 3 hours, overnight if desired. When ready to serve, decorate edges with remaining ¼ cup whipped cream. Toast remaining ¼ cup almonds and lightly place them in whipped cream edging. Serves 6.

Almond-Cranberry "Jelly" Roll

This makes a lovely party dessert, and, fortunately, may be made early on and forgotten until serving time. No last minute fussing in the kitchen.

3 *eggs, separated*
2½ *cups sugar*
½ *cup plus 2 Tbs. orange juice*
½ *tsp. grated lemon rind*
½ *tsp. grated orange rind*
¾ *cup cake flour, sifted*

1 *tsp. baking powder*
¼ *tsp. salt*
½ *cup powdered sugar*
3 *cups whole cranberries*
¾ *cup blanched almonds, slivered*
  thin

Beat egg yolks vigorously, until thick and lemony. Slowly add ½ cup sugar. Beat well. Then stir in 2⅓ tablespoons orange juice, lemon rind and ¼ teaspoon orange rind. Mix well. Beat egg whites stiff until peaky. Beat in ¼ cup sugar. Fold into the juice-egg yolk mixture. Sift flour with baking powder and ⅛ teaspoon salt. Fold into egg mixture and pour into shallow greased jelly roll pan that has been lined with wax paper. Bake in preheated 350° F. oven approximately 15 minutes or until done and golden in color. Sprinkle clean dish towel with powdered sugar. Turn cake on to the towel. Remove wax paper quickly and roll cake up into a roll (like a jelly roll). Let stand until completely cooled. Meanwhile, make filling: combine cranberries, almonds, remaining 1¾ cups sugar (more if necessary) and orange juice, salt and orange rind. Bring mixture to a boil in saucepan, lower heat and cook approximately 6 minutes, or until cranberry skins pop. Cool and chill before spreading. When filling is cool, unroll the cake from towel and spread filling evenly over it. Carefully roll cake up (without help of towel) and sift powdered sugar over it. Cover with wax paper and refrigerate *at least* 3 hours. Serves 6.

Cassata

The first time I served this elegant Sicilian cream cake, one of my guests looked at the candied fruit clustered throughout it and said, "Oh, we're having fruit salad for dessert." He stopped joking after he tasted it, and asked for seconds. Dieters beware! It is very rich.

10-*inch sponge cake*	1 *Tb. assorted chopped candied*
1½ *lbs. ricotta cheese*	*fruits*
1 *cup sugar*	¼ *cup semisweet chocolate bits,*
1 *tsp. vanilla*	*chopped*
1 *Tb. candied orange peel,*	2 *Tbs. cognac,* crème de cacao *or*
chopped	*rum*
	¼ *cup powdered sugar, sifted*

The sponge cake may be made from scratch, but, frankly, such light ones are available packaged at supermarkets, I generally use the store-bought type. Split the cake layers (it usually comes in two layers) in half, making four layers. Set aside. In a mixing bowl combine the ricotta with sugar and vanilla and mix well. You may use a blender, but I prefer a touch of texture left, so I do it by hand. When the mixture is quite creamy, add the candied peel and fruits and chocolate. Mix well. Then add liqueur. I prefer cognac or rum, but you may use any favorite liqueur. Mix again. Taste and add additional sugar if required. (The mixture should be sweet.) Spread the mixture on one layer of cake. Top with the second layer. Cover with ricotta mixture, and continue stacking until the mixture is used up. Chill the cake in refrigerator at least 4 hours, preferably overnight. Before serving, dust the top lightly with sifted powdered sugar.

NOTE: to keep the cake layers from sliding, I have found that a casserole of approximately the same size is useful. I simply build up the layers in the casserole. Then at serving time, turn the cake out of the casserole on to a serving plate and dust with powdered sugar. Serves 8.

Italian Cheese Cake

To be made in the morning (or evening before), long before party time, this dessert is a thing of beauty and a joy to eat.

3 *large packages cream cheese*
    (8 ozs. each)
6 *eggs*
1 *cup sugar*
1½ *tsps. vanilla*
2 *Tbs. flour, sifted*
1 *tsp. lemon juice*

1 *cup sour cream*
½ *cup Cheddar cheese, not too*
    sharp
1 *cup heavy cream, whipped*
12 to 15 *fresh strawberries, kept*
    whole

Leave the cream cheese and eggs at room temperature for about one hour. To begin, separate eggs. Beat cream cheese with egg yolks until smooth, adding yolks one by one. Slowly beat in sugar, vanilla, then flour. Combine lemon juice with sour cream and add to cream cheese mixture. Grate Cheddar and add. Whip egg whites until peaked, then fold them carefully into cheese mixture. Preheat oven to 325° F. Pour mixture into an ungreased 8 or 9-inch cheese cake pan or angel cake pan with spring-released sides and bottom. Bake approximately 1 hour, or until the center is moderately firm. Cool at room temperature at least 2 hours before cutting. For a creamier consistency, chill for at least 2 to 3 hours. When serving, top with whipped cream and dot with whole strawberries. A very rich dessert, this actually serves 12 if the slices are slender.

CAKE IMPROVISATIONS

There comes a time in every girl's life when the pressures of modern living become overwhelming. For instance, you have just discovered that it is the birthday of the guest you have invited for dinner, but you have a midafternoon dental appointment and hardly a spare minute between morning and evening to assemble a main course. Let alone an elaborate birthday cake for your old and dear friend. Time now for a quickie, and old friend Eloise will be delighted.

Hasty Rum Cake

1 *package lemon cake mix*	¾ *cup cooking oil*
1 *package lemon instant pudding*	2 *tsps. rum extract*
3 *eggs*	1 *cup powdered sugar*
1 *cup milk*	⅓ *cup rum*

Combine the cake and pudding mixes, and add eggs, milk, cooking oil and rum extract. Beat with electric beater at medium speed for 10 minutes. Grease an angel food cake pan on bottom and sides. Preheat oven to 350° F. and bake cake approximately 45 minutes. When done, remove cake immediately from pan by running a knife around the edges. While cake is still hot, cover with a light rum frosting, made as follows: mix powdered sugar with ⅓ cup rum until smooth, then swirl over the top and sides of the hot cake. As the frosting dries, it becomes a glaze. Delicious! No-one—least of all Eloise—will ever guess how improvised it was! Slice thin like pound cake. Makes 12 servings.

Chocolate Date-Nut Cake

This superrich dessert is deceptively easy to make and is a delicious punctuation point to a company dinner.

1 *cup dates, chopped and pitted*	1⅓ *cups flour, sifted*
1 *tsp. baking soda*	½ *tsp. salt*
1 *cup boiling water*	3½ *tsps. cocoa*
1 *cup sugar*	½ to ⅔ *cup chopped walnuts*
½ *cup butter or margarine*	½ *cup chocolate bits*
1 *egg, slightly beaten*	½ to 1 *cup heavy cream,*
1 *tsp. vanilla*	*whipped*

Step one: Mix the chopped dates with the baking soda and boiling water. Stir well and set aside until mixture cools.

Step two: Cream sugar and butter. Add egg and beat together. Add vanilla.

Step three: Sift flour with salt and cocoa.

Step four: Add date mixture to the sugar-egg-butter mixture, alternately with the sifted dry ingredients, little by little. When all have been added, fold in the nuts and chocolate chips. Pour mixture into a greased rectangular baking pan (approximately 9 x 13). Bake 30 to 35 minutes in a 350° F. oven that has been preheated. This cake can be set aside in the morning and served for dinner. Cut in squares and top with whipped cream. Serves 8.

Applesauce Raisin-Nut Cake

This very simple cake is light and lovely as a dessert for family or company dinner. In this diet-conscious era, I like to serve it unfrosted, though it is equally good with a Seven-Minute icing. The cake may be made a day ahead and keeps nicely, as it is so very light and airy.

1 *cup raisins*	2 *cups flour, sifted*
½ *cup margarine*	½ *tsp. salt*
1 *cup sugar*	1¼ *tsps. baking soda*
1½ *tsps. cinnamon*	1½ *tsps. baking powder*
¼ *tsp. cloves*	1 *cup (unsweetened) applesauce,*
¾ *tsp. nutmeg*	*strained*
1 *egg or 2 egg yolks, unbeaten*	1 *cup walnuts, chopped*

Cover the raisins with boiling hot water and set aside for 10 minutes to "plump up." Meanwhile, cream the margarine with the sugar until light and fluffy. Add the spices and mix well. Add the unbeaten egg and beat vigorously with an electric mixer. Sift all the remaining dry ingredients together and add to the creamed mixture alternately with the applesauce. Beat until smooth. Drain the raisins and mix them with the nuts. Add to the creamed mixture. Mix well. Pour into a greased oblong 9 x 12 baking pan and bake 45 to 55 minutes in a preheated 350° F. oven. Cool cake on rack, cover and set aside until needed. Serves 8.

Quick and Easy Orange Cake

1 *cup sugar*   1 *cup flour, sifted*
3 *eggs, separated*   2 *tsps. baking powder*
½ *cup orange juice*   1½ *tsps. vanilla*

Cream together the sugar and the egg yolks. Slowly add the orange juice. Sift the flour and baking powder together and add to the creamed mixture. Beat 3 egg whites until very stiff. Fold into the creamed mixture, along with the vanilla. Pour mixture into a greased angel food cake tin. Bake in a preheated medium (350° F.) oven approximately 30 minutes. Very light and fluffy, this cake is delicious served with ice cream or plain. No topping is really needed, but you may make a powdered sugar frosting if you insist. Again, happy birthday, dear Eloise! Serves 10.

Unbaked English Toffee Squares

This can double as a party dessert with whipped cream on top—very special. And incredibly quick and easy to make—the day ahead!

1 *cup rolled vanilla wafers*   3 *eggs, separated*
1 *cup walnuts or pecans,*   1 *tsp. vanilla*
   chopped   1½ *squares bitter chocolate*
¼ *lb. butter*   1 *cup whipped cream (optional)*
1 *cup powdered sugar*

With a rolling pin or mortar and pestle, roll the vanilla wafers into crumbs. Mix with the coarsely chopped nuts. Line the bottom of a greased oblong baking pan with half the wafer-nut crumbs. Cream the butter and sugar together. Slowly add the beaten egg yolks and vanilla. Melt the chocolate and add it too. Beat egg whites stiff and fold them in carefully. Pour into baking pan. Spread remaining nuts carefully over the top. Refrigerate overnight (or at least 8 hours). Cut in squares and serve cold, topped with whipped cream. Serves 6 to 8.

Pan Cookies

Any house with children in it is a cookie-eating house. My three sons seem to consume cookies as fast as jelly beans (Jelly Bean Cookies? Now there's a *bad* idea!). While cookie dough is a cinch to whip up, the entire process of baking tray by tray in stages can be quite time consuming—unless of course one has two ovens and four cookie trays. To simplify the process, I prefer to make pan cookies, which can be baked all at one time, like a cake, and then cut into squares when cooled. Like the fey old lady who collected trunkfuls of pancakes, I have through the years accumulated a number of delicious child-tested pan cookie recipes. *Voilà:*

Lemon Coconut Bars

½ cup butter or margarine
2 Tbs. powdered sugar
1 cup cake flour
1¼ cups brown sugar
2 eggs
2 Tbs. flour
1½ tsps. baking powder
¼ tsp. salt

1¼ tsps. vanilla
1 cup walnuts, chopped coarse
¾ cup moist shredded coconut
1½ cups powdered sugar
2 Tbs. butter or margarine
1½ Tbs. orange juice
1½ Tbs. lemon juice
¼ tsps. ground lemon peel

Grease an 8-inch baking pan, line with waxed paper and grease the paper. Mix together ½ cup butter and 2 tablespoons powdered sugar. Mix well, then add the cake flour. Mix and spread evenly in the baking pan. Bake briefly (10 to 15 minutes) in a 350° F. preheated oven. Remove when lightly browned. Meanwhile, beat the brown sugar and eggs until thick. Sift together the flour, baking powder and salt and add slowly to sugar-egg mixture. Mix well and add vanilla, nuts and coconut. Remove the lightly baked mixture from the oven and spread the coconut mixture evenly over it. Return to oven and continue baking it for 25 to 30 minutes or until set. Remove from oven and cool in pan. When cool, frost with an icing made with 1½ cups powdered sugar, 2 tablespoons butter, orange and lemon juice and lemon peel all thoroughly beaten together. Let stand until frosting thickens, then cut into cookie-sized squares. Makes 24 boy-sized cookies.

Raisin-Nut Bars

2 eggs, beaten
1½ cups sugar
1 cup butter or margarine
2 cups water
1 cup raisins
1 cup liquid from raisins

1 tsp. baking soda
2½ cups flour, sifted
1 tsp. cinnamon
1 tsp. salt
1 tsp. vanilla
¾ cup nuts (walnuts preferred)

Cream together the eggs and sugar and butter. Set aside. Boil 2 cups water and pour over the raisins. Pour off 1 cup of the raisin water and set aside to cool a bit. While still warm, though, add the baking soda to the cup of water. Sift together the flour, cinnamon and salt. Add the dry ingredients alternately with the raisin water to the egg-butter mixture. Mix well. Add vanilla, nuts and the drained raisins. Mix thoroughly. Spread evenly over a greased jelly roll pan or large rimmed cookie sheet. Bake in a moderate (350° F.) oven for approximately 18 to 20 minutes. Cool in pan, then cut into squares. I sometimes cut the squares a bit larger than cookie size and serve them warm with afternoon tea when a friend drops by. You may cover the cooled bars with a thin powdered sugar icing if you wish, but they are very light and delicate "as is." Makes 30 bars.

Caramel Squares

½ *cup butter or margarine*   1½ *tsps. baking powder*
2 *cups brown sugar*   1½ *tsps. vanilla*
2 *eggs*   1 *cup walnuts, chopped coarse*
1 *cup flour*   ½ *cup raisins, chopped (optional)*

Grease a jelly roll pan or large rimmed cookie sheet. Line the pan with waxed paper and grease the pan. Preheat oven to 350° F. Cream the butter and brown sugar until light. Add one egg at a time, beating well with each addition. Sift together the flour and baking powder and add to the creamed mixture. Mix well and add vanilla and nuts (and raisins if desired). Spread evenly over pan and bake approximately 12 minutes, or until the edges harden slightly. Remove from oven and allow to cool 10 minutes in the baking pan. Then cut into small squares, remove from pan and roll in sifted powdered sugar. Makes 20 squares.

Chocolate Peanut Butter Bars

4 *cups oatmeal, uncooked*   1 *tsp. salt*
¾ *cup butter or margarine,*   6 *ozs. chocolate bits, melted*
   melted   ⅓ *cup peanut butter (I like*
1 *cup brown sugar, packed tight*   *chunky for more texture)*
½ *cup white corn syrup*

Grease and lightly flour a 9 x 13 baking pan. Preheat oven to 425° F.

Mix together the uncooked oatmeal with the melted shortening. Add brown sugar and blend well, slowly adding the corn syrup and salt. Mix thoroughly and spread evenly in the pan, patting down well. Bake about 12 to 15 minutes, until golden in color. Meanwhile, have the melted chocolate bits and peanut butter well mixed together and ready to spread over the top of the pan, as soon as it comes from the oven. Set pan aside to cool. Then cut into 20 small bars or squares.

Chocolate Bars with Orange Glaze

1¼ cups flour, sifted	2 eggs, unbeaten
1 tsp. baking soda	½ cup orange juice
⅛ tsp. cinnamon	½ cup milk
½ tsp. salt	¾ cup walnuts, chopped coarse
¾ cup brown sugar, well packed	1½ cups powdered sugar, sifted
½ cup butter or margarine	2 Tbs. butter or margarine
1½ cups dates, chopped	2½ tsps. grated orange rind
½ cup water	2 to 3 Tbs. heavy cream
1 cup semisweet chocolate bits	

Sift together flour, soda, cinnamon, and salt. Place brown sugar and ½ cup butter in large saucepan. Cream together and add dates and water. Cook over low fire, but stir all the while, until dates become soft. Remove from heat and add chocolate bits. Stir and let cool 2 minutes. Beat in the eggs. Alternately add orange juice and milk with dry ingredients. Mix well after each addition. Stir walnuts in last, and spoon mixture into a greased jelly roll pan. Bake in preheated 350° F. oven for 20 to 30 minutes. Let stand on rack to cool. When completely cooled, cover with orange glaze, made as follows: Cream powdered sugar and butter together. Add grated rind. Mix well and add enough cream to make mixture spreadable. Spread evenly over the cooled chocolate mixture. Cut into 24 bars or squares and use as needed.

Oatmeal Fig Squares

1 cup dried figs	½ cup flour, sifted
1 cup water	½ cup brown sugar
1½ tsps. grated lemon rind	½ tsp. salt
1 Tb. lemon juice	1½ cups uncooked rolled oats
½ cup granulated sugar	¼ cup butter
2 Tbs. flour, sifted	¼ cup margarine
½ cup walnuts, chopped coarse	

Combine the chopped figs and water in a saucepan and simmer until soft (approximately 10 minutes). (If figs are too dry and tough to chop, pour boiling water over them to cover and allow to stand for 10 minutes. Drain and cut with kitchen shears.) Add the lemon rind and juice to the simmering figs. Combine the granulated sugar and 2 tablespoons flour and add to the mixture. Add a pinch (literally) of salt, and stir. Keep simmering until mixture is thick but clear, stirring frequently. When clear, add the nuts and remove pan from heat. Set aside to cool. While filling cools, make a crust as follows: Sift together remaining flour, brown sugar and salt. Add rolled oats and mix well. With your fingers, work in the butter and margarine until mixture is soft and crumbly. In an 8-inch square baking pan pat ½ the crumbly crust until it is smooth and even all over. Pour the fig filling smoothly over the crust. Then cover the filling with the remaining crusty crumbs. Bake in a medium (350° F.) oven for 30 minutes or until firm and golden brown on top. Remove pan from oven and allow the cookies to cool in pan. Then cut in 24 small squares. Can be kept in airtight container.

Pecan Bars

½ cup dark brown sugar

½ cup butter

1 cup flour, sifted

½ cup sweetened coconut

2 Tbs. flour

2 eggs

1 cup light brown sugar

1 cup pecans, chopped coarse

Pinch of salt

1 tsp. vanilla

Sifted powdered sugar

Cream the dark brown sugar and butter until smooth. Then add 1 cup flour and mix well. Mixture will be sticky. Pat it into a greased oblong cake or jelly roll pan. Bake in a 350° F. oven for 15 to 20 minutes or until *lightly* browned. Mix coconut with 2 tablespoons flour and set aside. Beat the eggs until frothy and add the light brown sugar. Continue beating until thick. Then add the coconut and chopped pecans, along with a pinch of salt and the vanilla. Mix thoroughly. Spread over the lightly browned mixture in the oven and continue baking for an additional 20 to 25 minutes, until well browned. While hot, sprinkle with sifted powdered sugar and cut into 30 bars or squares. Delicious!

Butterscotch Pecan Bars

1 *cup dark brown sugar*
¾ *cup butter*
1 *egg*
¾ *tsp. vanilla*
2 *cups flour, sifted*
½ *tsp. baking powder*

¾ *tsp. salt*
¼ *cup milk*
1 *cup pecans, chopped coarse*
1 *cup coconut*
1 *6-oz. package butterscotch bits*

Cream the sugar with butter and stir in the egg and vanilla. Sift the flour, baking powder and salt together. Add it to the creamed mixture alternately with the milk. Fold in the pecans, coconut and butterscotch bits. Spread the mixture on a greased cookie sheet—approximately 10 x 14. Bake in a moderate (350° F.) oven for 10 to 15 minutes. Cool, cut into 24 bars. Frost with butter or sugar frosting if you desire, but they are actually rich enough as is.

Chocolate Candy Cookie Bars

1 *cup butter*
1 *cup light brown sugar*
1 *egg yolk*
2 *cups flour, sifted*

1 *tsp. vanilla*
6 *1-oz. chocolate bars (without*
    nuts)
¾ *cup walnuts, chopped fine*

Cream the butter and brown sugar. Add a slightly beaten egg yolk, flour and vanilla. Mix well and spread ¼ inch thick in a long flat baking pan, preferably a jelly roll pan. Bake for 18 to 20 minutes in a 350° F. oven. Meanwhile, unwrap the candy bars and have them ready. Keep nuts separate. When the baked mixture is light golden brown, remove from oven and quickly spread the candy bars on top with a knife, working fast to melt and spread the chocolate evenly. Immediately sprinkle the nuts over the top. Cut while still warm. Yield: 30 bars.

Holiday Fruit Bars

I used to make this recipe at Christmastime, but it became so popular with my family that it is now a year-round holiday favorite. Try it sometime for the Fourth of July.

½ *cup soft butter*   ¼ *tsp. salt*
1 *cup sugar*   1 *cup walnuts, chopped*
1¼ *tsps. vanilla*   1 *cup pitted dates, cut in pieces*
2 *eggs*   ½ to 1 *cup candied citron*
⅔ *cup flour, sifted*   ½ *cup dried apricots, cut in*
1¼ *tsps. baking powder*   *pieces*

Cream the butter with the sugar until light. Add vanilla, then one egg at a time, beating vigorously after each egg is added. Sift dry ingredients together and add to the egg mixture along with the nuts and fruits. Mix well. Grease a square 8 x 8 cake pan and spread the batter in it evenly. Bake in preheated 350° F. oven until firm, approximately 30 to 40 minutes. Cool in pan for several hours or overnight. Then cut into 20 small squares or bars and roll each bar in finely grained granulated sugar. May be stored in airtight cannister for several weeks. (But I doubt if they last that long!)

Chocolate Brazil Nut Bars

¼ *cup soft butter*   2 *Tbs. flour, sifted*
1 *cup flour, sifted*   1½ *cups Brazil nuts, chopped fine*
¼ *tsp. salt*   1½ *tsps. vanilla*
¾ *cup brown sugar, tightly*   ½ *cup flaked coconut*
   packed   ¾ *cup semisweet chocolate bits*
2 *eggs, beaten*   ¼ *cup light corn syrup*
¼ *tsp. salt*   1 *Tb. water*
⅛ *tsp. cinnamon*

Cream butter. Add 1 cup flour and ¼ teaspoon salt, sifted together. Blend well and pat into a 9 x 9 baking pan. Bake in preheated 375° F. oven for 10 minutes—or until layer is cooked but not browned. Beat the sugar into the eggs. Add remaining salt, cinnamon, flour, 1 cup nuts, vanilla and coconut. Mix well. Remove pan from oven and spread this mixture over it evenly. Return to oven for 12 minutes—or until done. Cool in pan. Meanwhile, back at the stove, melt the chocolate bits in the top of a double boiler. Add corn syrup and water. Stir until smooth and thickening. Spread over baking pan. Sprinkle with remaining ½ cup nuts. Cool until chocolate is firm. Cut into 18 oblong bars. May be stored until needed.

Orange Bars

No, this is not a stand where you get oranges, but another delicious pan cookie.

1 *large navel orange*	2 *cups flour, sifted*
¾ *cup seeded raisins*	¼ *tsp. salt*
½ *cup butter, softened*	½ *tsp. grated orange rind*
1 *cup granulated sugar*	¾ *tsp. baking powder*
1 *egg, slightly beaten*	1½ *cups powdered sugar*

Cut orange in half and squeeze 2 tablespoons juice into a small bowl. Set aside. Put remaining orange, with its rind, and raisins through food chopper. Set aside. Cream together the butter and granulated sugar. Add egg and beat vigorously until light. Combine and sift together flour, salt, prepared orange rind, and baking powder. Add to egg-butter mixture and mix well. Add chopped orange mixture. Mix well. Pour into a greased oblong 9 x 12-inch baking pan. Bake in preheated hot (425° F.) oven for 20–25 minutes. Combine reserved orange juice with powdered sugar. Beat until smooth. Spread over baking pan right after you remove it from the oven. Cool in pan. When completely cool, cut into oblong bars, 1 x 3 inches.

Apricot-Pecan Sticks

These are really special—great as a party accompaniment to ice cream.

¾ *cup soft butter*	½ *cup apricot jam (more if*
2 *cups sugar*	*needed)*
2 *eggs plus 2 egg whites*	*Dash of salt*
3 *heaping cups flour, sifted*	1 *cup pecan halves*
1½ *tsps. vanilla*	

Cream the butter and combine with half the sugar and the 2 whole eggs. Beat with electric beater until light. Add all the flour except 1 tablespoon. Beat again. Add vanilla and mix well. Place the dough on a greased cookie sheet and cover with wax paper. Roll with rolling pin quite thin—to ¼ inch thick. Roll it so that it covers cookie sheet. When rolled flat, remove wax paper. Cover dough with the apricot jam spread thin. Preheat oven to 375° F. and bake dough for a brief 5 minutes. Meanwhile, beat egg whites with salt until very stiff. Combine remaining 1 cup sugar and 1 tablespoon flour and slowly add to egg whites. Fold in pecan halves. With a spatula, spread mixture over the layer of half-baked dough. Return to oven to bake an additional 15 minutes. Cool. Cut into 1 x 3-inch sticks, with a pecan in each—if possible. Will keep in airtight container. Yield: 24 sticks.

Hungarian Pecan Squares

One more for the pan cookie collection—and this is one of the richest and best.

2¼ cups flour, sifted	1½ Tbs. brandy
½ cup sugar	½ cup granulated sugar
¼ tsp. salt	¾ cup light brown sugar
1 cup butter (no substitutes, please!)	2 tsps. cinnamon
	3½ cups pecans, chopped fine
2 eggs, separated, plus 2 whites	¼ cup powdered sugar, sifted

Sift together flour, ½ cup granulated sugar and salt. Work in the butter evenly. Add the unbeaten egg yolks and brandy. Pat carefully into an ungreased oblong baking pan or jelly roll pan. Bake in pre-heated medium (350° F.) oven for 15 minutes. While this layer is baking, place in a heavy saucepan the remaining white sugar, brown sugar, cinnamon, nuts, and all 4 unbeaten egg whites. Mix well and cook over a low heat until the sugars dissolve. Stir frequently. Raise heat to medium and cook until mixture does not adhere to sides of pan. Remove baking pan from heat. Spread saucepan mixture evenly over it. Return to oven and bake an additional 15 minutes. Cool for 5 minutes and sift powdered sugar over the pan. Cut into 2-inch squares. Store in airtight container until needed. Yield: 20–24 squares.

Apricot Nut Bars

½ cup soft butter	2 Tbs. cornstarch
½ cup light brown sugar	2½ tsps. grated lemon rind
1 cup flour	2 tsps. grated orange rind
1½ cups dried apricots	⅛ tsp. cinnamon
⅓ cup light brown sugar	1¼ cups walnuts, chopped
¼ tsp. salt	2 eggs, well beaten
⅛ cup lemon juice	1 small can flaky coconut
⅛ cup orange juice	

Cream butter until light, add ½ cup brown sugar and cream until fluffy. (Use electric mixer if possible.) Blend in flour at low speed until smooth. Spread dough in bottom of an oblong 9 x 12-inch baking pan. Bake in preheated 350° F. oven until golden—about 10 minutes. Remove and let cool in pan for 20 minutes or so.

To make topping: barely cover apricots with water in saucepan and cook gently for 20 minutes, or until tender. Drain—but keep 2 tablespoons liquid in reserve. Let apricots cool a few minutes. Then cut into quarters. Return to saucepan, and add liquid, remaining brown sugar, salt, juices, cornstarch, fruit rinds and cinnamon. Bring to fast boil. Lower heat, let simmer 3 or 4 minutes, until liquid thickens. Add nuts and mix well. Spread mixture over cooled dough. Mix eggs together until light and frothy. Add coconut, mix well, and spread evenly on top of apricot-nut mixture. Return pan to oven and bake 20–25 minutes, until topping becomes firm. Remove from oven, cool, then cut into 24 oblong bars while still warm. Store in airtight container until needed.

Walnut Date Bars

1 8-oz. package dates, pitted	¾ tsp. nutmeg
1 cup walnuts, chopped coarse	¼ cup flour, sifted
2 eggs, beaten	1 Tb. lemon juice
1½ cups powdered sugar, sifted	½ tsp. grated lemon rind
½ tsp. salt	1 Tb. salad oil

Put the dates through a food chopper, or cut into very fine pieces with kitchen shears. Mix with nuts. Add beaten eggs, 1 cup powdered sugar, salt and nutmeg. Mix well. Add flour, lemon juice, lemon rind and oil. Mix again. Spread mixture into a greased 8 or 9-inch square baking pan. Bake approximately 25 minutes in a preheated 350° F. oven. Cool for 15 minutes and cut into oblong bars. Roll in remaining ½ cup of sifted powdered sugar and store in airtight container until needed. Makes approximately 36 bars.

Raspberry Layers

1¼ cups flour, sifted	⅔ cup thick raspberry jam
1½ tsps. baking powder	2 eggs
½ tsp. salt	1½ cups sugar
1 tsp. sugar	6 Tbs. margarine, melted
½ cup soft butter	1 Tb. vanilla
1 egg yolk	2⅓ cups flaked coconut
1½ Tbs. cognac	

Sift together the dry ingredients: flour, baking powder, salt and 1 teaspoon sugar. Blend in soft butter until well mixed. Add unbeaten egg yolk and cognac and mix well. Pat mixture into a greased oblong pan. (A jelly roll pan is ideal.) Spread jam over the top. Beat 2 eggs until thick and lemony. Add remaining sugar, melted margarine and vanilla. Keep beating with vigor. Add coconut and mix well. Spread evenly over the jam. Bake in a preheated 350° F. oven for 25–30 minutes. Cool in pan. Cut in 1-inch squares and store in airtight container until needed. Makes approximately 36 squares.

CHAPTER XI

Improvisations

The Emergency Shelf and How To Cope

While it isn't exactly a parallel to Eliot's Five Foot Book Shelf, a kitchen emergency shelf can be very helpful in times of domestic crisis (spelled Uninvited Guests, Stay-lates, Teen-age Drop-ins). Certain handy "standards" can help you fill out, expand or embellish at the last minute that meal-that-is-a'waiting.

In essence, an emergency shelf is merely a cupboard well-stocked with versatile staples. You can keep a year's supply of anchovy paste and canned pumpkin pulp to little avail. But cans of foods that adapt well to many dishes and combinations are a necessary complement to all kitchens (and often mean an extra compliment for the cook as well).

The following are the basis of a good emergency shelf, but you will want to add your own special handy dandys that mix and blend with other foods and assist you in the Waiting Game. I call the following canned foods my catalysts—combined with other foods they trigger some fascinating results.

Emergency Shelf (All canned or packaged foods)

Chick peas
Kidney beans
Pork and beans
Tomatoes
Pineapple rings
Crab meat
Tomato juice
Evaporated milk
Sweetened condensed milk
Tomato sauce
Tomato purée
Tuna fish
Clam juice
Creamed corn
Mushroom soup
Consommé
Tomato soup
Split pea soup
Cream of chicken soup
Chicken gravy

Beef gravy
Chicken broth
Beef broth
Canned ham
Assorted cake mixes (especially
        yellow and sponge cake)
Assorted flavors gelatin
Canned (or packaged) croutons
Assorted dried soups (most
        important being onion)
Boxed dried skim milk
Worcestershire sauce
Tabasco sauce
Maggi
Soy sauce
Lasagne, noodles, spaghetti,
        macaroni and other pastas
Bouillon cubes
Clear gelatin

Claret Consommé

This improvisation is so simple and yet so impressive I frequently serve it to company as a first course on a winter menu. I pass around a tray with Japanese cups (handleless) filled with the clear soup. Guests warm their hands on the cups as they sip. It's amazing how something so simple can seem so festive.

2 10½-oz. cans undiluted
    consommé
1 soup can claret wine
1 can water

Salt to taste (careful now!)
24 whole cloves
6 lemon slices, sliced thin

Combine the consommé, claret and water in a saucepan. Add salt if needed. Simmer over low heat 5–6 minutes. *Do not boil.* Stick 4 cloves in each lemon slice and place slice in each soup cup or bowl. Pour hot soup in bowls and serve immediately. (If you don't want to bother with the cloves-and-lemon, just put a sprig of fresh parsley in each cup. It's extraordinary, though, how impressed people are by the clove-stuck-lemon-slice trick. It looks like more work than it really is.) Serves 6.

Mystery Soup

This is so simple to fix ahead of time and always baffles guests. It makes a cool guessing game served as a starter during a summer heat wave.

2 10½-oz. cans undiluted beef consommé	2 leeks, trimmed and sliced thin
	1 bay leaf
2 10½-oz. cans undiluted cream of asparagus soup	3 cups milk
	2 Tbs. chopped fresh watercress

Place the 2 types of soup in large saucepan. Add the leeks, bay leaf and milk and bring mixture to a boil. Lower the heat and simmer for 6–8 minutes. Remove and cool. Refrigerate for 5–6 hours until well chilled. Serve cold with chopped watercress sprinkled over the top. Serves 6 to 8.

Corn and Turkey Chowder

2 cans turkey noodle soup	2 soup cans milk
1 can cream-style corn (8 ozs.)	1 Tb. minced fresh green pepper
½ tsp. salt	¼ tsp. black pepper
¼ tsp. celery salt	1 Tb. instant onion

Combine all ingredients in large saucepan. Mix well and heat over medium fire. Serve hot. Sprinkle paprika over the top. Serves 6.

Chicken-Clam Chowder, Instant Style

2 10½-oz. cans cream of chicken soup	¼ tsp. dried tarragon
	1 Tb. minced green pepper
2 10½-oz. cans consommé	1 large can clams, minced
2 Tbs. instant onion	6 sprigs fresh parsley

In a saucepan combine both soups, onion, tarragon and green pepper. Add liquid drained from clams. Mix well and heat over medium fire. Simmer gently 15 minutes. Add clams and cook an additional 5 minutes. Serve hot with parsley sprigs adorning the top. Serves 6.

Quick Spice Soup

1 *can pea soup*	1 *can tomato soup*
2 *cups light cream*	½ *tsp. dry mustard*
1 *tsp. curry powder*	½ *tsp. Worcestershire sauce*
¼ *tsp. dried chili peppers*	*Dash of Tabasco sauce*
½ *tsp. salt*	⅛ *tsp. cumin*

Place all ingredients together in blender. Blend at high speed for 2 minutes. Place in saucepan and simmer gently for 10 minutes or until hot. Serve immediately. Serves 6.

Immediate Borscht

A quick inspiration from the Emergency Shelf—tasty, too.

1 *lb. can Harvard beets*	¾ *cup sour cream*
2 *10½-oz. cans onion soup*	6 *sprigs fresh parsley*
2 *Tbs. lemon juice*	

Chop beets coarsely and place in saucepan with liquid. Add onion soup and mix well. Heat over medium fire. Add lemon juice to taste. Serve piping hot, with a glob of sour cream on top of each bowl. And a sprig of parsley on top of *that*. Serves 6.

Quick Curried Split Pea Soup

Another trip to the Emergency Shelf—for a fast and fancy soup.

2 *10½-oz. cans split pea soup*	½ *tsp. minced onion*
2 *soup cans milk*	2 *medium carrots, grated*
1 *tsp. curry powder, hot*	¾ *cup light cream, whipped*

Put soup into saucepan. Add milk (using empty soup can as a measure) and blend well. Heat over medium heat. Add curry and onion and mix thoroughly. When hot, serve in bowls with grated carrot on top and a big glob of whipped cream. Serves 6.

Herbed Cream of Chicken Soup

2 10½-oz. cans of cream of
  chicken soup
1½ cups chicken broth
¾ cup heavy cream

2 tsps. fresh tarragon
Salt to taste
½ tsp. chopped parsley

Place in a blender all above ingredients. Blend at high speed for 3 minutes or until smooth. Heat in saucepan over medium heat. Serve hot with chopped parsley on top of each bowl. Serves 6.

IMPROVISATIONS FOR CANNED OR FROZEN VEGETABLES

To dress up very fast a canned, drained heated vegetable, simply pour over it as you serve it, one of the following impromptu sauces:

Curried Mayonnaise

1½ cups mayonnaise, allowed to
  stand at room temperature
  ½ hour before serving

1 Tb. curry powder
¼ tsp. ground cumin

Mix thoroughly (or put in blender for 20 seconds) and toss lightly with hot vegetables (especially good with green beans, broccoli or Brussels sprouts). Yields: approximately 2 cups.

Yogurt French Dressing

1½ cups prepared thick French
  dressing, homogenized type
1½ cups plain yogurt
2 tsps. onion salt

½ tsp. black pepper, freshly
  ground
1 tsp. celery salt

Combine all ingredients and mix thoroughly. Put in blender 45 seconds until smooth and easily pourable. Pour over piping hot green beans or peas or other green vegetables. Yield: 2 cups.

Hasty Cheese Topping

1½ cups prepared French
    dressing
½ tsp. garlic salt

½ tsp. freshly ground black
    pepper
½ cup grated Parmesan cheese
¼ tsp. onion salt

Combine all ingredients. Pour over hot buttered spinach as you carry it to table. Good also for asparagus or cauliflower. Yield: 2½ cups.

Western Baked Beans

This quick trip West is even better (methinks) than the usual jazzing up you can do with a can of baked beans, onions, Worcestershire sauce and brown sugar. And it's made for improvising as you go along.

2 Tbs. butter or margarine
¾ lbs. ground beef
1 package onion soup mix
1 can kidney beans (1 lb.),
    drained
2 cans pork and beans (1 lb. each)

¾ cup catsup
2 Tbs. prepared mustard
½ tsp. black pepper
Dash of cayenne pepper
2 tsps. tarragon vinegar
¼ cup red wine

Melt shortening in large, heavy skillet. Brown beef lightly. Add soup, both types beans, and catsup. Stir until well mixed. Combine remaining ingredients and add to skillet. Mix well. Pour mixture into a deep crock or earthen casserole. Bake approximately 30 minutes until well heated and flavors are blended. Serves 6.

Slavic Baked Beans

This different version of baked beans is a quick one to prepare (and it's consumed even faster).

2 cans baked beans in tomato
    sauce (1 lb. each)
¾ cup sour cream
1 Tb. chopped parsley
½ tsp. salt

½ tsp. Maggi
1 tsp. garlic salt
½ tsp. black pepper
1 small onion, sliced

Pour beans into large mixing bowl. Add sour cream and mix well. Combine parsley and all spices, then add to bean mixture. Stir in onions until well mixed. Pour mixture into deep casserole. Bake uncovered in hot (400° F.) oven for 15–20 minutes, or until mixture bubbles. Serve with side dish of sour cream. Serves 6.

Quick Fruit Compote

This makes a marvelously refreshing dessert—and is so improvised it's almost embarrassing.

3 *oranges, peeled and sectioned*
  into boats
1 *can grapefruit with juice*
2 *large apples, peeled and diced*

⅛ *tsp. lemon juice*
½ *cup sour cream*
¼ *cup honey*
Sprigs of fresh mint

Combine all the fruits. Sprinkle lemon juice over top. Let stand 15 minutes at least. At serving time, place fruit in individual dishes. Put a big gob of sour cream on top and trickle honey over the sour cream. Decorate with sprig of fresh mint. Serves 6.

Quickie Fruit #Two

Also good, and particularly refreshing after a heavy Italian or Hungarian dinner.

1 *box frozen sliced peaches,*
  defrosted
1 *box frozen grapefruit, de-*
  frosted and drained
1 *box frozen mixed fruits,*
  defrosted

1 *box frozen strawberries,*
  defrosted
2½ *Tbs. lemon juice*
2 *Tbs. Cointreau or Kirsch*
¼ *cup pecans, chopped fine*
Sprigs of fresh mint

Put all fruits into large mixing bowl. Mix gently to keep from mashing fruit. Sprinkle lemon juice and liqueur over top. Let stand in refrigerator 30 minutes at least. Serve in individual dishes. Sprinkle chopped nuts over the top and trim with a sprig of fresh mint. Serves 6 to 8.

CHAPTER XII

A Few Words About Breakfast

It is widely known that many people of this world go to bed hungry.
It is less widely known that many Americans go to *work* hungry and
unfed. Staggering out of bed in predawn darkness, they bounce twice,
and like all automatons numbly fumble their way to their car, train or
bus. Zombie-like, they reach their office and hope that the coffee wagon
or loyal secretary will put a cup of steaming coffee into their trem-
bling, undernourished hands.

As the daughter of a German father who believed strongly in the
fuel of a hearty breakfast, I won't take time out to scold such
goings-on. They have been going on too long. And therein lies the
problem.

Breakfast is a state of mind. In most of Europe it means coffee and
a hard roll. In Asia it means rice and fish. And in the United States,
when it is eaten at all, it follows a rigid format: juice, cereal and

coffee, or juice, eggs and coffee. Sunday breakfasts vary the format only slightly: juice, omelet, coffee cake and coffee, or fruit, pancakes or waffles and coffee.

Lunch and dinner are such wonderfully flexible, versatile meals. Why do we adhere to such a taut list of foods for our breakfasts (when we do eat them)? Dietitians consider breakfast the most important meal of the day, and even *they* choose breakfast menus with blinders on. Eggs, cereal, toast, here we go again!

So why the carping? Do I have something better to suggest? You bet I do, though brace yourself for a revolutionary thought. My husband actually evolved it several years ago when he was suffering from the Commuter Doldrums, which are usually at their worst in the middle of a cold, dark, dismal January.

I had overslept and stumbled into the predawn, gloomy world of the Midwinter Commuter. There in the kitchen was my husband, calmly sipping his own breakfast. "What are you drinking?" I asked with a certain amount of wifely trepidation.

"Chicken noodle soup," he replied nonchalantly and continued sipping. Doesn't everyone? was evident in his tone of voice. Then he added, "I'm tired of hot cereal and thought this would be the very thing for that cold walk to the station." Hmmm. Well, why not?

Next morning I was late again, and there he was calmly eating a tuna fish salad sandwich on toast. "For breakfast?" I stared in disbelief.

"Why not?" he countered. "It's fuel. And a little protein in the morning is a good idea. Besides, I'm beginning to find eggs a bore."

Why not indeed? I found myself thinking again, and this led to a not-too-agonizing reappraisal of what breakfast is all about.

Since then, overnight visitors at our house have been startled to find anything from hot borscht to leftover lasagne on the breakfast table. One of our sons is particularly addicted to a toasted cheese sandwich (and don't think that hasn't caused a raised eyebrow or two at school when a teacher asked, "And what did you have for breakfast today, kiddies?").

Not everyone is up to (or down to) baked beans for breakfast, but I do think breakfast deserves some rethinking to make it a more interesting, nourishing meal than it traditionally has been.

And now you know why this is such a short chapter—because in MY book breakfast can be A N Y T H I N G. Hold on, Conservatives, there are a few suggestions that have nothing to do with tuna fish and soup, but are nourishing anyhow. Would you believe Weekday Waffles?

WAFFLES FOR THE WEEK

It is a custom in our house to have a large Sunday brunch of waffles, bacon or sausages, with syrup, sour cream and brown sugar accompaniment. I always make a quadruple batch, bake them all, and freeze the leftovers for quick weekday breakfasts. During the week it is a cinch to pop a frozen waffle into the toaster for a quick before-school filling breakfast. In making up the batch, I usually plan a variety, adding nuts to some of the batter, raisins to another portion, grated Cheddar cheese to another. In case we happen to have fresh blueberries, they make still another variety. But the following is my basic recipe, very light and crisp.

3 *eggs, separated*	1½ *cups flour, sifted*
¾ *cup milk*	½ *tsp. salt*
¼ *cup light cream*	1 *tsp. sugar*
6 *Tbs. butter, melted*	3 *tsps. baking powder*

Beat egg yolks until lemony and foamy, then add milk and cream slowly. Stir in melted butter. In a separate bowl, sift together flour, salt, sugar and baking powder. Mix well and add slowly to the egg batter. Stir lightly. Beat egg whites until stiff peaks are formed. Fold gently into batter. Batter may be made ahead of use, but if made hours ahead it may thicken. If so, add a little milk to make it thin enough to pour into the waffle iron. Makes 6 waffles.

To serve: for an adult brunch, I sometimes add 1 teaspoon rum to the syrup after it is heated. Instead of syrup, I sometimes spread sour cream on the buttered waffles, then sprinkle lightly with brown sugar.

Ginger-Flavored Waffles

Waffles being somewhat bland adapt beautifully to added flavors and ingredients. The following is sweet but delicious. For breakfast, try it with a topping of butter and sour cream. It also doubles as a dessert, with a scoop of vanilla ice cream or fresh fruit and whipped cream on top.

Basic waffle batter (above)	¼ *cup candied ginger, chopped*
½ *cup molasses*	*very fine*
1 *tsp. ground ginger*	

Prepare waffles as you regularly do, but substitute the molasses for ½ cup of the liquid specified in basic recipe. When well mixed, stir in ground ginger and chopped ginger bits. Bake in heated waffle iron as usual. May be frozen. Makes 6.

Butterscotch Walnut Waffles

This sweetie makes a pleasant adult dessert, served with sour cream, whipped cream or even ice cream as topping. Children like it for breakfast, though I find it a bit sweet for that early hour. No matter when you serve it, remember it, too, can be prepared ahead and toasted at serving time.

1½ cups sifted flour	2 large eggs, separated
¼ tsp. salt	1¼ cups milk
2½ tsps. baking powder	¼ cup melted butter or salad oil
2¼ Tbs. brown sugar	¾ cup walnuts, chopped coarse

Sift the flour, salt and baking powder together in large mixing bowl. Add brown sugar. Beat together egg yolks and milk. Stir in butter or oil. Combine with flour mixture in large bowl, beating only until smooth. Do not *over*beat. Fold in nuts. Beat egg whites until stiff, and carefully fold into mixture. Makes 6 waffles.

Oatmeal Pancakes

The batter for these unusual pancakes may be whipped up the night before, with only the beaten egg whites to be added the following morning. If batter has thickened overnight, add a little milk (carefully!) to thin it. Easy does it!

½ cup flour, sifted	3 cups milk
⅛ tsp. cinnamon	3 cups quick-cooking rolled oats
3 Tbs. sugar	3 eggs, separated
3¼ tsps. baking powder	¾ cup cooking oil
1½ tsps. salt	

Sift together the flour, cinnamon, sugar, salt and baking powder. Set aside. Heat, but do not boil, milk and pour it over uncooked oats. Allow to cool. When quite cool, beat egg yolks and add to oat-milk mixture. Stir gently. Add cooking oil alternately with dry ingredients to the oat mixture. Mix gently but well. When ready to use, beat egg whites until fairly stiff and fold into batter. Heat greased skillet or griddle and drop spoonfuls of batter on griddle. Turn when they bubble, as with regular pancakes. Serve them piping hot with syrup or sour cream or whatever you wish. Serves 6.

Rice Pancakes

This is a tasty way to add the daily grain supply to growing children's diets.

1 *large egg, beaten light*	1 *Tb. baking powder*
¾ *cup milk*	2½ *Tbs. sugar*
3 *Tbs. butter, melted*	1 *cup cooked rice*
1½ *cups flour, sifted*	2 *tsps. grated lemon rind*
½ *tsp. salt*	

Let milk and egg stand at room temperature ½ hour before using. Add milk to egg and beat lightly. Then add butter. Sift dry ingredients together (flour, salt, baking powder and sugar) and add to batter, mixing well. Add rice and lemon rind and stir vigorously but do not overbeat. Batter should be thin enough to pour, but not runny. Add a little milk, just enough to thin batter if necessary. Serves 6 (makes 12 large pancakes).

Baked Pancakes

Like the advertisements that proclaim, "I found my job through *The New York Times,*" I should give credit too. The inspiration for this recipe came from the *Times,* but it has been amended again and again. The basic beauty of it, though, is that it offers a soufflé-like pancake baked in the oven. No longer do you have to stand and wait and flip, and stand and wait and flip. With this recipe, even the cook gets to enjoy the pancakes. The recipe is so fast and easy to assemble, I do it quickly first thing, even on frantic weekdays. Then pop it into the oven, and spend the 15 minutes it takes to bake setting table, making school lunches or finding clean shirts for various family members. Then miraculously the pancake is ready when everyone else is!

4 *eggs, beaten lightly* ⅛ *tsp. nutmeg*
1 *cup milk* ½ *cup butter*
1 *cup flour* ¼ *cup powdered sugar*
½ *tsp. grated lemon rind* ¼ *cup lemon juice*

Mix together eggs and milk. Add flour, lemon peel and nutmeg and beat briskly but not long. Batter should be slightly lumpy. Melt half the butter in a large skillet with a heatproof handle. When sizzling hot, pour half the batter in the skillet. Remove skillet immediately to a preheated 425° F. oven. Bake approximately 15 minutes until pancake rises and lightly browns on top. Remove and sprinkle half the powdered sugar over top (this absorbs some of the butter). Return to oven for 3–4 minutes. Remove and sprinkle half the lemon juice over the top. Serve and cut into pielike wedges. Good with syrup or jelly over it. Return the still-hot skillet to the stove (watch out for that hot handle), heat remaining butter over high flame, pour in remaining batter, place in oven, and repeat procedures. Serves 6.

Mandarin Tangarin' Delight

This jellied fruit dish is refreshing at breakfast, but also makes a cooling dessert after a too-rich dinner. If you serve it as dessert, top it with a dab of whipped cream.

4 *cups canned tangerine juice,* ¼ *tsp. grated orange rind*
    chilled 2 *small cans mandarin oranges*
2 *packages orange gelatin* *(11 ozs. each), drained*

Heat 2 cups tangerine juice (do not let it reach a boil) until almost boiling. Put gelatin and orange rind in large bowl. Pour hot juice over it and stir until dissolved. Add remaining chilled juice and stir well. Refrigerate until gelatin is thickish, but not solid. Stir in mandarin oranges and return bowl to refrigerator. Chill until solid. Serves 6.

Fruit with Fresh Mint

Here's a way to revive lagging breakfast appetites. (It makes a pleasing, noncaloric dessert, too.) Make it the night before, just pull it out of the refrigerator in the morning and serve.

2 *oranges, peeled and sectioned*   3 *Tbs. chopped fresh mint*
2 *cups canned pineapple cubes*   ½ *tsp. lemon juice*
1 *cup canned apricot halves*   1 *Tb. sugar (more to taste)*

Combine fruits and mix well. Add crushed chopped fresh mint. Sprinkle lemon juice and sugar over top (taste as you go, for canned fruit will already have sweetening added). Refrigerate overnight. (Fresh grapefruit, canned plums, fresh melon or apples, bananas, almost any fruit may be used. But if you use apples or bananas, add them in the morning as they discolor if kept too long after being peeled.) Serves 6.

Pecan and Sour Cream Coffee Cake

Make this the night before. It will be light and delicate at the breakfast table. (Or reheat it in the morning if you prefer warm coffee cake.)

1 *cup butter*   1 *cup sour cream*
2 *cups sugar*   ½ *tsp. vanilla*
2 *eggs*   1 *cup pecans, chopped*
2 *cups flour, sifted*   1½ *Tbs. sugar*
¼ *tsp. salt*   1 *tsp. cinnamon*
1¼ *tsps. baking powder*   ⅛ *tsp. nutmeg*

Cream butter until fluffy, then add 2 cups sugar. Continue creaming. Beat in eggs, one by one. Beat very well. Sift together flour, salt, and baking powder. Alternately fold in the dry mixture to the butter mix, alternating with the sour cream and vanilla. Fold carefully until everything is well but gently mixed. Mix pecans with sugar, cinnamon and nutmeg, until nuts are well covered. Pour ⅓ of batter into a well-greased and floured tube pan. Spoon ½ nut mixture over batter. Spread remaining batter evenly. Sprinkle remaining nuts evenly over the top. Bake in preheated 350° F. oven for approximately 50 minutes or until toothpick comes out clean. Cool on rack immediately. When completely cooled, wrap cake in foil well and keep until needed. (Or serve immediately if you can't resist the fragrance.) Serves 6.

Homemade Herbed Sausages

This is a somewhat different breakfast treat—homemade pork sausages. Shades of frontier days!

2 *lbs. ground pork* *
⅛ *lb. pork fat, ground*
2½ *Tbs. chopped fresh parsley*
1½ *tsps. salt*
3 *Tbs. leaf sage, crushed*
½ *tsp. dried oregano*

¾ *tsp. dried thyme*
1 *tsp. black pepper, freshly*
  ground
½ *tsp. savory*
½ *tsp. dry mustard*

Combine the pork with the pork fat until well mixed. Mix together all seasonings. Add to pork and mix thoroughly. Refrigerate 2 or 3 hours. Then shape into 6 large or 12 small patties and chill overnight. In the morning, place in a cold heavy skillet. Cook over a low fire, turning often, until well browned and thoroughly cooked. Serve as accompaniment to Roman Eggs. Serves 6.

Roman Eggs

The title of this dish probably bears as much relation to Italy as hamburgers do to Hamburg, but never mind, the eggs are delicious no matter what you call them. An egg by any other name still tastes wonderful with bacon, ham, or Homemade Herbed Sausages—especially in the early A.M.

6 *eggs*
Salt to taste
½ *tsp. black pepper*

2 *tsps. butter*
1 *Tb. Worcestershire sauce*
6 *Tbs. milk*

Grease a muffin tin with 6 pockets. Break an egg into each pocket. Salt and pepper each egg. Put a dab of butter on top each egg. Add Worcestershire sauce and a tablespoon of milk. Bake in preheated 350° F. oven for 10–15 minutes until done. Use a knife to slip each egg out of its pocket. Serve on toasted and buttered cheese bread. It is possible to assemble this dish in the muffin pan the night before. Cover securely and refrigerate overnight. Uncover and bake quickly. Serves 6.

---

* Cajole your butcher into grinding it for you if possible.

Baked Ham and Eggs

Prepare this a night ahead, and simply get up a bit earlier to put it into the oven. Once in, you can set the timer and continue morning-as-usual chores until everyone is ready for breakfast. Then presto! a soufflé-like delight to surprise everyone, including perhaps yourself!

7 *slices stale bread*	8 *eggs, beaten slightly*
1 *cup cooked diced ham*	½ *tsp. salt*
1½ *Tbs. chopped chives*	½ *tsp. black pepper*
½ *tsp. dill weed*	3 *cups milk*

Trim the crusts off the bread slices. Put a layer of ham in the bottom of a greased casserole. Add a layer of the bread slices, broken into large pieces. Put another layer of ham, remaining bread, then sprinkle chives and dill weed over the top. Mix eggs, salt and pepper with the milk and pour over the casserole. Cover and refrigerate until needed (1 hour at least, overnight if you like). Bake in preheated 325° F. oven for 30–40 minutes. Serves 6.

Turkish Garlic-Poached Eggs

A robust Turkish friend insists that this is all he ever eats for break-fast and that he has never been ill in his life. There is no question that garlic has medicinal value, but I leave it to your own discretion whether you really want to eat it for breakfast or not. If not, would you believe lunch?

12 *eggs*	12 *pieces toast, halved*
6 *cloves garlic, minced*	1 *tsp. hot paprika*
2 *cups plain yogurt*	2 *Tbs. butter, melted*

Poach 12 eggs in the usual way. Meanwhile, mix the garlic with yogurt. Place poached eggs on toast halves. Pour yogurt over them. Smooth paprika into the melted butter and dribble butter over the yogurt sauce. Very invigorating. (This recipe may not really qualify in the make-ahead category, but it certainly qualifies as something *different* for breakfast.) Serves 6.

Index